INTERNATIONAL INVESTING MADE EASY

MARTIN J. PRING

INTERNATIONAL INVESTING MADE EASY

Proven Money-Making Strategies with as Little as $5000

McGRAW-HILL BOOK COMPANY

New York St. Louis San Francisco Auckland
Bogotá Hamburg Johannesburg London Madrid Mexico
Montreal New Delhi Panama Paris São Paulo
Singapore Sydney Tokyo Toronto

NOTE: Although masculine pronouns are used in this book with such terms as "reader," "investor," and "analyst," they are intended to cover both sexes. International investment activity concerns many people, and the participation of women as investors, traders, analysts, and observers cannot be overlooked.

Library of Congress Cataloging in Publication Data

Pring, Martin J
International investing made easy.

Bibliography: p.
Includes index.
1. Investments, Foreign—Handbooks, manuals, etc.
I. Title.
HG4538.P69 332.6′737 80-14897
ISBN 0-07-050872-0

1 2 3 4 5 6 7 8 9 0 DODO 8 9 8 7 6 5 4 3 2 1

The editors for this book were Kiril Sokoloff and Celia Knight, the designer was Elliot Epstein, and the production supervisor was Sally Fliess. It was set in Baskerville by Progressive Typographers, Inc.

Printed and bound by R. R. Donnelley & Sons Company.

To my parents and brother.

CONTENTS

PREFACE

International Investing Made Easy seeks to explain international investment strategy in terms of the familiar techniques used in domestic markets and current world economic information. Reading and studying this book should help make it possible for any investor with a working knowledge of and experience in the U.S. stock market to follow and participate in all or any of the world's major financial markets.

This book is directed to investors who have already had some experience in the equity or debt markets. In this respect the text assumes that the reader is familiar with such basic concepts as bond yields, bull markets, bear markets, etc. On the other hand, the discussion of technical analysis, financial futures markets, and overseas investment assumes no prior knowledge of these subjects.

The late 1970s saw greater coverage being given in the American press to foreign business news than ever before. This resulted not only from the poor performance of U.S. stock and bond markets in the 1960s and 1970s but also from the persistent decline of the American dollar and the sharp inflation of energy prices. These situations prompted the realization that world economic developments can and will continue to have a pervasive influence on the U.S. economy. If the market performances of the past two decades are an accurate indication of the future financial scene, investors must find ways of achieving diversification out of U.S. dollar–denominated assets.

Part One describes how the various financial markets relate to the business cycle, setting the broad background conditions that affect the specific markets. Chapter 3 describes characteristics of some of those markets within easy reach of American investors. In addition to foreign equity markets, the discussion will include the U.S. bond market, some overseas bond markets, currencies, gold, and gold shares. Since commodities are a relatively specialized area and carry greater risk, they will not be covered, although the basic concepts described also apply to commodities and there is no reason why the aggressive reader cannot extend these ideas to include commodities as well.

Part Two explains some important principles of technical analysis that can be used to determine what to buy and when to sell. Chapter 9, describing mechanical systems designed to "beat the market," concludes this discussion.

Part Three outlines the huge variety of international investment vehicles available, such as offshore mutual funds, interest rate futures, etc., and how and where they may be obtained. This discussion also covers some of the more practical aspects, such as leverage, transaction costs, minimum investment requirements, availability of quotations, etc. Chapter 12, "A Final Word," warns of some of the psychological pitfalls that trap most investors at one time or another. Possessing adequate information is one important factor in investing, but unless the information is applied in a commonsense and logical manner, potential for success is greatly diminished. While most of this book concerns practical knowledge of international investing, Chapter 12 offers some advice on using it properly.

A book on international investing cannot be complete without mention of the world's largest and most liquid capital markets, namely those of the United States. For this reason, a substantial part of the text has been devoted to the U.S. debt and equity markets, the rapidly developing interest rate futures market, and the opportunities that exist for investors to buy, sell, and switch no-load U.S.-oriented mutual funds. After all, the prime objective of an internationally oriented investor is to maximize profits by choosing from the best of a number of promising situations. To exclude U.S. markets from this process is therefore counterproductive.

While every effort has been made to ensure the accuracy of the information contained in this book, the reader should always recheck the sources for himself in view of the speed with which some of the new futures markets, mutual funds, tax laws, government regulations, margin requirements, etc., are changing.

Martin J. Pring

ACKNOWLEDGMENTS

I would like to thank the many organizations for permission to reproduce charts and other figures. A particular debt goes to my colleague Tony Boeckh, editor and publisher of *The Bank Credit Analyst, The International Bank Credit Analyst,* and *The Interest Rate Forecast* (1010 Sherbrooke St. W., Montreal, P.Q., Canada), for permission to use many charts from these publications, and to Linda La Roche and Cindy Jones for their help in constructing the charts.

I would also like to thank Peter DeHaas and Kiril Sokoloff for their constructive suggestions, but above all my deepest debt is to my wife, Danny, for typing the manuscript and for her helpful ideas on rearranging the material.

M. J. P.

INTRODUCTION

As a result of accelerating global price inflation and differing responses of individual governments in dealing with it, huge price swings developed in the world's financial markets in the 1970s. This volatility offered investors a large number of profitable opportunities, provided they did not hold out for the long term. Concurrent with the emergence of these opportunities, the value of American financial assets was being destroyed, necessitating the adoption of a new, international approach. In the past an isolationist philosophy combined with governmentally inspired impediments have worked against such a possibility.

For years the field of international investment was popularly assumed to be the preserve of the so-called Gnomes of Zurich, those invisible Swiss bankers who manage vast amounts of portfolio money for their anonymous clients. In recent years, however, three important developments have opened up these markets for average American investors and made it much easier to diversify from the traditional havens of American savings capital which performed so badly in the 1970s.

The first development was the de facto abandonment of the Bretton Woods fixed exchange rate system in 1971. It was a decisive event in the creation of an American-based currency futures market which has since expanded into eight major contracts. American investors now have the opportunity to trade 64 different currency relationships. At the same time these new markets can be used with far greater flexibility to virtually eliminate the currency risk previously associated with foreign investments.

The post-Bretton Woods floating exchange rate system also encouraged huge international flows of speculative capital which exacerbated both the magnitude of business cycle fluctuations and the volatility of financial markets everywhere, creating substantial profit opportunities for anyone willing to abandon the "buy-hold" approach and play the cyclical swings to which all financial markets are subject.

The second development was removal of the Interest Equalization Tax which was payable on the purchase price of most foreign stocks and bonds bought by American residents. This tax was an obstacle to overseas debt and equity investment by Americans, and effectively closed the American capital market to most foreign borrowing.

The third development was legalization of gold ownership for Americans, which opened up another entire area of profitable investment opportunities by creating several American-based futures contracts, as well as encouraging direct ownership of gold bullion.

The major factor inhibiting many investors so far from participating in these markets has been inertia due to a general lack of knowledge. The objectives here are to point out the opportunities available along with the associated risks, to explain some simple techniques of technical analysis that can be used to make profitable investment decisions, to outline the process of buying and selling these international markets, and to indicate where information on the various markets can be obtained.

INTERNATIONAL INVESTING MADE EASY

PART ONE
INTRODUCTION TO INTERNATIONAL INVESTING

1

WHY INTERNATIONAL MARKETS?

Excessive creation of paper money by the governments of the world in the postwar period has resulted in a global financial disequilibrium characterized in most countries by high interest rates, rampant inflation, and enormous swings in the external values of their currencies.

Inflation is usually thought of as an increase in the general price level, but in a more subtle sense the dynamics of the inflationary process alter the relative prices of goods and services, setting up dislocations that accentuate the price performance of individual financial markets within a country. When these dislocations are aggravated by large currency swings, it can be appreciated how relative stability in the world's financial markets has been replaced by volatility as surplus investment capital constantly flows from one country to another in search of emerging investment opportunities. Long-term investment has therefore been replaced by short-term expediency, for in effect the stagflation environment of the 1970s extending into the 1980s means that there is no long term any more. Consequently, most serious investors today are more concerned with maintaining the purchasing value of their capital assets than with making money.

For the average American investor the precedence given to survival over growth has been nurtured by nearly two decades of rather disastrous investment results in both debt and equity markets. Between January 1966 and December 1978 the American stock market, as measured by the Dow Jones Industrial Average (DJIA), fell about 20 percent from the 1000 to the 800 level. When adjusted for price inflation the decline was even worse, the Dow having fallen from 1000 to the equivalent of less than 400. While overall performance during this period was disappointing, it did encompass three major bull markets, so nimble investors could have improved upon this performance by playing the major swings successfully.

Investments held in American corporate AAA-rated bonds would have fared no better during this period. Interest rates on these instruments rose from under 4½ percent to almost 10 percent by 1978, significantly destroying the nominal capital value of 20- and 30-year debt instruments. By early 1980 long-term rates had risen well into double figures.In real dollar terms, i.e., after adjusting for ravages of inflation, investments in long-term debt securities fared even worse than equities.

In view of this poor performance, it is little wonder that one of the most significant investment developments in recent years has been the growing awareness among American investors of the profitable opportunities available in other domestic and international financial markets. The actual number of individuals and institutions that have actually placed money abroad is small in comparison to the broad spectrum which participates in the two traditional havens for investment dollars, namely the American debt and equity markets. However, in response to the poor overall returns that have been achieved in these two traditional areas in the post-1966 period, this small number has been growing rapidly in recent years.

In addition to the international financial markets, frustrated American investors have also turned to financial futures, a new and rapidly developing set of investment vehicles. Futures contracts cover currencies, gold, and American interest rates, both for long- and short-term maturities. These three markets have greater appeal to debt and equity investors than most other commodity markets, since they are less risky, yet they still offer the leverage associated with the futures markets.

One important feature of these markets is that it is just as simple to make money in a period of declining prices as it is in a period of rising ones. This is particularly helpful in these inflationary times where debt markets appear to spend more time in a bear phase than in a bull trend. In view of these appealing characteristics, futures markets will be considered within the scope of international investing.

In this context the whole world should be viewed as one gigantic market, with the markets of each individual country being looked at in the same way that IBM or General Motors is considered as part of the American stock market. In this way investors can move from one market to another as conditions dictate, investment positions rarely being taken for less than 3 months or more than 24.

In contrast to a program concentrated on the traditional American debt and equity markets, where a good opportunity presents itself only once every 2 or 3 years, adoption of a large universe of market situations makes it possible to identify at least three or four outstanding buying opportunities each year.

SOME INVESTMENT COMPARISONS

The drawbacks of confining an investment program to one financial market can be more fully appreciated by evaluating the experience of investors in the American stock market during the period from 1966 to 1978, and by considering some other investment performances.

In February 1966 the DJIA, which is usually a good proxy for the market as a whole, was selling at 977 on a monthly average basis. By November 1978 it had fallen to 804 for a net loss of 18 percent. During that same period, this widely followed market average had undergone three complete cycles. Investors who used some timing techniques to buy and sell at bottoms and peaks would have fared far better than those who held onto their investment throughout this period. In reality there is no technique which enables investors to get in and out at exact turning points, but even allowing for a 10 percent margin of error at turning points,[1] a net gain in the 1966 to 1978 period of $177 would have been realized on an initial investment of $977 (i.e., $1 for every Dow point), compared with a $173 loss for the "buy-hold" approach. While such gains appear more acceptable at first sight, this performance would also show a net loss in real purchasing value. The real decline in the value of equities during this 12-year period is illustrated more dramatically in Chart 1-1, which shows the monthly DJIA adjusted for the rise in U.S. wholesale prices.

This example has been chosen to illustrate the poor experience of investors in the American stock market during the 1966 to 1978 period. It in no way implies that the American stock market will always be outperformed by the Wholesale Price Index. Indeed, there have been many periods in American financial history when the stock market has offered substantial inflation-adjusted capital gains.

The essential point is that investors should not continue to concentrate on this one market alone, for there are now many other potentially profitable investment opportunities within easy reach. Investments should no longer be held indefinitely, but should be bought and sold as

[1] Based on monthly average figures.

CHART 1-1 Dow Jones Industrial Average 1965–1978 Deflated by Wholesale Prices

Courtesy of *The Bank Credit Analyst.*

conditions change. For example, between late 1974 and 1977 the British equity market was the world's best performer. In 1978 it was the French market that rose 70 percent and should have been bought. Gold bullion rose from $38 in 1968 to $850 in early 1980, compared to a flat or declining American stock market, depending on which index is used.

Potential returns on investments made in international equity markets over the past 20 years would have been far higher than those confined to the U.S. market alone. This is shown in Chart 1-2, which compares the performance of the S&P 500 Composite with an index con-

from the best-performing stock market in specific periods. Reference to this chart show that the S&P Composite stocks rose from 55.78 in 1960 to 125 in 1980 for a twofold rise. On the other hand, the international investment shift approach showed the potential for a rise from 55.78 to over 4300, a phenomonally greater increase in the same period.

Quite clearly it is unlikely that an investor would have consistently selected the best-performing market in advance, so the performance of the World Stock Index has been far better than could reasonably be expected. However, what Chart 1-2 really demonstrates is that diversifying

CHART 1-2 Standard & Poor's 500 Composite versus a Potential International Performance

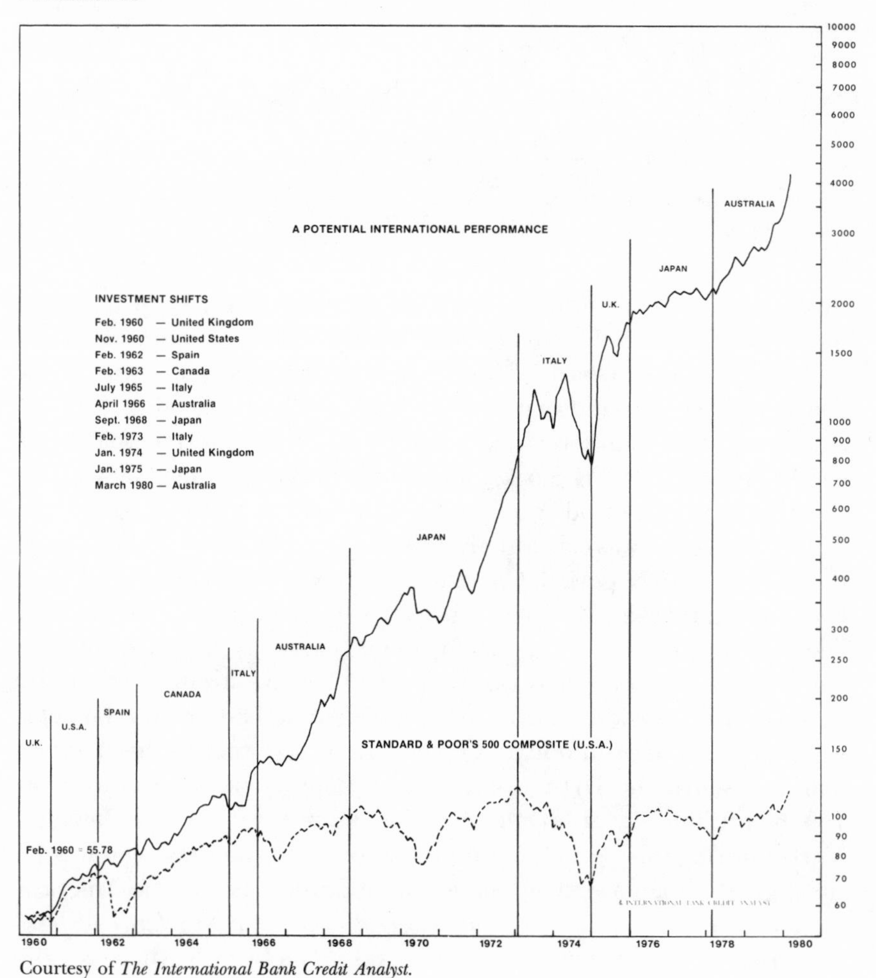

Courtesy of *The International Bank Credit Analyst.*

CHART 1-3 Relative Strength of DJIA against the World Stock Index

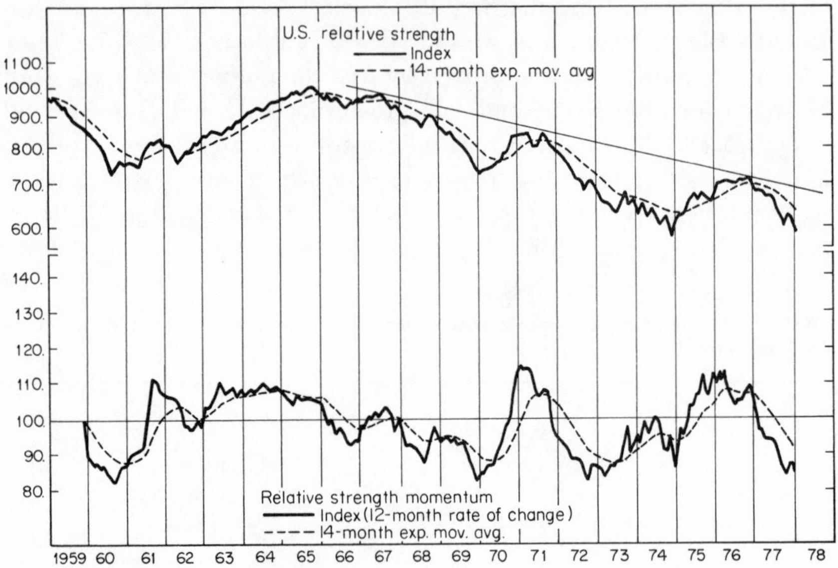

Courtesy of *The International Bank Credit Analyst.*

investments among world markets offers substantially greater profit potential than does confinement to one national market alone.

A comparison of Chart 1-3 and Chart 1-4 provides an example of the advantages of this international approach. Chart 1-3 illustrates the American stock market (DJIA) relative to The International Bank Credit Analyst's World Stock Index. This declining index shows that, apart from brief periods such as 1970 to 1972 and 1975 to 1976, the American market was consistently outperformed by the rest of the world in the 1965 to 1978 period. Chart 1-4 compares the Japanese stock market to the American stock market between 1971 and 1978. Wherever the line is rising it means that the Japanese market is outperforming its American counterpart, and vice versa. This relative strength (RS) index also takes into consideration currency fluctuations between the Japanese yen and the American dollar. The benefit of investing in the Japanese market vis-à-vis the DJIA is self-evident. The index, which rose from 100 to 350, shows that (dividends aside) an investment in the Japanese market during this period would have appreciated at a rate that was 3½ times greater than a similar amount of money invested in the American stock market. *The conclusion should not be drawn that these relative performances will be repeated.* They may or may not, but obviously there is a distinct advantage to having the choice of investing in foreign markets as well as in the traditional American financial markets.

For investors who feel more comfortable with fixed income securities, favorable comparisons between United States and foreign bond markets can also be made. For example, the American bond market reached a bull market high in December 1976, and by November 1978 yields on 20-year U.S. Treasury issues had risen 135 basis points from 7.30 percent to 8.75 percent, while over the same period both German and Japanese bond yields had fallen. In Japan, for example, long-term Telephone and Telegraph bonds, an important bellwether, declined in yield from 8.90 percent to 6.70 percent between December 1976 and November 1978. Long-term German bond yields also fell in this period from 7.20 percent to 6.40 percent.

The idea of putting money overseas may constitute an insurmountable stumbling block for some investors, but this does not preclude diversifying investments. As discussed later, for example, gold bullion and gold shares often move in an opposite direction to stock and bond markets. To take an example: Between January 1973 and December 1974 the DJIA was in a bear market, falling from 1050 to 570. During the same period gold bullion rose from about $75 to $200. At that time it would have paid to switch into stocks as the Dow advanced from 570 back to 1000 in September 1976, while the price of gold fell by half to $100 (August 1976). In the following 3 years the stock market essentially

CHART 1-4 Relative Strength of Japanese Market versus DJIA, Adjusted for Yen

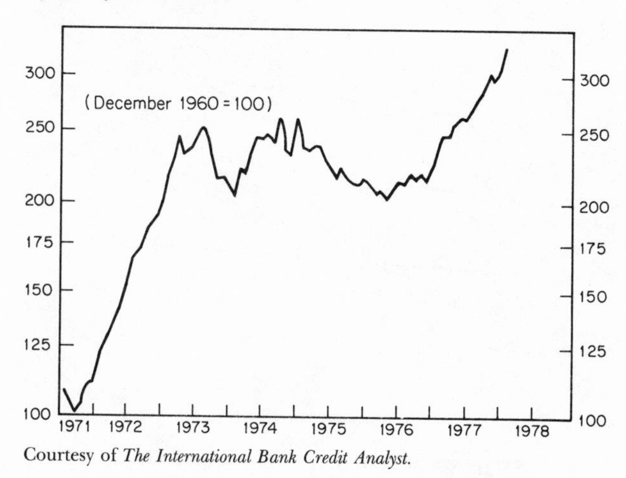

Courtesy of *The International Bank Credit Analyst.*

moved sideways, while gold ran up well over $400 and later in excess of $800.

Investors can also diversify without putting money abroad by finding money-making alternatives to the stock market through participation in domestically based international currency and interest rate futures markets. These markets are nowhere near as volatile as other commodity markets, yet they still offer substantial leverage to those willing to undertake the associated risks. Between September 1976 and March 1978, for example, when the DJIA fell from 1000 to around 750, the Japanese yen, Swiss franc, and German mark rose 26 percent, 33 percent, and 22 percent, respectively, against the U.S. dollar.

Some rather extreme examples have been cited above to make the case for an international approach to investing, and the unlikelihood of an investor selecting them all should be noted. Indeed, the objective is not to follow every market at all times and pick every single buying opportunity. Expecting to always find the best opportunity is hardly reasonable. However, it certainly is possible to find investment alternatives to the U.S. stock and bond markets by following several different markets in order to recognize significant buying opportunities.

Looking at the 3 years between September 1976 and September 1979 shows that it is also advisable. The U.S. stock market was moving sideways and the U.S. debt markets were declining. Both were outper-

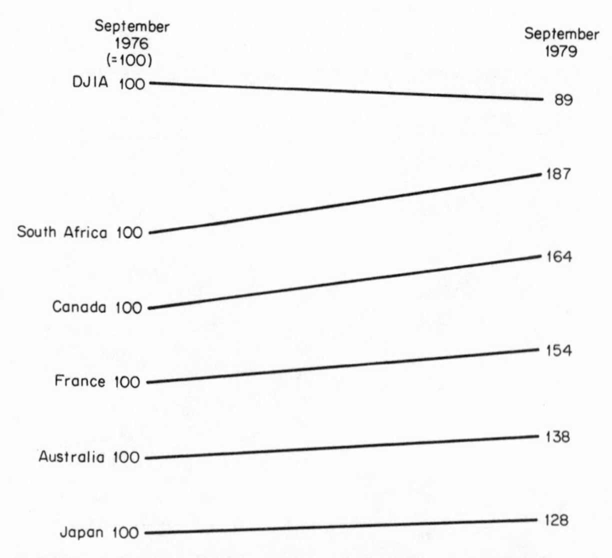

FIGURE 1-1 Dow Jones Industrial Average versus selected foreign stock markets, September 1976–September 1979.

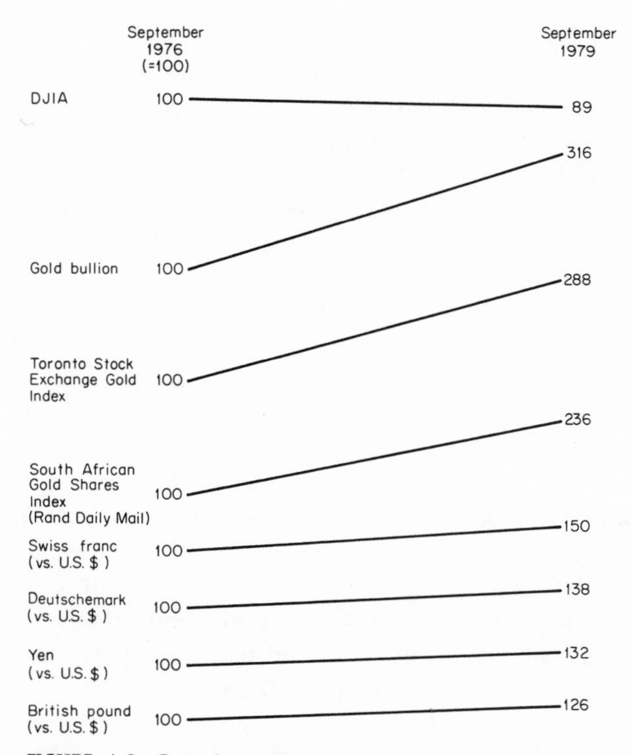

FIGURE 1-2 Dow Jones Industrial Average versus selected international financial markets, September 1976–September 1979.

formed by several other markets during this period, as Figure 1-1 and Figure 1-2 show. At this time it was also possible to invest in the recently developed financial futures markets, which presented new investment alternatives. Incidentally, September 1976 and September 1979 did not mark the extreme high and low points for the different financial markets (the British stock market reached its low in October 1976 and the Japanese yen its high in October 1978), so these comparisons understate their superior performance.

This international approach has great appeal, but of course important queries arise:

- How is it possible to follow a substantial number of these overseas markets in detail from an American base?
- What specific investments should be made?
- Where can suitable investment vehicles be obtained?

In practice, it is not possible for most investors to follow all the fundamentals of the various markets. Even if timely information were available in English, which for many countries it is not, considerable time would have to be spent analyzing data on various economies, industries, and companies, if a responsible investment program were to be followed. The only practical way in which such a project can be undertaken by most investors possessing limited resources is to use the tools of technical analysis. Such tools enable investment decisions to be taken on the basis of the price action of markets themselves, but more of that later.

The problem of individual stock or bond selection can be overcome through investment in mutual funds, for there are many mutual funds around the world that have been developed to attract investment in the debt or equity market of specific countries. Since performance of such funds fairly closely matches the markets in which they are invested, it is therefore possible to more or less "buy the market" with one transaction. In addition, the organizations concerned are also fully conversant with local security regulations and tax laws, and problems of dividend collection, certificate deliveries, and safekeeping are eliminated. Names and addresses of such funds, including commission costs, performance, investment policy, etc., are given in Appendix 3.

TECHNICAL ANALYSIS

As discussed above, the approach to international investing described here is based on technical analysis. While fundamental analysis is concerned with goods in which markets deal, technical analysis concentrates on the action of markets themselves. The technical analyst assumes that all the knowledge of all potential or active market participants is reflected in the price at any given time. Since this price represents the knowledge of all buyers and sellers, the "market" by definition is much smarter than any of its participants.

This assumption would be of little use, however, were it not for the fact that all financial markets move in trends. The whole point of technical analysis is therefore to identify such trend reversals at an early stage and participate in that movement until a reversal in the opposite direction takes place. Such an approach never results in a purchase at the exact bottom or a sale precisely at the top, except in the most fortuitous of circumstances. However, its careful and persistent application normally enables the investor to participate in the major part of a move, and puts the odds of success strongly in favor of any who adopt this approach.

Since successful technical analysis is based on the recording and analysis of price trends, all the investor needs are weekly quotations of the various financial markets. Weekly quotations are preferred over daily prices, not only because less work is involved, but also because weekly data is more readily available from the American financial press. A further advantage of basing investment decisions on weekly prices is that investors are less likely to get caught up in day-to-day market swings and are therefore better prepared psychologically to take a longer view, which is normally a more profitable time frame for investment purposes in any case.

What makes this international approach even more interesting is that it is becoming much easier for the average American investor to follow and participate in the many financial markets around the world. *Barron's* and *Business Week,* for example, are two of many financial publications that have expanded their international coverage. Development of currency, gold, and interest rate futures contracts on American commodity exchanges, and the introduction of many foreign and offshore mutual funds in recent years, have also made trading in these international financial markets extremely easy for the American investor. How to approach international trading, practical information regarding international investment vehicles, and other factors to consider are covered in the chapters which follow.

2

FINANCIAL MARKETS AND THE BUSINESS CYCLE

Although the basic concern here is with analysis of the technical trends of financial markets, it is important first of all to understand how various markets relate to the business cycle, the forces that propel them, and the type of economic conditions that are normally consistent with major turning points. This chapter will also explain in general terms some of the reasons why the world financial markets have become more and more volatile since the mid-1960s.

THE DISCOUNTING MECHANISM OF FINANCIAL MARKETS

The trend of all financial markets is essentially determined by investor expectations of movements in the economy, and the effect those changes are likely to have on the price of the asset in which a specific financial market is dealing. Market participants typically anticipate future economic and financial developments and take action by buying or selling the appropriate asset, so that normally a market will reach a major turning point well ahead of the occurrence of an actual development. This process is known as discounting.

Since an expanding level of economic activity is normally favorable for stock prices, a weak economy bullish for bond prices, and an inflationary economy favorable for gold and gold-related assets, these three markets are often moving in different directions at the same time. Moreover the debt, equity, and currency markets for individual countries can also vary, for although it can be empirically shown that most economies move in concert with the world trade cycle, the exact position of the business cycle in each country can still vary considerably from country to country. This is because monetary and economic policies of different governments rarely coincide, due not only to heterogeneous political conditions but to different economic structures. As a result of these factors, it can be appreciated that a wealth of profitable opportunities are continually being created as various financial markets are simultaneously moving in different directions in response to these changing economic and financial conditions.

Since an economy is rarely stable but is either expanding or contracting, financial markets are in a continuous state of flux. A hypothetical economy, as shown in Figure 2-1, revolves around a point of balance known as *equilibrium*. Roughly speaking, equilibrium can be thought of as a period of zero growth when the economy is neither expanding nor contracting. In practice, this state of affairs is rarely if ever attained, since an economy as a whole possesses tremendous momentum, either in the expansionary or contractionary phase, so the turnaround rarely occurs at the equilibrium level. In any event the "economy" consists of a host of individual sectors, many of which are operating in different directions at the same time. Thus, at the beginning of the business cycle leading economic indicators such as housing starts might be rising, while lagging indicators such as capital spending or employment levels could still be falling. Investors in financial markets are not concerned with periods of extended stability or equilibrium, for such periods do not produce volatile price swings and opportunities to make quick profits.

Since the financial markets lead the economy, it follows that greatest profits can be made just before the point of maximum economic distortion, or disequilibrium. Once investors realize that an economy is changing direction and returning toward the equilibrium level, they discount this development by buying or selling the appropriate asset. Obviously, the more dislocated and volatile an economy becomes, the greater is the

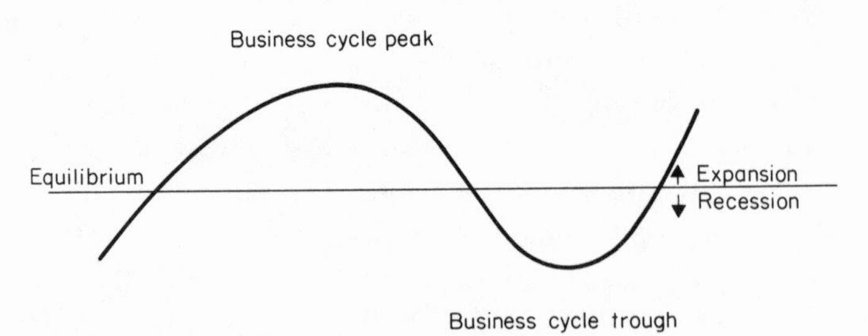

FIGURE 2-1 Hypothetical business cycle.

potential, not only for a return toward the equilibrium level but for a strong swing well beyond it to the other extreme. Under such conditions the possibilities for making money in financial markets are greater because they too will normally become subject to wider price fluctuations.

GROWING TREND OF VOLATILITY

In recent years these swings above and below the equilibrium level of both individual countries and the global economy as a whole have escalated. A number of factors have generated this growing volatility.

In the first place, during the postwar period governments around the world adopted Keynesian monetary and fiscal policies. This was a reaction to the global depression of the 1930s and represented an attempt to modify the painful effects of recessions by stimulating the various economies through government expenditure and easy money policies before business activity contracted too deeply. As far as the short run was concerned, such policies did tend to moderate recessions and were initially very successful, especially in a political sense for the governments in power.

However, one of the economic functions of a recession is to weed out and improve the productivity of businesses that have become inefficient during a period of prosperity. Since the world economies were not allowed to correct themselves adequately in this way, these aggressive easy money policies resulted in fewer bankruptcies and improvements in efficiency than would otherwise have been the case. On the premise of saving jobs, for example, the governments of Britain and France took over large companies that would otherwise have gone into liquidation. Such policies tend to produce a long-term effect of taxing efficient sectors of the economy and using the money to subsidize inefficient sectors.

This in turn helped foster an expectation that governments would bail out the economy whenever hard times threatened. Therefore, people felt there was less risk of unemployment or bankruptcy, so the tendency was to dip into savings and accumulate more and more debt.

Given these distortions and inefficiencies in the system, governments of the major countries in the world found it necessary to increase the amount of stimulation in each succeeding business cycle in order to get their economies moving again. In a sense, this situation can be compared to a heroin addict forced in time to take larger and larger doses in order to reach a high. The longer the addiction lasts, the more painful the withdrawal process will be. In the case of the economy, this stimulation in most countries has resulted in price inflation and interest rates both tracing a series of higher peaks in each succeeding postwar business cycle, and ascending troughs during each recession. These trends point up the long-term structural and financial deterioration that has taken place. Policies that attempt to redress these imbalances, and the implied misallocation of resources, almost certainly invoke very painful side effects in much the same way as the withdrawal process does for the unfortunate heroin addict.

Secondly, the postwar period has been characterized in virtually every country by a rapid development of wealth transfer payments and an escalation of government interference in the private sector through taxation policies and overregulation. As a result, the proportion of people who actually produce goods has shrunk considerably, while the number of those who basically consume (such as burgeoning government bureaucracies) has increased.

In spite of the decline of producers in relation to consumers, standards of living in industrialized countries have nevertheless risen in the postwar period. This is due in part to substantial productivity gains resulting from technological innovation, and partly to increased borrowing, both at private and governmental levels.

This situation can be compared to a family breadwinner who finds himself increasingly burdened with dependents. In order to maintain his standard of living he must either finance his expanding needs by becoming more efficient and earning more money, or by borrowing larger and larger amounts of money. Eventually his growing indebtedness will catch up with him and he will have to begin repaying his debts, or his credit will be withdrawn or severely curtailed. In both cases his standard of living will eventually decline unless he can offset these deflationary effects by sharply reducing the number of his dependents or directing them into income-producing areas. The essential difference between the breadwinner and the economy as a whole is that governments are able to accumulate much more debt over a far longer period before their day of reckoning arrives.

These growing debt burdens and rising servicing costs in both private and public sectors are another reason why governments have found that greater stimulation has been necessary in order to promote economic growth in each succeeding business cycle. Thus, once the global business cycle has peaked out, governments have been boxed into a policy dilemma. If their economies are permitted to contract naturally without resort to Keynesian demand stimulants, the process of correcting imbalances built up during the postwar period would undoubtedly result in a sharp global recession or even an actual depression. On the other hand, the existence of these deflationary forces necessitates the use of progressively larger doses of monetary and fiscal stimulation in order to promote a new cycle of economic growth. As noted above, however, this in turn results in escalating rates of price inflation. It is these crosscurrents of deflationary and inflationary forces which have been responsible for the rapid changes in the level of global economic activity in recent years.

Given this advanced stage of financial and structural disequilibrium, it is not difficult to appreciate that financial markets are likely to continue to exude volatility for some time to come. Moreover, since the economic structure of each country is not only inherently different from others but also differs in the degree of long-term financial deterioration, any given global event such as a sharp rise in commodity prices will affect each economy and its financial markets in different ways and to varying degrees. The relative price performance of each financial market is thereby accentuated. While it would be preferable to live in a more stable and predictable world, these tremendous market movements should be accepted and welcomed as presenting positive buying opportunities.

This examination of the reasons for volatility in financial markets has of necessity been greatly oversimplified. However, bearing in mind that the major objective here is to identify and capitalize on market swings, it must suffice to provide a general background.

MARKET MOVEMENT AND BUSINESS CYCLES

The major movements of interest rates, equities, and gold prices are related to movements in the level of business activity. Figure 2-2 represents a typical business cycle which normally has a life of between 3 to 5 years. As in Figure 2-1, the horizontal line reflects a level of zero growth, above which are periods of expansion, and below which are periods of contraction. Thus, after the peak has been experienced, the economy continues to grow but at a declining rate until the line crosses below the equilibrium level and an actual contraction in business activity takes place.

Periods of expansion generally last longer than those of contraction, so for this reason bull markets in equities and gold, and bear markets in bond prices, generally last longer than bear markets in equities and gold, and bull markets in bonds.

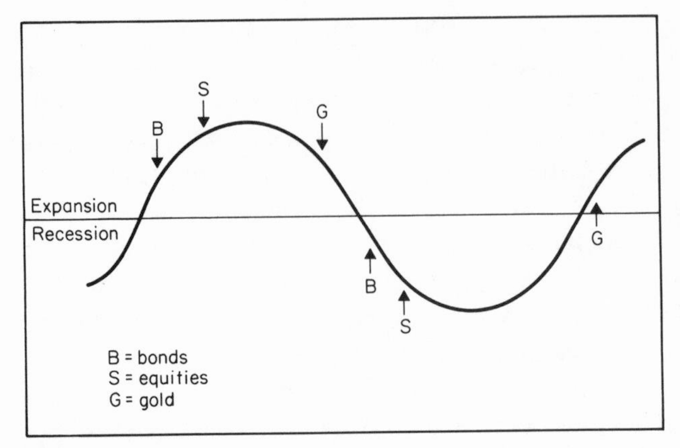

FIGURE 2-2 Hypothetical business cycle showing peaks and troughs of financial markets.

Figure 2-3 also shows how the three markets of interest rates, gold, and equities relate to the typical business cycle. In the example, interest rates have been plotted inversely to correspond with bond prices. Consequently, a bull market for bonds is represented by a rising line, and a bear market by a descending one. The bond market is the first financial market to begin a bull phase. This usually occurs after the growth rate in the economy has slowed down considerably from its peak rate and is quite often delayed until the initial stages of the recession. Generally speaking, the sharper the economic contraction, the greater will be the potential for a rise in bond prices (i.e., fall in interest rates). Alternatively, the stronger the period of expansion the smaller the amount of economic and financial slack, and the greater will be the potential for a decline in bond prices (and rise in interest rates).

Following the bear market low in bond prices, economic activity begins to contract more sharply. At this point participants in the equity market are able to "look through" the valley in corporate profits, which are now declining sharply because of the recession, and begin accumulating stocks. Thus, because the equity market discounts developments ahead of time, it bottoms out ahead of the trough in business.

During the relatively early stage of the business cycle, the economic and financial slack that developed as a result of the recession is gradually absorbed, putting upward pressure on the price of money, i.e., interest rates. Since rising interest rates mean falling bond prices, the bond market peaks out and begins its bear phase. On the other hand, since a substantial amount of excess plant and labor capacity still exists, rising business activity results in improved productivity. Consequently, the outlook for profits remains favorable. Since the stock market discounts trends in corporate profits, it continues to advance until participants sense that the business expansion is sufficiently mature to develop distortions and curtail the potential for improvements in profits. At this point there is less reason to hold equities, since their price potential has been realized and they in turn enter into a bear phase.

The price of gold is determined basically by the interaction of two types of market participants. The first group deals in gold as an industrial commodity affected by demand and supply relationships, the second invests in gold for its own sake or as a hedge against inflation. Essentially, the level of business activity has a more or less identical effect on both types of gold market participants, since the level of industrial demand and the growth rate of price inflation are both normally rising during a business cycle expansion, and falling during a contraction. The price of gold and gold-related assets therefore discounts trends in business activity, but lags equity prices. This is because both forms of market demand for gold, i.e., commodity and investment demand, are oriented to lagging indicators of an economic cycle. For example, since gold is considered to be a good store of value, its investment demand depends substantially on the rate of price inflation. Since the peak rate of price inflation is typically experienced around the beginning of the recessionary stage of the business cycle, the peak in the price of gold should theoretically be achieved 6 to 9 months ahead of the point where the rate of price inflation turns down. For its part, the stock market discounts trends in corporate profits which are a leading indicator of the economic cycle, so the stock market peak would naturally be expected well before the peak in gold prices. The same relationship should hold at market bottoms with equities troughing out well before gold.

On the other hand, gold shares discount profits of gold mines, and since earnings of these companies are determined by factors other than the price of gold, their cycle falls between those of industrial equities and the gold price itself. Since bullish factors for gold (i.e., rising business activity) are bearish for interest rates, the gold and gold assets markets are generally moving in the opposite direction to the bond market. This interaction is shown more clearly in Figure 2-3. Figure 2-4, on the other hand, shows how these turning points developed during the 1966–1978 period.

A typical business cycle is therefore composed of three individual cycles for interest rates, equities, and gold, all of which are influenced by the same economic and financial forces, but with different effects.

An investor who participates in all three cycles instead of concentrat-

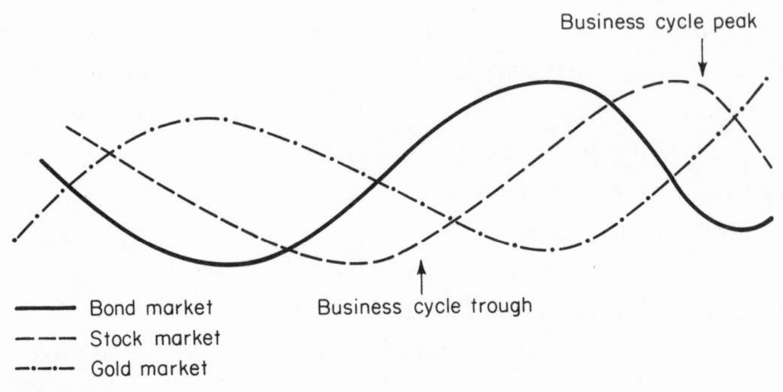

FIGURE 2-3 The interaction of financial markets during a typical business cycle.

ing solely on the equity market normally finds three major buying opportunities within the 4-year business cycle instead of just one. It should be stressed, however, that an actual cycle in the marketplace will not necessarily correspond to the conceptual description outlined above, in view of the fact that special circumstances can affect a particular market and cause it to reverse at an earlier or later point than might be expected from a study of the business cycle. For example, in the 1970–1974 cycle most commodities peaked during the spring of 1974, but the American dollar price of gold bullion made its cyclical high later in the year because the legalization of gold purchases for American residents in December 1974 had the effect of delaying the bearish phase of the cycle.

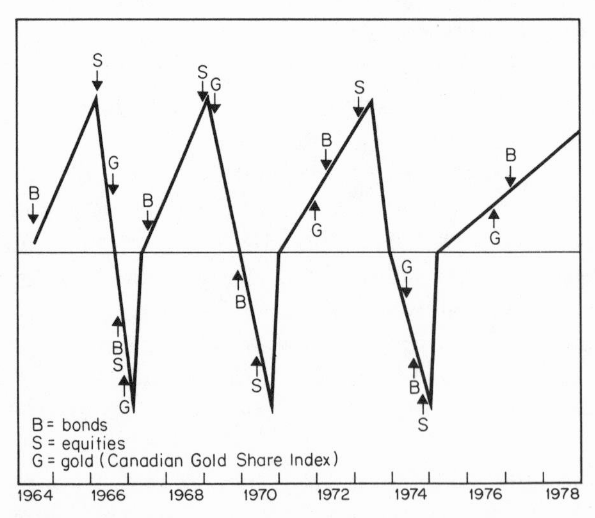

FIGURE 2-4 Peaks and troughs in U.S. financial markets in three business cycles.

CURRENCIES

Trends in the price of a country's currency do not fall into a regular pattern so far as the business cycle is concerned. This is because a currency is a relative value between the monetary unit of one country versus the monetary unit of another. There are many factors which affect the value of a currency but it is ultimately determined by the interaction of forces of supply and demand, as with any other commodity. In this respect, the most potent factor affecting long-run currency relationships is differential money supply growth rates. Quite obviously, if a country is expanding its stock of money at a faster rate than other countries, other things being equal, a surplus of that currency is likely to develop, thereby pushing down its price. As well as this direct effect, there is also an indirect one arising from the relationship between money growth, economic growth, and price inflation.

Generally speaking, a rapid increase in the supply of money will, after a lag, result in faster economic growth. Normally an economy that is expanding rapidly will also increase its volume of imports and transfer productive resources toward the fast-growing domestic market and away from foreign markets. This chain of events then adversely affects the balance of payments which, other things being equal, puts downward pressure on the currency.

As business activity expands still further, plant and labor capacity become used up, so the third effect of a rapidly increasing money supply results in accelerating price inflation, thereby reducing the purchasing parity of that currency against others and adding still more downward pressure on its external value. The direction and magnitude of international capital flows, which are largely determined by interest rate differentials, are a final determinant of currency values.

3
CHARACTERISTICS OF THE MARKETS

The four types of financial markets which will be discussed here are debt, equity, gold, and currency markets. Although it is not possible to give adequate individual coverage to each of the world's financial markets, the basic investment principles described later can be extended to them all.

The markets under consideration have been chosen because they meet four important criteria:

1. Timely data is available so that investors can track the various markets personally, or subscribe to a service that charts the data.
2. There is a sufficient amount of intermediate and long-term volatility to create profitable opportunities.
3. Adequate liquidity exists to facilitate buying and selling the investment vehicle concerned, reducing the risk of being "locked in."
4. A suitable investment vehicle encompassing the whole market rather than a specific stock is accessible.

The markets will be discussed in the order in which they develop in relation to the business cycle, i.e., interest rates, equities, gold, and gold-related assets. Although currencies have a tendency to rise during periods of economic contraction and fall during expansions, as discussed above, they cannot be readily positioned in the business cycle. Currency markets will therefore be discussed separately at the end of the chapter.

DEBT MARKETS

The level of interest rates or their reciprocal bond prices is determined by the demand for, and supply of, money. At a relatively early stage of an economic expansion much of the surplus economic and financial slack is used up and growing demand for credit, which is used to fuel the expansion, puts upward pressure on interest rates. In a cyclical sense it is only when economic activity contracts that surplus liquidity builds up and interest rates can begin to fall. Unlike the stock market where prices are determined by opinions on and attitudes to economic trends, cyclical movements in bond markets are determined by basic flows of money in the economy. Only to a limited degree can bond markets be said to discount future trends in the economy. Transactions based on expectations can alter the course of the bond market for short periods but can rarely reverse a cyclical movement by themselves. This is because money is still flowing in and out of the market as a result of government policies, mortgage demand from the level of housing activity, corporate demand due to capital spending plans, etc. Since bond prices are determined more by the basic flow of funds in the economy than by psychological factors, their trends are generally far more stable and easier to predict than those of equities.

International trading in interest rates can only be profitably achieved at the long end of the market where prices swings are sufficient to make cyclical moves worthwhile. United States futures contracts in 30-day and 90-day commercial paper and 3-month Treasury bills, which will be discussed later, are the exception for although price fluctuations are small relative to long-term bonds, the leverage that can be obtained from these vehicles more than compensates.

For most of the postwar period bonds were considered to be an unexciting vehicle for making money compared to the stock market. In recent years, however, violent swings in bond prices in most countries of the world have offered some excellent investment opportunities. Even so, fluctuations in bond prices, which usually range from 10 to 15 percent over a typical cycle, are normally still far less substantial than those of stocks.

On the other hand, this relative price stability enables purchases to be made with far less margin than stocks. It is possible, for example, to buy $100,000 of U.S. Treasury bonds with as little as $10,000 of equity. Given this substantial leverage factor, a 10 to 15 percent rise in bond prices would translate into a 100 to 150 percent return on the $10,000 actually invested. Foreign bonds can also be purchased on margin although financing will probably involve less leverage and will have to be arranged on an individual basis. In view of a general lack of knowledge of financial conditions overseas and the possibility of currency risks, it is unlikely that domestic branches of U.S. banks will offer much support in this area unless an investor is particularly well-heeled and has an excellent working relationship with his bank.

While bond prices normally fluctuate less than their equity counterparts, the gearing effect of the margin debt can result in equal if not greater movements in capital actually invested. The disadvantage, of course, is the fact that leverage works both ways, so that the degree of risk undertaken is also proportionately larger.

Most of the major industrialized countries have reasonably developed bond markets. Normally they can be divided into two categories: government bond markets and corporate bond markets.

Although interest rates paid by governments are invariably lower than those paid by corporations, the government sector is recommended for trading purposes, as a general rule. This is because government bonds can be bought and sold far more easily, since there is a ready domestic market for them in virtually every country. This liquid aspect of government bonds also makes them cheaper to buy and sell. The difference between the bid and ask price of an infrequently traded bond is much greater, since the dealer who positions them runs the risk of rapidly changing markets in an item that may have to be held in inventory for a long time. In this respect the bond business is no different from any other. For instance, the profit margin in a supermarket with a high turnover of inventory is far less than that of a furniture store with a very low turnover. In an extreme circumstance, such as a financial crisis, it is often impossible to find a bid at virtually any price for some poorer quality bonds; therefore it is best to deal only in high-quality vehicles.

UNITED STATES

The United States has the largest and most developed bond market in the world. There are basically three ways in which investors or traders can participate in the American bond market: by the purchase of bonds, mutual funds, or interest rate futures contracts. The mechanics of charting, buying, and selling the first two vehicles are discussed in Chapter 10.

INTEREST RATE FUTURES AND FUTURES MARKETS

The description of futures contracts here deals specifically with debt markets, but the basic principles apply to all futures markets including currencies and gold.

An interest rate futures contract is an agreement between a buyer and a seller. The seller agrees to make available to the buyer a fixed amount of a given debt instrument on a specific day, the buyer agreeing to pay an agreed price in consideration. In theory, no money should change hands until the date on which the contract comes due. In practice, the exchanges require that a cash deposit be put up by both buyer and seller in case either should default on their obligation. This security deposit is known as *margin,* and usually forms a very small part of the total outstanding value of the contract. For example, the margin requirement on a $100,000 Treasury bond is about $2500. It can therefore be appreciated that futures contracts offer investors substantial leverage. For example, a 2½ percent rise in a Treasury bond contract, (i.e., $2500), will double the return on the $2500 put up as margin. On the other hand, a decline of 2½ percent would completely wipe out the investment and either require that additional collateral be put up, or mean liquidation of the contract.

In view of this substantial leverage, it is important that potential investors in such markets first gain investment experience in cash markets, and secondly ensure that they have sufficient capital (well in excess of the minimum margin requirement) with which to back up the position taken. Margin is usually put up in the form of cash, but most exchanges also permit use of U.S. Treasury bills, which are issued in minimum denominations of $10,000. Use of Treasury bills allows the investor to earn interest on the money which would otherwise remain idle.

The face amounts to be delivered vary from contract to contract, and are listed in Table 10-2. Contracts are arranged for delivery in 3-month intervals, usually extending out over a 1½- to 2-year period. Thus, if today's date is January 15th, 1979, the contract schedule for 3-month T-bill futures in the financial section of a newspaper would reveal contracts for March, June, September, and December of 1979; and March, June, September, and December of 1980. If interest rates undergo a substantial rise between the time of purchase of the T-bill contract and its delivery date, the value of the contract will fall, and vice versa.

When trading in a new delivery month begins, there are no contracts in existence. Contracts can only be created when a buyer and seller complete a transaction. The number of contracts outstanding at any particular time is known as the "open interest."

One important difference between futures and cash markets is that in the cash market some form of delivery of the item in question is always made. Futures contracts, on the other hand, are often created where either the buyer, the seller, or both, have no intention of giving or taking delivery of the physical asset. Such transactions are of course speculative in nature and have the effect of greatly influencing the open interest figure. Generally speaking, a rising market should be accompanied by an expanding open interest and a falling one by a decline in the open interest. A sharply rising open interest can sometimes indicate an overenthusiasm by investors and is often followed by a sharp price setback.

An investment in interest rate futures has two advantages over an investment in the cash bond market. First, it is possible to obtain far greater leverage because of the smaller margin requirement. Second, it is easier to capitalize on periods in which interest rates are rising, i.e., when bond prices are falling, since the procedure for selling a futures contract is just as easy as for buying. The seller, for example, simply puts up the required margin and sells a contract. If his judgment is correct and interest rates do in fact rise, he can then buy back the contract at the resulting lower price and pocket the difference. This process of selling a contract that is not owned is called *short selling*. From a practical viewpoint the only difference between buying and "shorting" is that in the shorting process the sale transaction occurs before the buy side.

Since futures prices are linked with the spot or cash price for debt instruments, their major movements usually correspond to those of the spot rates. However, since expectations play a significant part in the pricing of futures contracts, from time to time it is possible to experience diverging trends between the far-out contracts and those nearby. If, for example, during a cyclical rise in interest rates, participants in the futures markets were anticipating a peak in yields in 12 months' time but new evidence caused a change in view by bringing forward those expectations by 6 months, there would be a change in the price of the far-out contracts, even though the spot rate remained unchanged. It should be pointed out that differences between nearby and far-out contracts can also develop due to alterations in the yield curve of the cash market, which opens up arbitrage[1] possibilities in the futures markets.

[1] Arbitrage is the process of taking advantage of price discrepancies of an identical asset in two markets by buying in one market and selling in the other.

An example of changing expectations and their influence on the futures markets occurred in mid-1979. Charts 3-1 through 3-4 represent the price action of T-bill futures in late 1978 and early 1979. During mid-1979, market expectations of the trend of T-bill yields became more positive. Reference to these charts shows that in February 1979 all the contracts were trading at approximately the 90.5 level. Although they began to diverge slightly over the next few months, it was not until late May that a substantial change in expectations developed, since the prices of the far-out contracts moved up substantially more than the nearby months. Throughout this period the cash market for 90-day T-bills remained basically unchanged, yet by June 1 the June bills were just over 90.5; by September, 90.9; by December, 91.2; and the March 1980 contract was at 91.4.

Such dramatic swings are unusual but they do stress the fact that the relationship between the cash and futures markets is not always identical, and that positions in far-out contracts should be based on an analysis of both the price action of these contracts themselves and those of the cash market.

Investors in interest rate futures who wish to follow cyclical or primary trends in interest rates can minimize these problems to a large ex-

CHART 3-1 Treasury Bill Futures and Changing Expectations (June 1979, Chicago, at 13-week intervals)

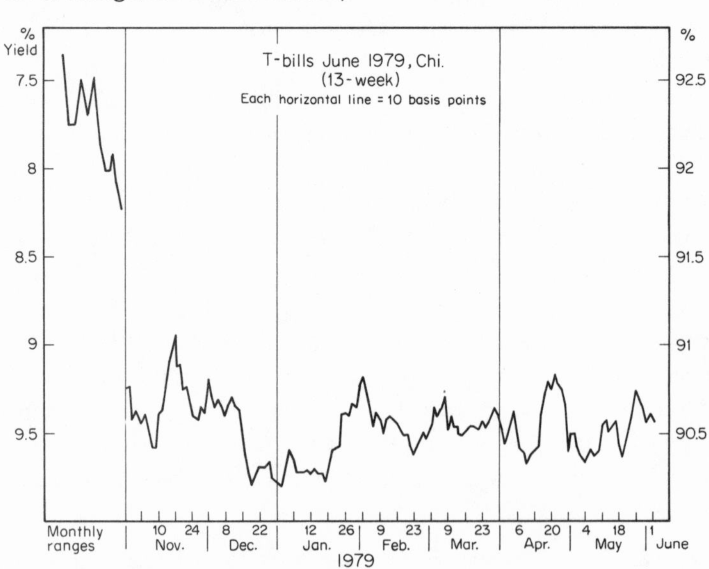

SOURCE: Commodity Research Bureau, Inc.

CHART 3-2 Treasury Bill Futures and Changing Expectations (September 1979, Chicago, at 13-week intervals)

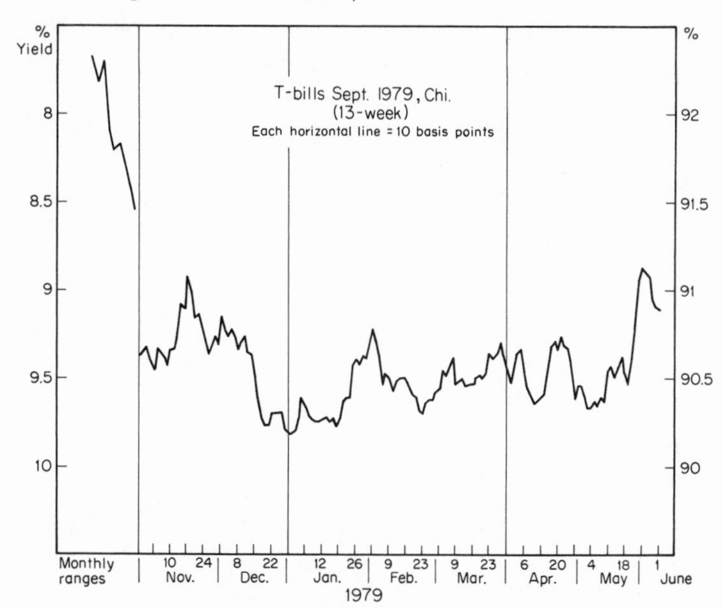

SOURCE: Commodity Research Bureau, Inc.

CHART 3-3 Treasury Bill Futures and Changing Expectations (December 1979, Chicago, at 13-week intervals)

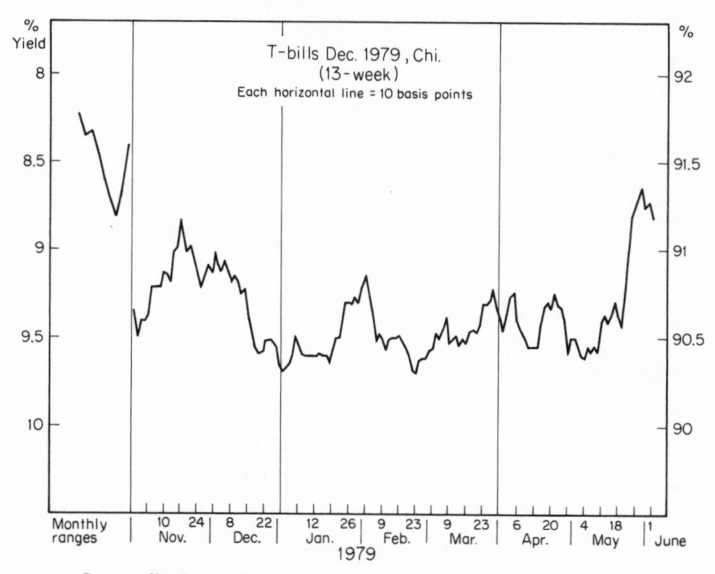

SOURCE: Commodity Research Bureau, Inc.

CHART 3-4 Treasury Bill Futures and Changing Expectations (March 1980. Chicago, at 13-week intervals)

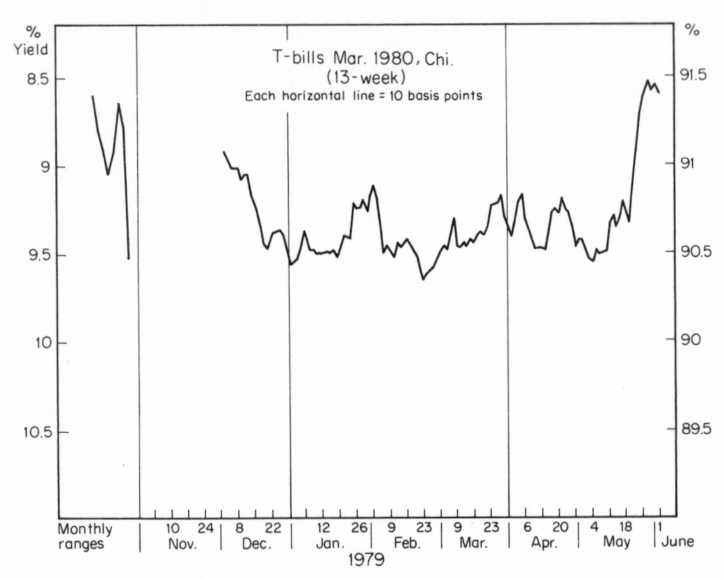

SOURCE: Commodity Research Bureau, Inc.

tent by investing in the nearby contracts (i.e., 3- or 6-month futures), which will be less subject to such distortions. Positions can be maintained by rolling over the contract into the new nearby position just prior to the expiration of the old one. One disadvantage to this procedure arises from the tax treatment of capital gains achieved in futures markets. This is because capital gains in commodity markets are realized within a 6-month holding period and are classed as ordinary income for tax purposes, whereas gains realized over a longer holding period are treated as capital gains for tax purposes, therefore qualifying for the reduced rate. Unfortunately, all gains resulting from short positions are treated as ordinary income, regardless of the time period over which they were made.

Another characteristic of interest rate futures, as with all futures markets, is that on rare occasions an unexpected economic or financial development may have a substantial effect on the price level. The spot or current price adjusts immediately, but the futures market may be unable to because the various exchanges post a limit as to how much the price of each contract may move in a particular day. "Limit" moves for specific contracts are included in the information tables in Chapter 10. Usually, interest rate movements are generally stable, so this problem of being locked in does not occur very often, but it is an additional risk factor that must be taken into consideration when dealing with these investment vehicles.

BRITISH BONDS

Appendix Chart A1-8 illustrates the British bond market in historical perspective. It shows that the 1970s have witnessed some fairly substantial swings. The index is the Financial Times 20-Year Government Bond Yield Index, and it has been plotted inversely to correspond with bond prices.

In Britain, government bonds are also known as gilt-edged securities, or "gilts." There are essentially two ways to acquire British gilts, either through purchase of a mutual fund or through purchase of a specific bond. The actual buying or selling of these instruments is discussed in Chapter 10. Unlike the American market, margin and other leveraging facilities such as a futures market are not available, nor is it generally possible to take advantage of a declining bond market through short selling. Gilt prices are not generally published in the American press, but are of course quoted in depth in the *Financial Times* of London.

CANADIAN BONDS

Canada has a reasonably well-developed bond market. Although liquidity in corporate and provincial bonds is quite good, foreign investors are probably better advised to concentrate on bonds issued by the government of Canada.

Since the Canadian economy is closely integrated with that of America, Canadian interest rates usually move fairly closely to American rates. On some occasions, though, conditions are sufficiently different to warrant participation in the Canadian market, especially when the Canadian dollar is in a rising trend against the American dollar. It is then possible to make a profit from both bonds and currency. Normally, Canadian rates are higher than those for the United States because of the country's continual need to import capital.

Chart A1-10 shows weekly government of Canada yields (which have been plotted inversely).

OTHER DEBT MARKETS

Unfortunately, data on foreign domestic debt markets, other than those already discussed, is difficult to obtain unless a local, non-English financial publication is subscribed to. For this reason, and because of the tax advantages, the Eurobond market for deutschemark, yen, Swiss franc, and French franc denominated bonds is recommended and is discussed in more detail in Chapter 10.

Chart 3-5 shows the inversely plotted yields for the bond indexes of a bellwether bond for the major industrialized countries. Reference to the chart shows that while most bond yields move in tandem most of the time, there are periods of substantial divergence. Note, for example, the sharp rise in German bonds between late 1974 and 1978, compared with the bear market that was going on in Italy at the time.

EQUITIES

As discusssed in Chapter 2, the world stock markets discount movements of global economic activity. Chart 3-6 shows The International Bank Credit Analyst's World Stock Index and a year-over-year rate of change of OECD Industrial Production. This economic measure in its raw form is considered to be a coincident indicator of global business activity. The construction of a rate-of-change index brings out cyclical swings in this index and also speeds up its turning points. The chart clearly demonstrates the close relationship between global economic activity and equity prices.

The lead time between the bull market top of the World Stock Index and the peak in business activity varies, as indeed it does for individual countries. Normally, it approximates 6 to 9 months but there have been times, such as in 1929, when the American stock market actually lagged the peak in U.S. business activity, or 1921, when it lagged the trough by 1 month.

The World Stock Index shown in Chart 3-6 is an average of the stock indexes of twelve industrialized countries weighted by gross national product (GNP). The arrows above and below the index represent the primary peaks and troughs of bull and bear markets, which seem to occur at approximately 4-year intervals. The arrow is shown at the 1965 peak rather than the higher 1966 top, since most markets peaked out prior to 1966.

Although the World Stock Index is a good proxy for the average level

CHART 3-5 World Bond Markets* (Showing markets in Australia, Canada, France, Germany, Italy, South Africa, and United Kingdom)

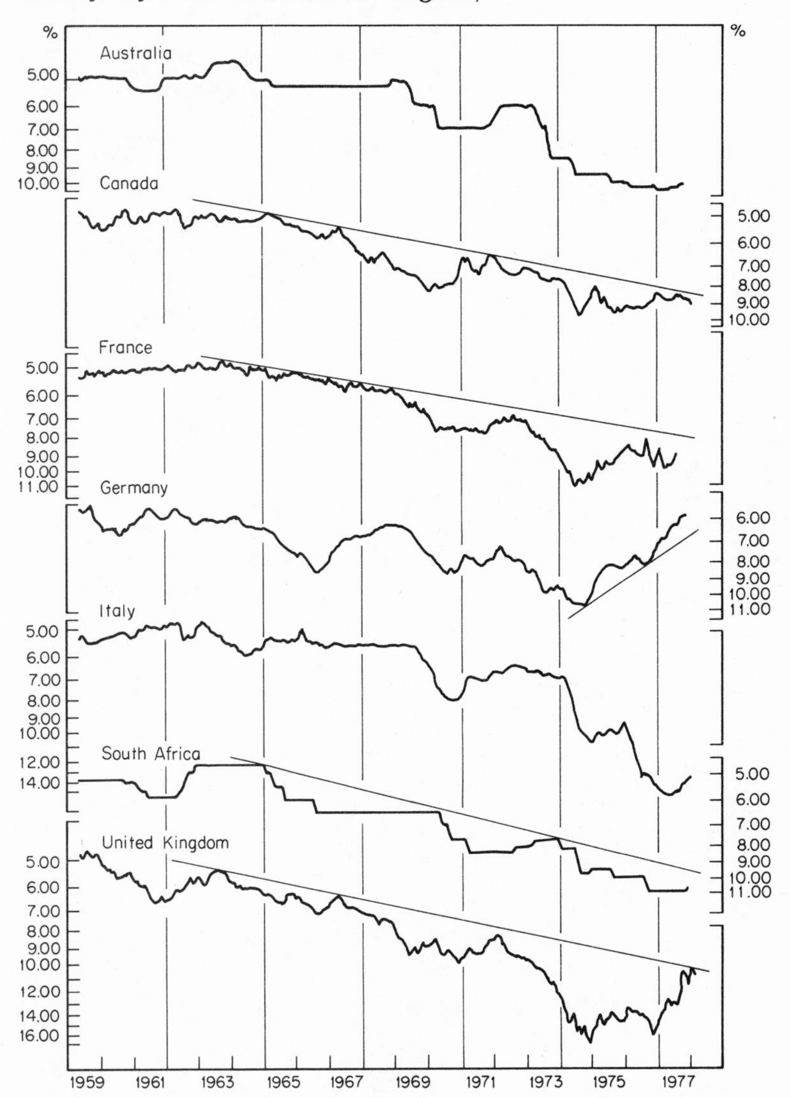

* Long-term government bond yield.

Courtesy of *The International Bank Credit Analyst.*

CHART 3-6 World Stock Index versus Global Industrial Production

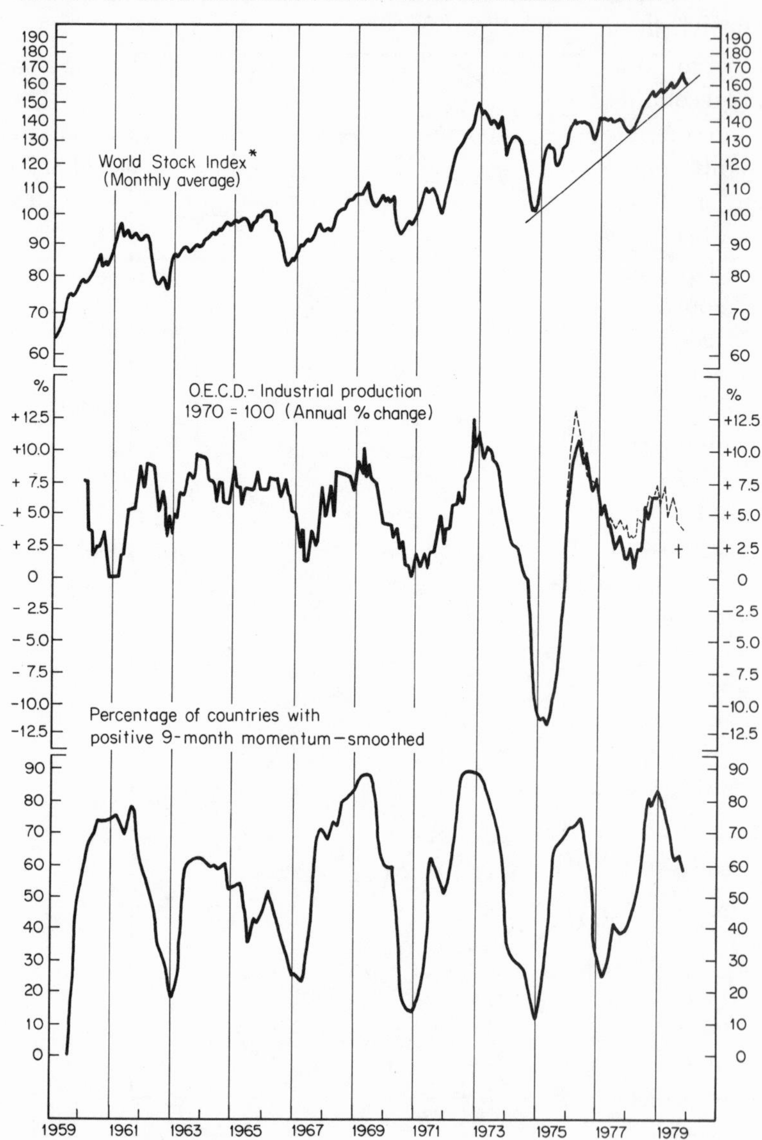

* Weighted by GNP: United States, Japan, Germany, France, United Kingdom, Italy, Canada, Australia, Netherlands, Spain, and Sweden.

† Weighted by GNP: United States, Japan, Germany, United Kingdom, Canada.

Courtesy of *The International Bank Credit Analyst.*

of global equity prices, some markets are usually in a different phase from the World Stock Index itself, some leading and others lagging. This is because the economic structure of each country and the monetary and economic policies of individual governments vary, so that swings in economic activity and major movements in the stock markets are also different. No country consistently leads or lags the World Stock Index. If anything, the British market has historically had a tendency to lead the world cycle. This is perhaps because of that country's periodic balance of payments crises, which forced succeeding governments to tighten monetary policy and turn the economy into a contractionary phase earlier than might otherwise have been the case. When Britain gets its economic house in order, such leading characteristics may no longer occur, so it would be a mistake to assume that this relationship could continue indefinitely.

Charts 3-7 and 3-8 show 12 leading stock markets between 1960 and 1978. Shaded areas on the charts represent periods when the World Stock Index was in a primary bear market. In spite of some notable exceptions, it is apparent that the various markets have generally fitted quite well into the global equity cycle. The primary producing countries, Australia, Canada, and South Africa, normally have a strong tendency to lag at market peaks. Also noteworthy is the countercyclical characteristic of the Italian market, which appears to form a top whenever the World Stock Index is approaching its bottom. This occurred in 1966, 1970, and 1974. On the other hand, the Italian market bottomed out in 1968 and 1972, at a time when the World Stock Index was approaching its cyclical peak. To a more limited extent, the Spanish stock market has also had a tendency to move in a countercyclical manner.

While most of the world's equity markets are fluctuating in conjunction with the global trade cycle, reference to Charts 3-7 and 3-8 shows that there are enough differences, both in terms of the timing of major turning points and the magnitude of the moves, to present a substantial number of good investment opportunities. In some cases, a specific market may only participate in a world bull market to a very limited extent, due to particularly adverse economic and financial conditions. In retrospect, such situations often look like giant bear markets and usually represent the most outstanding buying opportunities when such "double" cycles are completed. Two such examples occurred in Japan and the Netherlands in the early 1960s. Similarly, a market may almost completely fail to participate in a world bear phase, as was the case in Spain during the 1960s. When that strong uptrend does break, however, such markets are usually best avoided.

CHART 3-7 Six Stock Markets versus the World Equity Cycle (Showing the principal stock price indexes of Australia, Canada, France, Germany, Italy, and Japan)

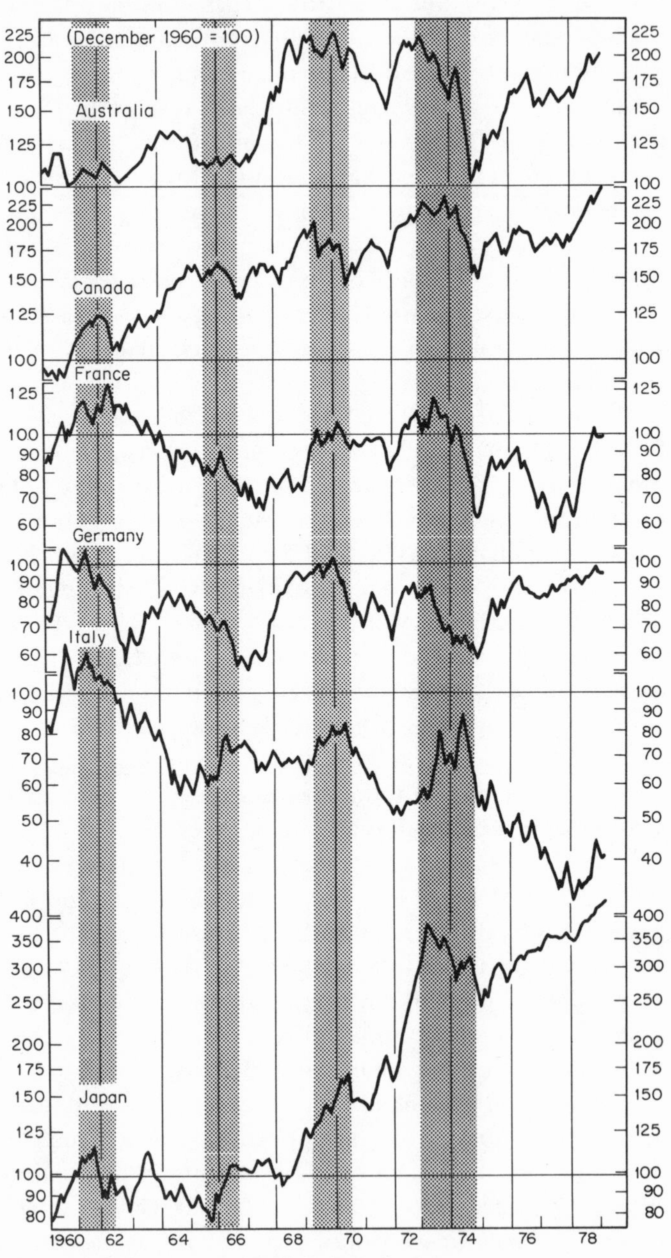

Courtesy of *The International Bank Credit Analyst.*

CHART 3-8 Six Stock Markets versus the World Equity Cycle (Showing the principal stock price indexes of Netherlands, South Africa, Spain, Sweden, United Kingdom, and United States)

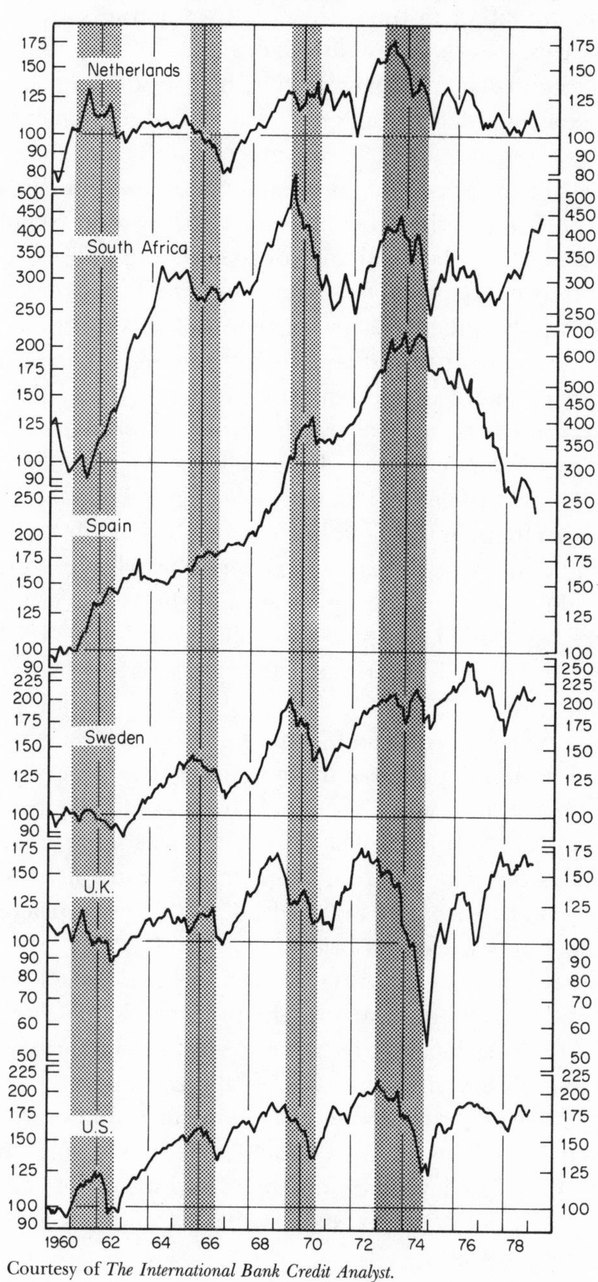

Courtesy of *The International Bank Credit Analyst.*

GOLD AND GOLD-RELATED ASSETS

There are essentially two ways to participate in the gold asset markets—purchasing bullion either in the cash or futures markets, or acquiring gold mining shares. It is also possible to buy gold coins such as American double eagles, South African Krugerrands, British sovereigns, etc.

Gold has been regarded throughout history as the ultimate form of money, despite many attempts by governments in the ancient as well as the modern world to reduce or even eliminate its role in this regard. Gold has obtained this position because it is virtually indestructible and its new production in relation to the outstanding supply is relatively small. It is therefore impossible to "print" more gold, unlike paper currencies whose supply is theoretically inexhaustible.

For trading purposes gold bullion should therefore be regarded as another currency. There is one important difference and that is that gold bullion pays no interest. In contrast, it is always possible to purchase debt obligations for any currency. Generally speaking, cyclical investment in gold is only profitable when the price of gold bullion is expected to rise at a faster rate than the yield that can be obtained in a good-quality debt instrument. In practice, the gold price usually responds positively to a period of accelerating inflation since this is also a time when bond yields are rising and bond prices are falling. Under such conditions the interest on the bond is often more than outweighed by the capital loss.

When the rate of price inflation is falling, the purchasing value of a currency is still declining but since this also tends to be a period of high but falling interest rates, investors switch from gold bullion to bonds where a higher overall return will be achieved. At the same time, the implied weakness in the economy from falling interest rates also results in a lowering of fabricator demand for gold bullion, thereby placing additional downward pressure on its price.

One of the most notable characteristics of the gold bullion market is its extreme volatility. Quite frequently the price of the metal will give a technical signal suggesting that its price trend has changed direction, only to reverse itself and move in its original direction.

Gold mining shares almost always change the direction of their trend ahead of gold bullion. This happens because investors in gold shares anticipate the profits of gold mining companies, and since these are largely determined by the price of gold, the shares have a tendency to anticipate price trends in the metal.

It is almost mandatory when investing in gold markets to record and chart bullion and at least one gold share index to understand the overall trend of the gold asset market. It is not always necessary to chart individual gold shares, since such charts can be obtained from subscriptions to chart services (see Table 10-1) and are discussed in Chapter 11.

CURRENCIES

Since the breakdown of the Bretton Woods monetary system of fixed exchange rates, virtually every currency in the world has been allowed to float freely to find its own value. In effect, the floating is rarely left to market forces, as central banks, for political as well as economic reasons, often intervene in the market to promote stability. Such intervention does not nor cannot reverse the basic cyclical trend of a currency, so central bank support operations have to some extent the effect of smoothing out short-term fluctuations which act to the benefit of technical analysis, since trend reversal signals become much more reliable.

On the other hand, when a central bank insists on pegging at a specific price for too long and finally gives up, market forces propel the currency's movement with far greater momentum than would otherwise have been the case, in an effort to make up for lost time. This of course offers an additional risk to investors who might be positioned on the wrong side of the market.

Currencies are traded in three forms: the spot or cash market, the forward market, and the futures market.

The cash or spot market of a currency is determined by the interaction of buyers and sellers in the marketplace, who for a variety of reasons find it necessary or desirable to convert one currency to another. It may be the completion of a business or financial transaction as a result of a central bank support operation or simply a prospective international tourist purchasing vacation money.

The forward transaction on the other hand is an outright purchase or sale of one currency against another with delivery designated for a specific date ranging from 3 days to 5 years after the transaction date. The price at which the forward transaction takes place will usually differ from the spot rate due to both market expectations and to arbitraging opportunities that arise from different interest rate levels between the two countries concerned. Currencies therefore are either at a discount for the forward maturities (i.e., forward price below the spot price) or at a premium price to the spot (i.e., forward price above the spot).

The currency futures markets operate on basically the same principles as the interest rate futures markets, but since there is a well-developed forward market for currencies, prices of currency futures more or less reflect price fluctuations of the forward markets, since any difference is quickly arbitraged out.

Since currency movements are generally rather small relative to other financial markets, they do not by themselves usually represent good vehicles for capital gains. On the other hand, if a stock or bond investment is made in a foreign market and both it and the local currency appreciate, the gain in the currency enhances the overall profit. If a decision is taken to invest in British bonds, for example, and it is also felt that the pound is in a position to rise against the American dollar, it might be possible to make a gain in both bonds and currency. As a general but not invariable rule, a country with a strong stock and bond market is normally associated with a rising trend in its currency. Since there have been plenty of exceptions to this rule for various economic and financial reasons, it should never be assumed that the trend of the currency will always move with that of debt and equity markets. Each market should be assessed separately using the principles outlined in Chapters 6 and 7.

If a firm opinion is held on the future trend of a currency, the best way to capitalize on that movement is through participation in the currency futures market rather than the spot market, where it is possible to obtain substantial leverage, and either sell short or go long. One nonspeculative use of the currency futures markets is to hedge a long position in an equity or bond market against a short position in the currency. For example, if the technical structure is indicating the possibility of a sharp rise in the German stock market, but an analysis of the deutschemark does not leave any clear indication of its trend, then the purchase of German stocks can be offset by the sale of a futures contract in that currency.

If the stock market rose by 30 percent and the currency were to fall by 10 percent, the net gain from an unhedged position would only be 20 percent (i.e., 30 percent − 10 percent). On the other hand, if the purchase of shares denominated in deutschemarks is offset by a short sale in the currency, it is then possible to cash in on the full 30 percent appreciation in the German stock market. Where a futures currency is trading at a discount against the spot rate, it will not be possible to offset all the currency risk through a short sale, since the value of the futures contract must by definition equal the spot rate when it matures.

The main difference between currency markets and other financial markets is that a movement in one currency is always offset by movement in another. In other words, for American investors purchase of the French franc is in effect a sale of the American dollar. If it is felt that the French franc is likely to rise, it is not always the best policy for an investor to limit his action to purchase of the French franc, for although the franc may be expected to be a strong currency relative to the American dollar, the American dollar in turn may be stronger than several other currencies, such as the Canadian dollar, for instance. The investor will then be able to maximize his profit in this situation, since the French franc contract will appreciate against the American dollar, and the Canadian dollar contract will decline against its American counterpart.

Since currency values are essentially bilateral relationships, it is difficult to obtain an overall index from the point of view of deciding whether a currency is in a rising or falling trend against the rest of the world. The most useful proxy is a trade-weighted measure index. This index is constructed by taking the price of a currency against a basket of other currencies and weighting the price of each component by the amount of trade each country does with the country for which the trade-weighted measure is being constructed.

Clearly, maximum profits are obtained when it is possible to identify a currency for which the trade-weighted index is strong, and one for which the trend is weak. It is also important, of course, to chart the specific relationship. Thus, if the Swiss franc were the strong currency in question and the pound sterling the weak one, it would be necessary to record and chart Swiss francs in terms of pounds sterling to act as a confirmation of the trade-weighted analysis.

4
WHAT TO LOOK FOR AT MAJOR TURNING POINTS

While the major part of this book is oriented to the technical approach to investing in financial markets, it is also worthwhile to point out some of the characteristics, developments, and news background present around major cyclical turning points. This will offer a useful adjunct to the technical approach. Even with the expanded news coverage given to overseas economies and financial markets, there is still a considerable lack of good factual information. However, the kind of developments associated with cyclical market peaks and troughs tend to be rather basic, are often fairly dramatic, and are of the type that frequently find their way into U.S. overseas financial reporting.

The following is a brief summary of the sort of developments that tend to occur at these important turning points. In using these guidelines it should be remembered that not all of them will be present or apparent at each turning point. The list is therefore suggested only as general background to be used to help spot potential opportunities.

EQUITY MARKETS

BULL MARKET PEAKS

1. Bull market peaks are almost always preceded by a rise in interest rates. This is certainly true of the United States, and most other countries as well. The lead time in the period between the low point in interest rates and the top in stock prices can vary from as little as 1 month to as long as 24

months. Unless interest rates have begun to rise, it is *normally* safe to assume that the bull market is intact.

2. In a similar vein, look for rises in the discount or rate of interest charged by the central bank. A rise in this rate after a long series of declines indicates a reversal in government policy toward monetary restraint. Such a decision is not taken lightly, so that while the stock market may continue to rise, a hike in the discount rate is an indication that it is rapidly reaching maturity.

3. After the market has been advancing for 2 to 3 years or more, be alert for extremely optimistic predictions, or for feature articles on a particular country's equity market in leading financial publications. When the American popular press is reporting such developments, the good news is out and since equity markets discount the news, it is often a good indication of an impending top.

4. Equally important to look for are reports of a booming economy. These indicate that things cannot get much better, again implying that the good news has already been discounted by the market.

5. If commodity prices have had a very sharp run up, the chances are that most of the world stock markets have reached their peaks, since commodity prices are a lagging indicator. Equity markets of the primary producing countries such as Canada, South Africa, and Australia are often reaching their peaks around the time of the peak in commodity prices, whereas countries such as the United Kingdom, Germany, and the United States have already started to turn down.

Bull market tops in equities are generally preceded by a long, strong rise in stock prices, sufficient to create overconfidence and carelessness, and success stories begin to hit the front pages of the popular press.

BEAR MARKET BOTTOMS

1. Bear market bottoms develop under exactly the opposite conditions described above. For instance, the economic news will be very dismal. Reports of bankruptcies, large layoffs, in-

creasing unemployment, etc., will abound. Interest rates will have begun to decline, and government policy will turn to one of ease, as indicated by a reduction in the central bank lending rate.

2. Commodity prices will already have fallen, as will the price of gold.
3. The rate of inflation as measured by the Consumer Price Index will also have peaked out.
4. The market will probably have experienced a final sharp sell-off, bearish sentiment will prevail, and predictions of very much lower price levels will abound.

BOND MARKETS

PEAKS

1. The first sign of a bond market peak is marked by a reversal in the declining rate of price inflation. This indicates that business conditions have recovered sufficiently to use up a considerable amount of economic and financial slack in the economy, thereby putting upward pressure on interest rates.
2. Turning points in long-term interest rates either coincide with or are more normally preceded by turning points in short-term rates, so look to see what the money markets are doing. Short rates have a tendency to lead long rates, not only because they are more sensitive to business conditions, but also because government monetary policy is easier to put into operation at the short end. Foreign short-term interest rates can easily be followed through the *Financial Times* of London on a daily basis if necessary.
3. An initial rise in the central bank lending rate (discount rate) usually confirms that a rise in interest rates is already under way and is a clear indication of a major policy reversal by the authorities. The discount rate usually lags other rates, since for political reasons the government is often reluctant to force up the general level of rates.
4. A further indication that bond prices have peaked out is given by signs that a strong business recovery is under way. This

would be signaled by reports of a significant decline in unemployment levels or a turnaround in capital spending.

5. In some countries central banks have a declared target for monetary growth, since excessive monetary creation eventually translates into higher rates of price inflation. When these targets are exceeded, the central bank is often forced to raise the price of money, i.e., interest rates.

6. Substantial external pressures on a country's currency will often force the authorities to raise interest rates in order both to attract capital into the country and to deflate domestic demand, and therefore improve the balance of payments. A persistent decline in the external value of a currency is therefore likely to put upward pressure on interest rates.

BOTTOMS

1. Often the first sign of an interest rate peak, i.e., a bond market low, is a reduction in the central bank lending rate, for just as the authorities are reluctant to raise rates they are very quick to seize the opportunity to lower them.

2. Lows in the bond market are usually preceded by a peak in short-term interest rates, so it is a good idea to monitor the progress of short rates.

3. Bond market lows occur around the beginning or middle of a recession. Consequently, weak business conditions such as rising unemployment, a sharp decline in consumer expenditure, etc., represent reliable signs of an impending bottom.

4. An excessively strong currency is not necessarily indicative of a major low in bond prices, but it does hint that the authorities are likely to relax rather than tighten monetary conditions, since exports will suffer a competitive disadvantage if the currency becomes too expensive.

GOLD BULLION

BULL MARKET PEAKS

1. Due to the fact that the price of gold bullion has only been allowed to freely react to market forces since the late 1960s

there have not been many cyclical peaks from which to establish useful benchmarks.

2. The bull market top in 1974 was associated with a blowoff in commodity markets and a peaking in the rate of price inflation in most countries. At that time newspapers were full of stories of the general public entering the market. "Gold fever" was therefore rampant.

3. Another pointer to assess is whether the peak in the bullion price is confirmed by a new high in major gold share indexes (e.g. Barron's Gold Stock Index, the Toronto Gold Share Index, etc.). Since gold is a commodity and therefore a lagging indicator, look at the Commerce Department's composite of leading indicators, which is published regularly in the U.S. press to see if they have started to decline. If they have not, then chances are that any decline in the price of gold represents a temporary interruption of the major trend.

4. Most financial markets end their bull phase with a sharp rally. Gold, being a very emotional commodity, is no exception so look for an explosive rally far greater than any seen previously, as this will likely mark the terminal phase of the bull market. Also watch for the emergence of wild forecasts well above current prices. Quite often such predictions can only filter through to the press when everyone is convinced that gold is going higher.

BEAR MARKET BOTTOMS

1. The 1976 bear market low in gold was made at a time when market sentiment was decisively negative and projections for sharply lower prices were rampant. Reports concerning the demonetization of the metal gained more significance while the number of advertisements promoting gold bullion, gold coins, etc., shrank considerably from the number at the December 1974 peak.

2. Another characteristic of the low in the price of bullion is the failure of the various gold share indexes to confirm the new trough in the price of the metal itself.

3. Economically, it would be expected that global recovery would be well under way to the extent that there would be a noticeable pickup in the rate of consumer price inflation.

Also, many commodities will have bottomed out, and bond and stock markets would have been in bull phases for at least 6 months.

4. While it has been typical for the U.S. dollar and the price of gold to move in opposite directions, for economic and financial reasons this is not always the case. A weak dollar is therefore a useful indication for strength in the gold markets, but by no means a necessary one.

CURRENCY MARKET TURNING POINTS

Major turning points in currencies are a lot more difficult to spot since their prices are determined by the interaction of a number of different economic and monetary factors.

However, one fairly sure guide to a major turning point in currencies is the appearance of the progress of any currency in the popular press. This is because economic or financial conditions have usually reached an extreme at such times, causing a sharp movement in price. This dynamic price change attracts attention and since the press is always likely to come up with a reason for market movements, it is able to link these two very newsworthy factors. As discussed earlier, major market turning points occur at financial extremes, so a prominent display by the press is therefore a good indication of a terminal phase of a major currency trend.

A good example occurred in late 1976 when the British government was forced to raise the bank rate by a significant amount in order to reverse the decline in the pound. At that time the almost vertical fall in the currency put it in excellent shape to respond to such strong measures. Similarly, in October 1978 the sharp fall in the U.S. dollar was halted by dramatic measures taken by President Carter. On the other side, stringent currency controls were instituted by the Swiss government in 1978 to discourage investment in Swiss francs, which had been rising dramatically against other major currencies, especially the U.S. dollar.

Clearly, cyclical lows in a currency are established at a time of financial crisis when it seems that the balance of payments is going to deteriorate forever, or when growth in a country's money supply appears to be out of control. Governments are then, usually belatedly, forced to take draconian moves such as raising interest rates or announcing huge foreign loans with which to support the currency.

One factor that separates a temporary peak from a cyclical peak, however, is a government announcement of central bank support operations without some indication of monetary restriction, for it clearly does not make sense to be buying your currency on one hand and permitting money to grow on the other through a policy of monetary expansion.

The characteristics of major turning points in the various markets described above should be used as rough background parameters in the decision-making process. Actual timing should be determined from the principles of technical analysis which are described in Part Two. If an assessment of the background fundamentals is used in conjunction with the technical approach, the probability of superior investment results should be enhanced.

5
ESTABLISHING A GAME PLAN

While it is important to understand the principles of technical analysis which are discussed in Part Two and used in the decision-making process of what and when to buy and sell, it is equally important to establish a general investment philosophy and set some objectives. This approach offers a general framework within which to work and can also be used as a check to make sure everything is going according to plan as far as possible.

1. DETERMINE CAPITAL TO BE INVESTED

The first decision obviously is to determine how much capital is to be invested—and the answer is to invest no more than you can afford to lose. Any market is a very emotional animal, and risking money that you can ill afford to lose interferes with the investment decision-making process. For example, if you are undercapitalized in a particular investment and that investment goes against you, this unexpected development may well cause you to liquidate out of fear, whereas a better financial position will enable a more objective, and therefore correct, decision to be taken.

2. DETERMINE TYPE OF RISK TO BE UNDERTAKEN

Since various markets differ in their degree of volatility, it is useful to determine the type and amount of risk that should be undertaken. Even though financial futures markets are generally less volatile than other futures markets, they are clearly not for everyone. Similarly, some investors may have a reluctance to invest in countries such as Italy which have a reputation of being relatively less stable than other industrialized countries. It is therefore very important to be comfortable going into an investment, otherwise the slightest movement against the position will stimulate an overly emotional response.

3. CHOOSE AN AREA OF SPECIALIZATION

It is important to realize that it is impossible to follow all the various financial markets described here, so do not try. A more sensible approach is to select an area of specialization, such as global stock markets, currencies, or financial futures, and get to know that field well. As you develop knowledge and experience, entry into new markets will come naturally but should never be rushed. Clearly, the area of specialization will depend on personal affinities for risk, but it should be one that is found interesting and should not be chosen just because it offers a greater return on capital or because that particular market is in fashion.

When an investor is considering branching out into new areas, it is a good idea to research well ahead of time the type of investment vehicles available and where they may be obtained. In this way you will find out more about that type of market, and whether or not you have an affinity for it. You will also be in an ideal position to make a move when the time appears appropriate.

Later chapters list many of the chart services available for the various markets. Usually they can be obtained on a free sample or cheap trial basis. Virtually all these services are tax-deductible, so their purchase represents a relatively cheap and efficient way to familiarize yourself with some new markets without the commitment of time.

4. DECIDE ON YOUR INVESTMENT GOAL

One important investment decision that should be taken prior to an investment commitment is to ask yourself what price objectives you have in mind, and over how long a period you intend to hold a particular investment. You should also decide on a cutoff point at which to liquidate your holdings if they should go against you unexpectedly.

Since markets are notoriously difficult to predict, it is more or less impossible to set and achieve specific objectives and time horizons at all times. However, it is possible to make a decision as to whether the investment is likely to be held for 10 or 12 weeks (i.e., for an intermediate period) or whether a longer hold of 6 months to 2 years is more suitable.

5. KEEP TO A REGULAR SCHEDULE

Once the decision to invest has been taken, it is more or less mandatory to decide what information is needed to adequately follow the progress of the investment, and then to set aside 15 or 20 minutes each day without fail to accomplish the necessary charting. It is also a good idea periodically to check your performance against your objectives, and make changes where appropriate. But do not at any time try and make your schedule more complicated than you can adequately handle. If you do, you are clearly overextending your productive capability and should therefore make an attempt at reducing your work load.

6. RECOGNIZE YOUR LIMITATIONS

As you gain experience you should begin to learn whether you are overextending yourself in terms of investments held, time taken to keep up your charts, undercapitalization, etc. It is important to adjust for these factors. The best investment decisions are those made objectively. Only you know how much emotion you can live with. If you find you are following the markets too closely, consider investing for longer periods with longer-term price objectives. In this way you will be able to ride out price corrections with little emotional damage and retain your decision-making reserves for important decisions.

Also remember that technical analysis is an art, not a science. It is far from infallible and depends to a large degree on correct interpretation. If your interpretation proves to be incorrect, or if you are faced with a false signal, reverse your position quickly. Remember also that technical analysis cannot tell you the best market to buy, but it can tell you which markets you are likely to make money in.

PART TWO

TECHNICAL ANALYSIS IN THEORY AND PRACTICE

6
IDENTIFYING TRENDS

This chapter deals with some of the basic principles of technical analysis that are useful for determining *when to buy or sell* a particular financial market. Since technical analysis is really the process of identifying price trends, these principles can be applied to all the financial markets. The outline of technical analysis described here is sufficient to help investors participate successfully in international markets, but further study is recommended if more extensive knowledge of the subject is required.[1]

THREE STAGES OF PRIMARY BULL AND BEAR MARKETS

It may be recalled from Chapter 1 that all markets move in trends, of which there are three types: major, sometimes known as the primary or cyclical trend, which lasts from 1 to 4 years; the intermediate or secondary trend running counter to the major trend and which can last from 3 weeks to as long as 6 months. Finally, there is the day-to-day, or minor trend which is too short to warrant serious investment consideration.

For most markets the major, or primary trend consists of three phases, separated by two intermediate or secondary reactions. These are shown in Figure 6-1.

The first stage occurs when the fundamentals for any given financial asset are still negative. In the case of stocks, for instance, profit reports will still be poor; for gold the rate of price inflation will still be falling; and for a currency the trend in the balance of payments is still likely to

[1] Martin J. Pring, *Technical Analysis Explained,* McGraw-Hill, New York, 1980.

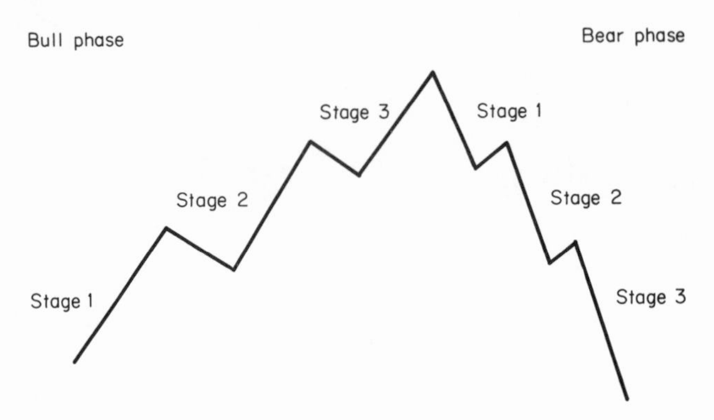

FIGURE 6-1 Stages of cycle.

be negative, and so on. Despite these adverse developments and accompanying bad news, investors at this point are anticipating better times to come and begin accumulating the financial asset in question. This first phase of the bull market quite often follows the last panic stage of the bear market, where forced liquidation due to margin calls and other institutional factors cause prices to fall sharply. In such an environment it is very difficult to accept the fact that the bear market is over, so the first bull market rally is received with widespread disbelief.

Following this initial rally a reaction of an intermediate proportion usually sets in. This secondary movement, which runs counter to the main trend, normally takes the form of a decline but can be represented by a horizontal movement. During this period, predictions of an extended decline taking prices below their previous bear market lows abound, and are usually believed since the news background at this time is poor. Given this discouraging environment, the very fact that the market does hold together during this corrective period is in itself a positive sign that a new bull market is underway.

The second leg of the bull market is fueled by the fulfillment of previous expectations. In the case of the stock market, profits will have started to rise; in the case of gold, the rate of inflation will be accelerating; for interest rates, the economy will be in a recessionary phase. This secondary bull market phase is also followed by a corrective period as doubts about the continuation of the main trend are raised, often as a result of some isolated incident or aberration in some economic or monetary statistics.

The final bull market phase is usually based on a general raising of expectations beyond reality, such as greater profits for equities, more deflationary conditions for bonds, and more inflationary conditions for gold. In this way prices move well ahead of the fundamentals, setting up the potential for considerable disappointment when these expectations fail to materialize. This final stage is often characterized by carelessness and overconfidence on the part of investors who have experienced 1 to 3 years of a rising market and are extrapolating this trend further into the future. This speculative phase is accompanied by a very favorable news background. The fundamentals are usually very favorable too, so it is a time when wild forecasts of substantially higher prices are being made.

Such an environment is typical of a market top. As it becomes clear that such expectations are totally unjustified, the initial downward phase of the bear market begins.

This first down leg is terminated by the development of a bear market rally which is normally extremely deceptive, since the fundamentals and the news background are usually still reasonably favorable at this point. This rally, which is typically quite sharp in nature, peters out as it becomes obvious that the fundamentals are deteriorating, and a renewed decline begins which is in effect the second down leg. This leg is also followed by a substantial rally, which in turn gives way to the third down leg. In most cases, this third phase is characterized by a sharp panic sell-off as the fundamentals deteriorate to a point not previously expected. In the case of interest rates, corporations are placed in a liquidity squeeze since their sales revenues, which are very sensitive to economic conditions, are falling at a faster rate than inventory levels and these can only be adjusted after a considerable time lag. This kind of action puts considerable upward pressure on interest rates as corporations are forced to finance their cash deficiencies at literally any price. With stocks, sharp price declines, associated with the terminal phase of the bear market, reduce the equity in margin accounts, usually resulting in forced liquidation. In the case of gold, economic activity proves to be much weaker than expected and the rate of price inflation declines sharply, sending panic among gold market participants. This final dramatic decline terminates the bear phase, and a new cycle then begins.

While this description typifies the primary movement of prices for financial markets, most of the time there are many exceptions. Occasionally, for example, a final speculative run-up is absent, or a panic phase might occur at the end of the second bear market down leg. The three-phase concept thus should not be used as an inflexible chain of events, but as a basic framework in which to work as it offers a rough guideline to the position of a financial market in its particular cycle. The principles of technical analysis are used to identify the turning points of these primary and intermediate turning points in order to profit from the major portion of each move.

PRICE PATTERNS

So far two trends have been discussed, a rising or bull movement and a declining or bear movement, but there is also a third type of trend and that is a horizontal one. Markets do not normally move straight up and then come straight down again, because changes in the direction of important trends are usually separated by a period when prices fluctuate in a narrow trading band in which buyers and sellers are more or less in balance.

Such a situation is shown in Figure 6-2 where the price action at the bull market peak is contained between two parallel lines constructed by joining the peaks and troughs of the price index in question. Over the years, market technicians have observed that these transitional periods can be identified from the formation and completion of clearly definable price patterns.

The example shown in Figure 6-2 is a price pattern known as a rectangle. The rectangle in effect represents a period in which supply and demand are in balance. Once prices move below the lower boundary of the rectangle, which is known as a *breakout* (line *BB*), the outcome of the battle becomes clear as sellers predominate and prices begin to fall.

Price patterns which separate rising and declining trends are known as *reversal* patterns. Had the outcome in the case described above been decided in favor of the buyers as in Figure 6-3, then the rectangle would really have represented a consolidation of previous gains. Consequently, price patterns that temporarily interrupt a trend are known as *continuation* or *consolidation* patterns.

The examples shown so far have occurred during bull markets, but reversal and continuation patterns also develop during bear markets. Figure 6-4 shows a reversal at the end of a bear market. Since reversal patterns can occur at both ends of a move, they are classified as two types. Where a pattern separates a rising from a falling trend, i.e., at a

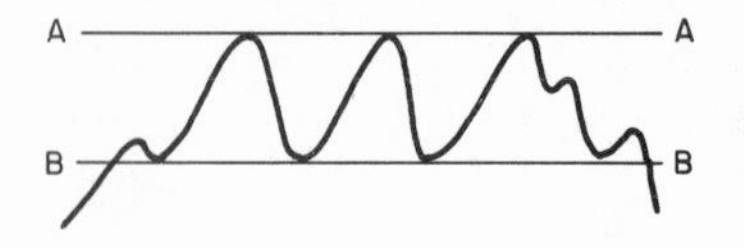

FIGURE 6-2
From *Technical Analysis Explained* by Martin J. Pring. Copyright © 1980 by McGraw-Hill, Inc. Used with the permission of the McGraw-Hill Book Company.

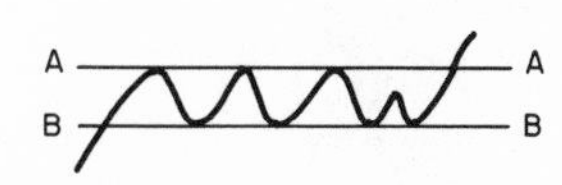

FIGURE 6-3
From *Technical Analysis Explained* by Martin J. Pring. Copyright © 1980 by McGraw-Hill, Inc. Used with the permission of the McGraw-Hill Book Company.

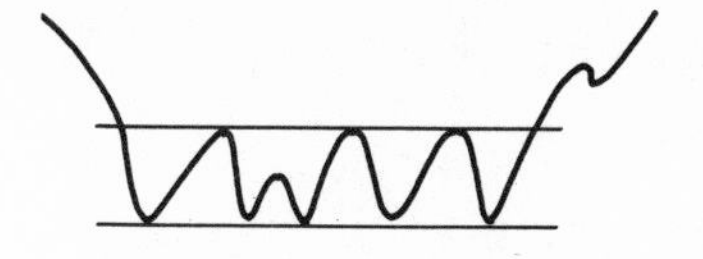

FIGURE 6-4
From *Technical Analysis Explained* by Martin J. Pring. Copyright © 1980 by McGraw-Hill, Inc. Used with the permission of the McGraw-Hill Book Company.

market peak, it is known as a *distribution* pattern. Its counterpart at a bear market bottom is known as an *accumulation* pattern. Distribution implies the transfer of stock or other financial assets from informed holders to the relatively uninformed. The accumulation process consists of such assets moving from weak or unsophisticated hands to more knowledgeable investors, who are prepared to look through the bad news that is inevitably coming out at the time, and who purchase stocks, bonds, or currencies in anticipation of better times.

Figure 6-5, Examples *a* and *b*, illustrates this transitional phase where market forces are roughly in balance. Buyers and sellers in this situation can be compared to two armies engaged in trench warfare. In Figure 6-5, "example *a*, two armies A and B are facing off. Line *AA* represents army A's defense, and *BB* is army B's line of defense. The arrows indicate the forays between the two lines as both armies fight their way to the opposing trench but are unable to penetrate the line of defense. In the second example army B finally pushes through A's trench. Army A is then forced to retreat and make a stand at the second line of defense (line AA_2)."[2]

In the case of financial markets, the two trenches represent the outer

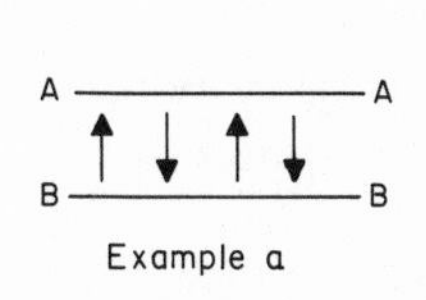

Example a

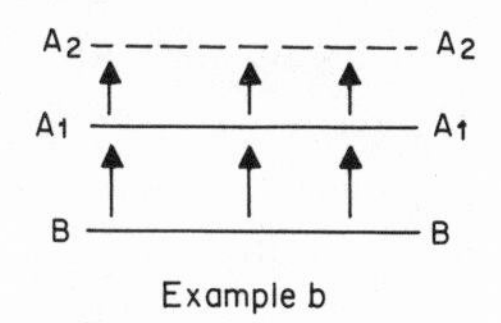

Example b

FIGURE 6-5
From *Technical Analysis Explained* by Martin J. Pring. Copyright © 1980 by McGraw-Hill, Inc. Used with the permission of the McGraw-Hill Book Company.

[2] Martin J. Pring, *Technical Analysis Explained,* McGraw-Hill, New York, 1980, pp. 24–25.

boundaries of the price pattern, the successful penetration of which signals a change in the balance between supply and demand.

In addition to the rectangle there are four other types of reversal pattern that frequently occur. These are the head and shoulders, the double top or bottom, the triangle, and the broadening formation. Before discussing them in more detail it is worth outlining some basic principles which apply to them all.

Pattern Significance The importance of a pattern is a consequence of its size. In effect, the larger a price pattern is in terms of its size (i.e., the time taken to complete it) and its depth (i.e., the degree of price fluctuation between high and low points of the pattern), the greater is its significance. For example, a rectangle that takes only 2 to 3 weeks to complete is unlikely to be separating a primary bull and bear market, in contrast to one that is formed over a longer period such as 6 months or more, which indicates that a very significant battle has taken place between buyers and sellers. When one side is able to overcome the other, the event is therefore of far greater importance.

Measuring Implications Most tools used in technical analysis indicate the direction of prices, not the magnitude of the swing. In the case of most price patterns, however, it is possible to derive certain measuring implications. It should be emphasized that such price objectives are only minimum objectives, for quite often prices extend much further. Figure 6-6 shows the measuring formula for a rectangle. This is derived by taking the vertical distance between the two parallel lines and extending that same distance down (or up in the case of a bull market) from the point at which prices break out of the rectangle. Quite often such objectives prove to be support or resistance levels in subsequent moves, as shown in Figure 6-6, Example *c* and Example *d*.

A support level may be defined as "Buying, actual or potential, sufficient in volume to halt a downtrend in prices for an appreciable period,"[3] and resistance as ". . . selling, actual or potential, sufficient in volume to satisfy all bids and hence stop prices from going higher for a time."[4]

In effect, a support level represents a *concentration* of supply. The

[3] Robert D. Edwards and John Magee, *Technical Analysis of Stock Trends,* John Magee, Springfield, Mass., 1957.

[4] Ibid.

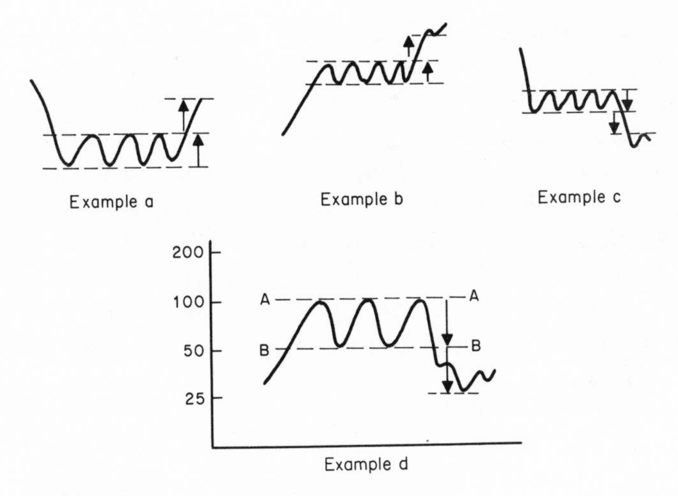

FIGURE 6-6
From *Technical Analysis Explained* by Martin J. Pring. Copyright © 1980 by McGraw-Hill, Inc. Used with the permission of the McGraw-Hill Book Company.

word "concentration" is stressed because supply and demand are always in balance, but it is their relative strength or concentration which determines the price level. The outer boundaries of price patterns can be said to represent support and resistance levels, the violation of which indicates that the concentration of demand or supply has effectively been overcome.

One significant aspect of support or resistance points worth noting is that former support levels, once penetrated, become resistance areas on any rally, and resistance levels turn into support levels during reactions. This characteristic is shown in Figure 6-7.

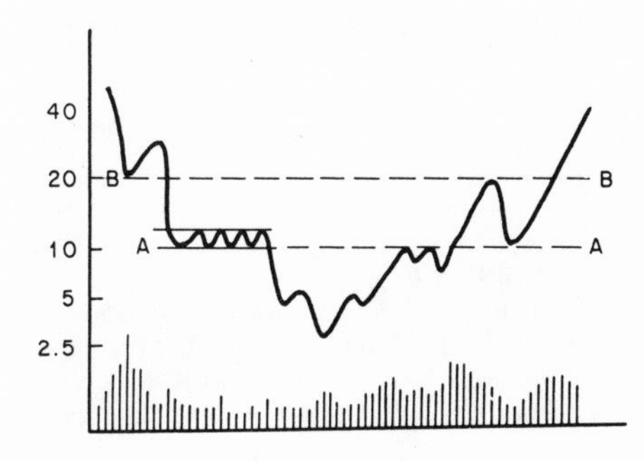

FIGURE 6-7
From *Technical Analysis Explained* by Martin J. Pring. Copyright © 1980 by McGraw-Hill, Inc. Used with the permission of the McGraw-Hill Book Company.

Confirmation of a Valid Breakout It has so far been assumed that any move out of a price pattern, however miniscule, has constituted a valid signal of a trend reversal (or a resumption if the pattern is one of consolidation). Since misleading moves known as "whipsaws" occasionally develop, it is important to set up certain criteria in order to minimize or filter out such misrepresentations of the genuine trend.

In this connection it has been found empirically useful to wait for a 3 percent penetration of the boundaries of price patterns before drawing the conclusion that the breakout is valid. Although the signals are by definition less timely, this procedure usually filters out a substantial number of such misleading moves and therefore results in a more profitable overall strategy.

Return Moves In a substantial number of cases, the initial breakout from a price pattern is accompanied by a reaction in the opposite direction to that indicated by the breakout itself. This correction, known as a "return move," is quite normal and gives investors the additional opportunity to purchase or liquidate the financial asset concerned before the main trend begins in earnest. A prime characteristic of such movements is the sharp contraction in volume. Examples of return moves are illustrated in Figure 6-8.

Volume Characteristics Where volume figures are available, they should also be used in the analysis. Volume in technical analysis is usually thought of as a relative concept. Consequently, volume is considered to be high only in relation to a recent period.

In 1978, for example, 30 million-share days on the New York Stock Exchange were not uncommon, yet compared to turnover 50 years before of less than 5 million, 30 million shares would appear substantial. For technical analysis such comparisons are of little significance. However, if the volume during formation of a price pattern were to rise from

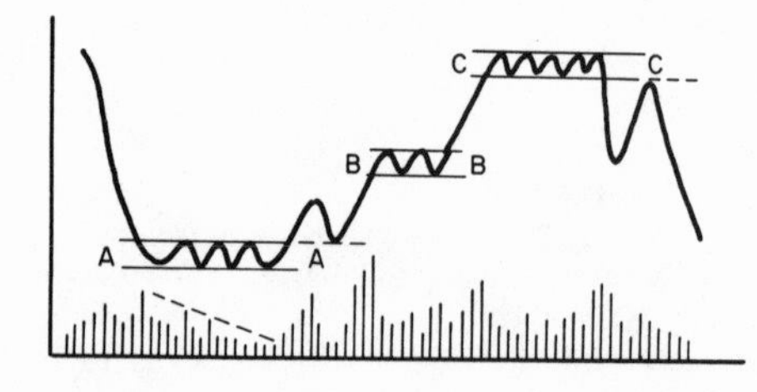

FIGURE 6-8
From *Technical Analysis Explained* by Martin J. Pring. Copyright © 1980 by McGraw-Hill, Inc. Used with the permission of the McGraw-Hill Book Company.

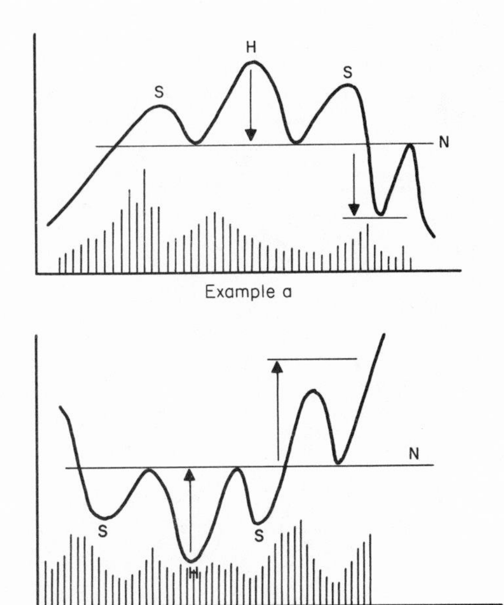

FIGURE 6-9
From *Technical Analysis Explained* by Martin J. Pring. Copyright © 1980 by McGraw-Hill, Inc. Used with the permission of the McGraw-Hill Book Company.

20 to 30 million shares, for instance, this would be regarded as heavy volume, and vice versa. As a general principle volume goes with the trend and, consequently, rising prices should be accompanied by expanding volume. If a rally is accompanied by a falling level of volume, this is normally a bearish sign. Alternatively, if an initial decline takes place on expanding volume, this is also abnormal and adds to the bearishness of the decline, whereas expanding volume after substantial price weakness has set in often indicates a selling climax, which usually marks a temporary bottom at least.

HEAD AND SHOULDERS PATTERN

Perhaps the most notorious and reliable reversal pattern is the head and shoulders formation. This pattern occurs at both bull market peaks and bear market bottoms. At major bottoms it is known as an inverted head and shoulders pattern. Both types are shown in Figure 6-9, Examples *a* and *b*. The head and shoulders distribution pattern consists of a "head" (the final bull market rally and first bear market decline) separated by two smaller rallies, the left and right shoulders. In effect, the right shoulder is the first bear market rally. When prices break below the line join-

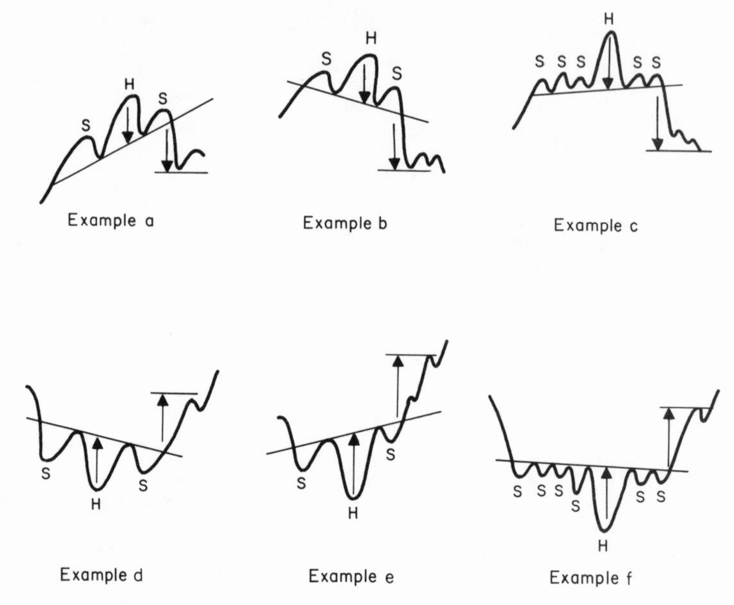

FIGURE 6-10
From *Technical Analysis Explained* by Martin J. Pring. Copyright © by McGraw-Hill, Inc. Used with the permission of the McGraw-Hill Book Company.

ing the bases of the two shoulders (known as the "neckline"), a signal of a reversal in trend is given. The measuring objective for a head and shoulders pattern is the distance between the top of the head and the neckline projected downward from the neckline in the case of a distribution pattern. In the case of an inverted head and shoulders, the distance between the head and the neckline is projected upwards. These measuring objectives are shown in Figure 6-9.

Examples *a* and *b* in Figure 6-9 show head and shoulders patterns with horizontal necklines, but such formations can also develop from rising or falling necklines (Figure 6-10). The patterns are valid as long as the head is higher (or in the case of an inverted head and shoulders, lower) than the two shoulders. It is not necessary for the pattern to be perfectly symmetrical, i.e., the two shoulders having equal height or proportion.

Occasionally a head and shoulders pattern appears to be forming, or actually is formed, and then prices reverse direction and continue along their previous trend. Such situations where a head and shoulders pattern "does not work" are usually indicative that a final move in the prevailing trend is about to take place. Such a move is usually sharp and dynamic. In bull markets they often represent the final, speculative blow off stage, or in the case of an inverted head and shoulders failure, the resulting decline represents a final bear market selling climax or panic stage. Such failures are rare, but when they occur they should be treated with the utmost respect.

During the formation of a head and shoulders top, volume is heaviest during the development of the head and left shoulder. The right shoulder is almost always accompanied by a notable decline in volume which indicates a lack of enthusiasm by buyers. The downside breakout below the neckline can be accompanied by either high or low volume, but the return move toward the neckline almost always occurs on low volume. For an inverted head and shoulders, the most important factor is that the upside breakout should occur on high volume. Such a development emphasizes that the balance between buyers and sellers has decisively turned in favor of buyers. A breakout on low volume is therefore suspect.

DOUBLE TOPS AND DOUBLE BOTTOMS

Examples of a double top and double bottom are shown in Figure 6-11, Examples *a* and *b*. A double top (Example *a*) is essentially two rallies separated by a reaction. When the reaction from the second peak moves below the previous decline, a reversal in the price trend is indicated. The second peak may be slightly higher or lower than the first, but it is usually accompanied by distinctly lower volume. The measuring objec-

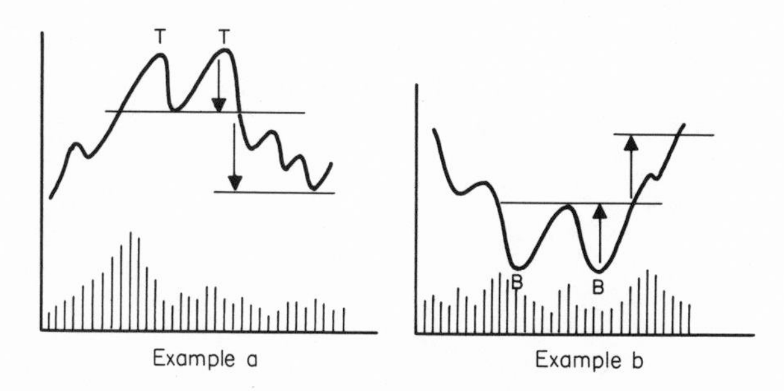

FIGURE 6-11
From *Technical Analysis Explained* by Martin J. Pring. Copyright © 1980 by McGraw-Hill, Inc. Used with the permission of the McGraw-Hill Book Company.

tive is the distance between the highest peak and bottom of the reaction separating them projected downward, as indicated in Figure 6-11.

A double bottom (Example *b*) is really the opposite of a double top. The second bottom is often accompanied by substantially lower volume than the first in a similar manner to that which characterizes double tops. Figure 6-11, Example *b*, also illustrates the measuring implication for a double bottom, which is derived by taking the distance between the lowest bottom and the peak of the rally separating the two reactions, and projecting that upward from the peak of that rally.

BROADENING FORMATIONS

Broadening formations occur where a series of three or more price fluctuations widen out in size so that the peaks and troughs can be connected by two diverging trendlines, as shown in Figure 6-12. In a sense, the broadening formation is the opposite of a symmetrical triangle (discussed later) where the lines converge.

There are basically two types of broadening formation, the "orthodox," as shown in Figure 6-12, and the "flattened" variety, illustrated in Figure 6-13, Examples *a* and *b*. Orthodox formations occur only at market peaks, and are relatively difficult to detect until sometime after the final top has been formed, since there is no clearly definable level of support whose violation could serve as a benchmark. In view of the violent and emotional nature of price swings, a breakout is difficult to pinpoint, but if the formation is reasonably symmetrical, a 3 percent move below the declining trendline (*AA* in Figure 6-12,) usually serves as a timely warning that an even greater decline is in store.

The flattened variety, which is easier to detect, occurs far more frequently and is usually extremely reliable. The patterns shown in Figure 6-13, Examples *a* and *b*, are similar to the head and shoulders variety, except that the "head" of the broadening formation is always the last to

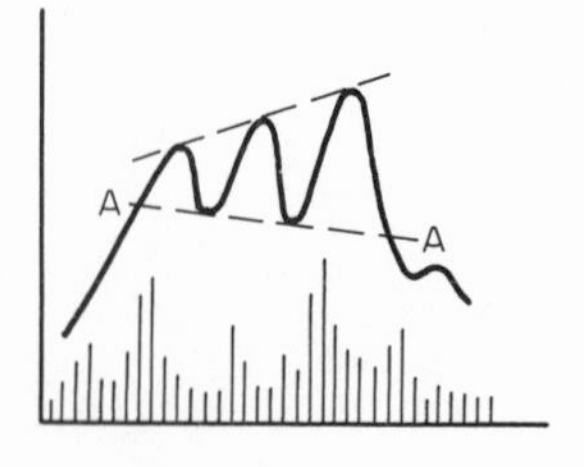

FIGURE 6-12
From *Technical Analysis Explained* by Martin J. Pring. Copyright © 1980 by McGraw-Hill, Inc. Used with the permission of the McGraw-Hill Book Company.

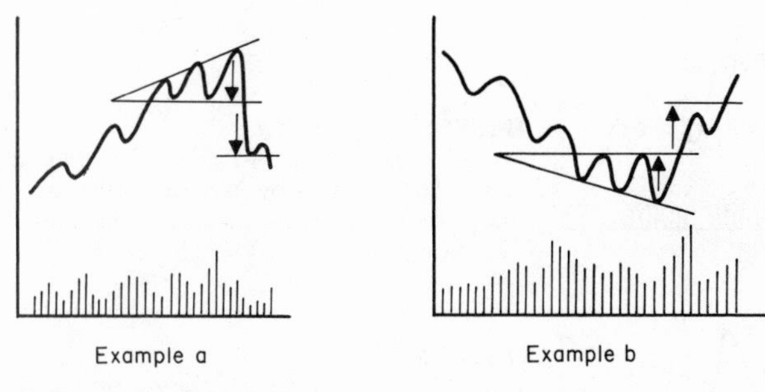

FIGURE 6-13
From *Technical Analysis Explained* by Martin J. Pring. Copyright © 1980 by McGraw-Hill, Inc. Used with the permission of the McGraw-Hill Book Company.

FIGURE 6-14
From *Technical Analysis Explained* by Martin J. Pring. Copyright © 1980 by McGraw-Hill, Inc. Used with the permission of the McGraw-Hill Book Company.

be formed. Breakouts occur when the "flattened" trendline is violated. In the cases of both types of reversal pattern, the breakout usually signals that a very sharp and powerful move (commensurate with the size of the pattern) is about to take place. Broadening formations can also occur as continuation patterns, as shown in Figure 6-14.

TRIANGLES

For purposes of analysis triangles are divided into two groups, symmetrical and right-angled. The following passage from *Technical Analysis Explained* describes their behavior.[5]

[5] Extract from *Technical Analysis Explained* by Martin J. Pring, pp. 47–48. Copyright ©1980 by McGraw-Hill, Inc. Reprinted by permission of the McGraw-Hill Book Company.

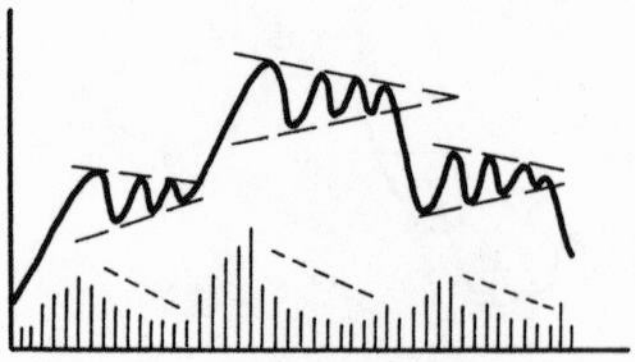

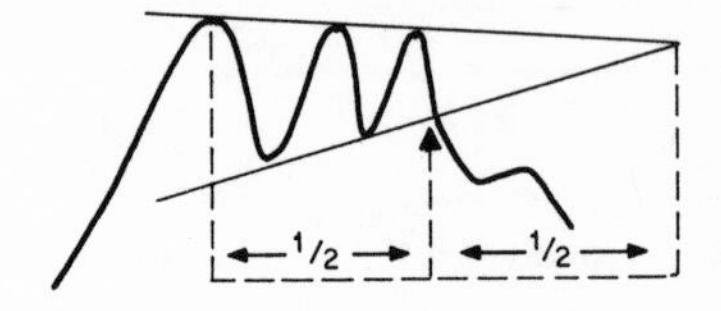

FIGURE 6-15
From *Technical Analysis Explained* by Martin J. Pring. Copyright © 1980 by McGraw-Hill, Inc. Used with the permission of the McGraw-Hill Book Company.

FIGURE 6-16
From *Technical Analysis Explained* by Martin J. Pring. Copyright © by Martin J. Pring. Copyright © 1980 by McGraw-Hill, Inc. Used with the permission of the McGraw-Hill Book Company.

Symmetrical Triangles A symmetrical triangle is composed of a series of two or more rallies and reactions where each succeeding peak is lower than its predecessor [see Figure 6-15] and the bottom from each succeeding reaction is higher than its predecessor. A triangle is therefore the opposite of a broadening formation, since the trendlines joining peaks and troughs *converge,* unlike the (orthodox) broadening formation, where they *diverge*.

These patterns are also known as "coils," for the fluctuation in price and volume diminishes as the pattern is completed. Finally, both price and (usually) volume react sharply, as if a coil spring had been wound tighter and tighter and then snapped free as prices broke out of the triangle. Generally speaking, triangles seem to "work" best when the breakout occurs somewhere between half and three-fourths of the distance between the widest peak and rally and the apex (as in [Figure 6-16]).

The volume and 3 percent confirmation rules used for other patterns are also appropriate for triangles.

Right-Angled Triangles Right-angled triangles are really a special form of the symmetrical type in that one of the two boundaries is formed at an angle of 90 degrees, i.e., horizontal to the vertical axis. (These triangle variations are illustrated in [Figure 6-17].) Whereas the symmetrical triangle gives no indication of which way it is ultimately likely to break, the right-angled triangle, with its implied level of support or resistance and contracting price fluctuations, does. One difficulty in interpreting these formations is that many rectangles begin as right-angled triangles,

Example a

Example b

FIGURE 6-17
From *Technical Analysis Explained* by Martin J. Pring. Copyright © 1980 by McGraw-Hill, Inc. Used with the permission of the McGraw-Hill Book Company.

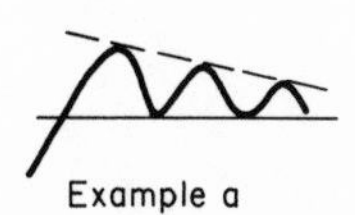

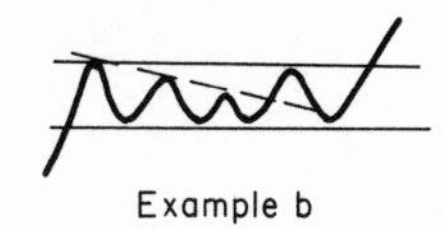

FIGURE 6-18
From *Technical Analysis Explained* by Martin J. Pring. Copyright © 1980 by McGraw-Hill, Inc. Used with the permission of the McGraw-Hill Book Company.

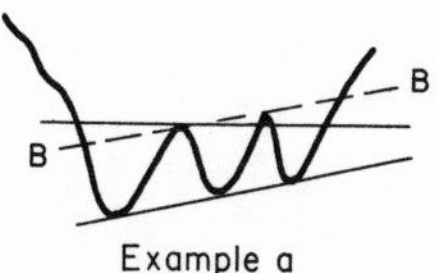

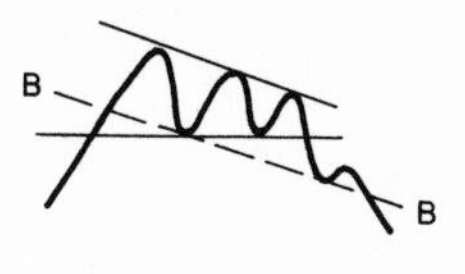

B B
Example b

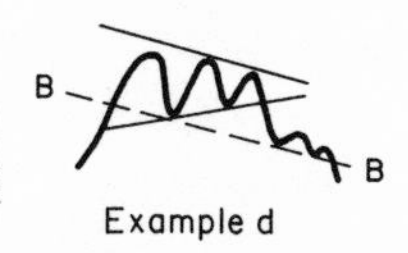

FIGURE 6-19
From *Technical Analysis Explained* by Martin J. Pring. Copyright © 1980 by McGraw-Hill, Inc. Used with the permission of theMcGraw-Hill Book Company.

so considerable caution should be used when interpreting these elusive patterns. Such a situation is shown in [Figure 6-18] where a potential downward sloping right-angled triangle in example (*a*) develops into a rectangle in example (*b*).

Measuring objectives for triangles are obtained by drawing a line parallel to the base of the triangle through the peak of the first rally. This line [*BB* in Figure 6-19] represents the price objective which prices may be expected to reach or exceed.

The reverse procedure at market tops is shown in examples *c* and *d*. The same technique is used to project prices when prices are of the consolidation variety.

7
MORE PRINCIPLES OF TREND DETERMINATION

Some further devices for determining price trends will be described in this chapter. The investor can use these to analyze all financial markets. The techniques discussed here help to clarify the decision-making process where investment opportunities are concerned. The concept of "relative strength" is used to indicate *what* to buy and sell, while other techniques described below answer the question *when* to buy and sell.

TRENDLINES

Close observation of the price action of any financial market will indicate that in a rising (falling) market it is often possible to join the bottoms (tops) of succeeding troughs (rallies) with a line. These lines, known as trendlines, are indicated in Figure 7-1, Examples *a* and *b*. When a price reaction in a bull market takes an index below its rising trendline, the implication is either that the trend itself has been reversed or that a period of consolidation will take place, which will eventually result in the resumption of the previous trend but at a reduced rate.

Figure 7-2 Examples *a* and *b*, demonstrates these possibilities. Unfortunately, there is no way of knowing at the time whether the trendline break is of the reversal or consolidation type. Quite often, valuable clues can be gleaned from some of the principles governing trendline analysis which are discussed below, or by observing the maturity of the primary bull or bear market. Clearly, the longer the primary trend has been operating, the greater is the likelihood that the trendline break indicates a major reversal. Should the break prove to be a temporary interruption

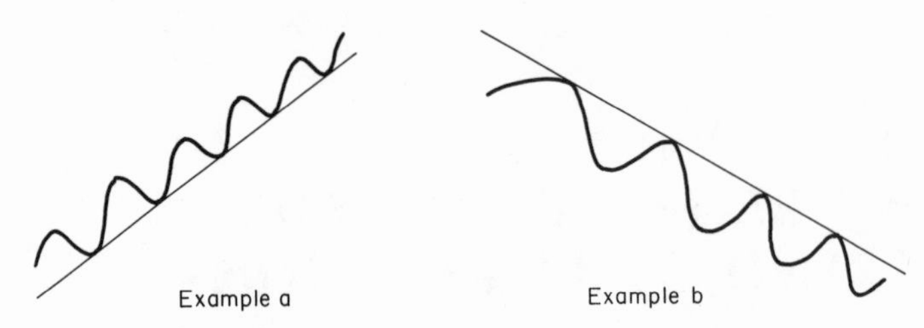

FIGURE 7-1
From *Technical Analysis Explained* by Martin J. Pring. Copyright © 1980 by McGraw-Hill, Inc. Used with the permission of the McGraw-Hill Book Company.

of the main trend, then whenever the index in question achieves a new cyclical high, a new trendline is drawn from the bottom of the bear market to the bottom of the most recent reaction. This is shown as the dashed line *AB* in Figure 7-2, Example *b*. The reverse is of course valid for bear markets.

Sometimes a trendline break occurs at the same time as the breakout from a price pattern. In such cases it is more apparent that the trendline violation is the reversal rather than the consolidation type, so that the price pattern and trendline breaks have the effect of reinforcing each other. Figures 7-3, 7-4, and 7-5 show such phenomena for bull and bear markets.

As with price patterns, trendline breaks are often accompanied by return moves. If the trendline is extended beyond the point of violation, the return move will often be reversed as it again touches the extended trendline. Such instances are illustrated in Figure 7-6, Examples *a* and *b*.

Trendlines can also offer a form of measuring objective. The potential price movement is obtained by ascertaining the vertical distance be-

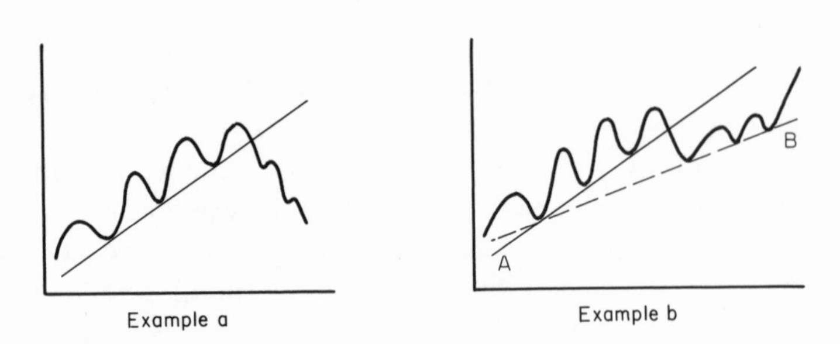

FIGURE 7-2
From *Technical Analysis Explained* by Martin J. Pring. Copyright © 1980 by McGraw-Hill, Inc. Used with the permission of the McGraw-Hill Book Company.

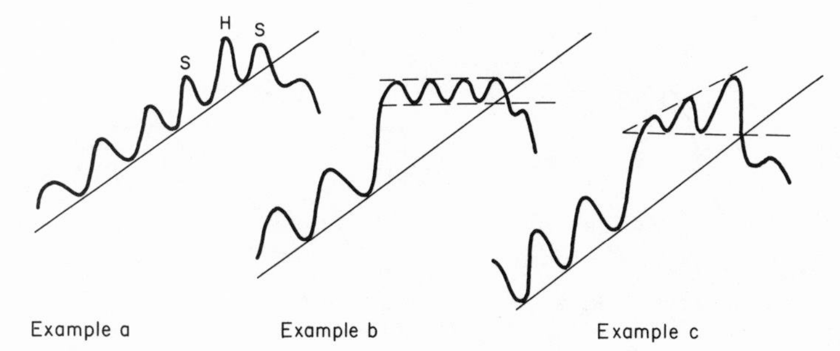

FIGURE 7-3
From *Technical Analysis Explained* by Martin J. Pring. Copyright © 1980 by McGraw-Hill, Inc. Used with the permission of the McGraw-Hill Book Company.

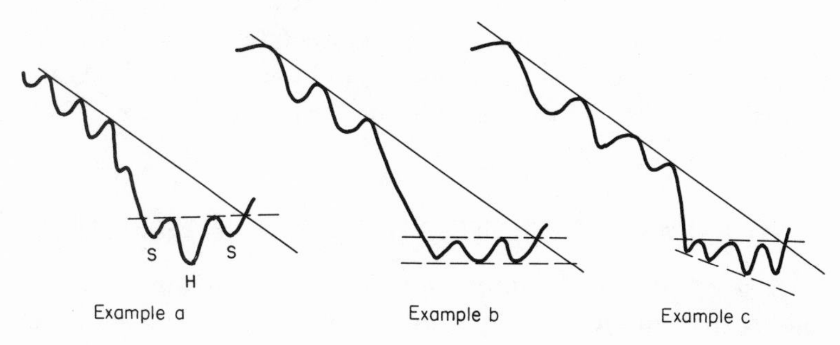

FIGURE 7-4
From *Technical Analysis Explained* by Martin J. Pring. Copyright © 1980 by McGraw-Hill, Inc. Used with the permission of the McGraw-Hill Book Company.

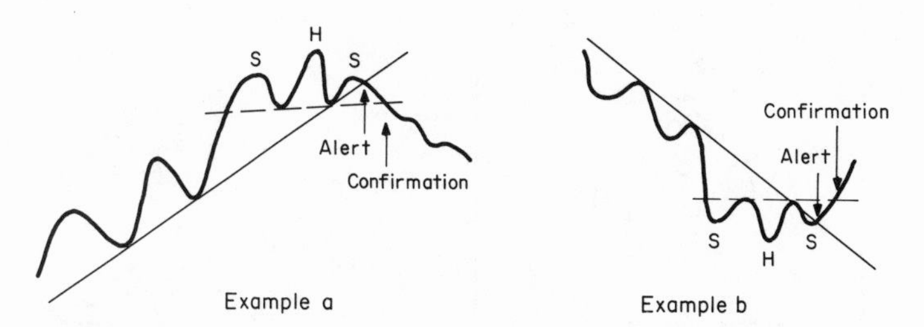

FIGURE 7-5
From *Technical Analysis Explained* by Martin J. Pring. Copyright © 1980 by McGraw-Hill, Inc. Used with the permission of the McGraw-Hill Book Company.

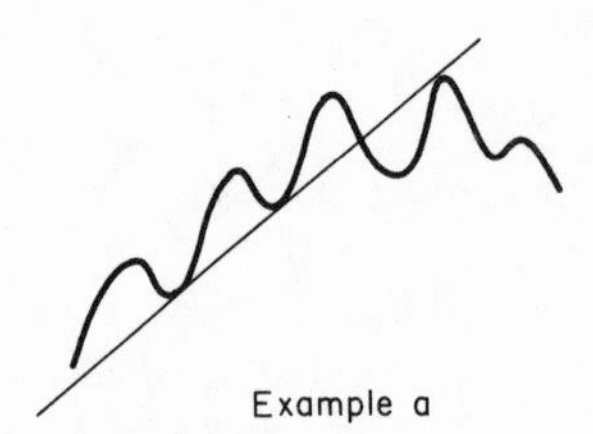

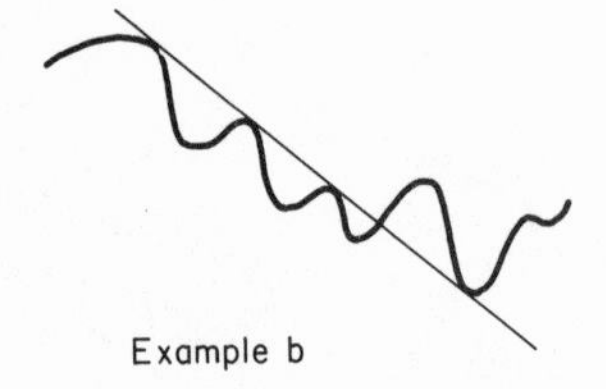

FIGURE 7-6
From *Technical Analysis Explained* by Martin J. Pring. Copyright © 1980 by McGraw-Hill, Inc. Used with the permission of the McGraw-Hill Book Company.

tween the highest peak of the index in a bull market and the trendline at that particular point, and projecting that vertical distance downward at the point where the trendline is violated. Figure 7-7 illustrates some examples for both bull and bear markets. Note how prices can often exceed their objectives, but the subsequent reaction is then reversed at the theoretically projected objective, which then becomes an important support or resistance point. Examples *a* and *b* in Figure 7-7 show this.

Trendlines obtain their significance from three aspects.

NUMBER OF TIMES A TRENDLINE HAS BEEN TOUCHED

Since a trendline is a simple device for identifying a price trend, it follows that the greater the number of times it has been touched, the more likely it is to represent a true reflection of that trend. Violation of a line that has been touched three or four times is therefore of far greater significance than one that has only been touched twice. The fact that prices inevitably react a number of times on contact with the trendline in effect demonstrates that the line itself is a significant support or resistance point.

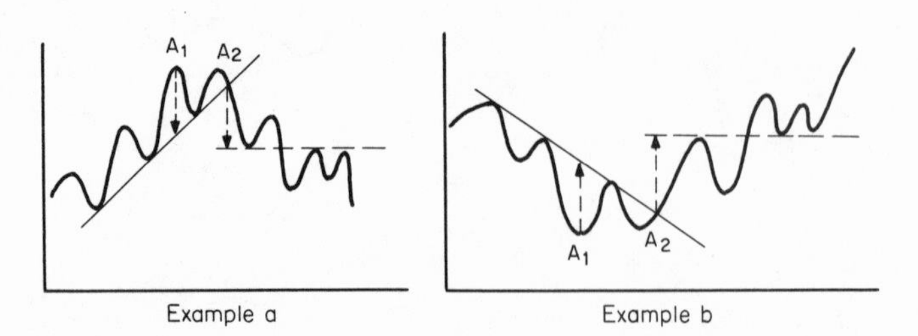

FIGURE 7-7
From *Technical Analysis Explained* by Martin J. Pring. Copyright © 1980 by McGraw-Hill, Inc. Used with the permission of the McGraw-Hill Book Company.

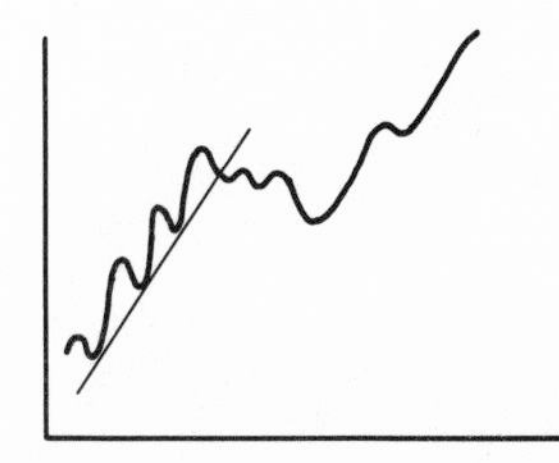

FIGURE 7-8
From *Technical Analysis Explained* by Martin J. Pring. Copyright © 1980 by McGraw-Hill, Inc. Used with the permission of the McGraw-Hill Book Company.

STEEPNESS OF A TRENDLINE

Generally speaking, the steeper a trendline is, the less sustainable the trend it is measuring is likely to be. Consequently, violation of a steep trendline does not carry the same significance as one with a more gentle slope. Such penetrations tend to be of the continuation rather than of the reversal type. Steep trends often occur during the critical initial stages in a bull market, as shown in Figure 7-8. The low point of the subsequent reaction is then used as a basis for the construction of a less steep, but more sustainable trend.

LENGTH OF A TRENDLINE

Significance of a trendline penetration depends on the length of time it has remained intact. This rule arises from a basic technical principle that the longer and greater a price movement is, the longer and greater the corresponding trend in the opposite direction is likely to be. Since a trendline identifies the length of a trend, it follows that the significance of its penetration will be a direct function of its length. Thus, violation of a trendline that has been in existence over a 2- to 3-year period will likely signal a reversal in the primary trend, whereas penetration of a trendline based on a 10- to 12-week movement, being of shorter duration, will suggest an intermediate or secondary reaction.

A trendline is perhaps the easiest technical tool to understand, but its construction and interpretation require a considerable amount of practice. Generally speaking, the significance will be greater in relation to how obvious the construction is.

MOVING AVERAGES

A moving average (MA) is a statistical technique used for smoothing out price fluctuations of financial markets. The objective of moving average calculation is identical to that of trendline construction, i.e., to isolate a

TABLE 7-1*

Date		*Index*	*10-week total*	*Moving average*
Jan.	8	101		
	15	100		
	22	103		
	29	99		
Feb.	5	96		
	12	99		
	19	95		
	26	91		
Mar.	5	93		
	12	89	966	96.6
	19	90	955	95.5
	26	95	950	95.0
April	2	103	950	95.0

* From *Technical Analysis Explained* by Martin J. Pring. Copyright © 1980 by McGraw-Hill, Inc. Used with the permission of McGraw-Hill Book Company.

price trend and to find a reliable method of identifying its reversal at an early stage.

A moving average is constructed by totaling a set of data, and dividing that total by the number of observations. The resulting number is known as the *average* or *mean average.* In order to get the average to move, a new item of data is added, and the first item on the previous list is subtracted. The new total is then divided by the number of observations, and the process is then continually repeated.

For example, if the calculation of a 10-week moving average was required, the method would be as shown in Table 7-1.

On March 9 the total of the weeks ending on that date was 966, and 966 divided by 10 results in an average of 96.6. On March 19 the number 90 is added, and the observation of 101 on January 8 is deleted. The new total of 955 is then divided by 10 and plotted on the chart.

Changes in the direction of a trend are identified when the price index crosses above or below its moving average. If the MA is flat or has already changed direction, its violation by the price index in question is fairly conclusive proof that the previous trend has been reversed.

If the violation occurs while the MA is still proceeding in the direction of the prevailing trend, this development should really be treated as a preliminary warning that a trend reversal has taken place. Confirmation should await a flattening or change in direction in the moving average itself, or should be sought from an alternative technical source.

Since a moving average is an attempt to identify a trend, it will often act as a support or resistance level, as in the case of an important trendline. Violation of a moving average will therefore have greater significance the more times that it has been touched by the price index.

Moving averages can be constructed to cover any time span, but the longer the period for which an MA is constructed, the longer the trend that it is monitoring, and therefore the greater will be the significance of its penetration.

Crossovers from moving averages constructed from some time spans have historically produced more reliable signals than those constructed from others. Usually 40-week or 30-week MAs have proved useful for identifying cyclical or primary movements, and 13-week or 10-week MAs for intermediate or secondary movements.

RATE OF CHANGE OR MOMENTUM

So far the trend determination techniques discussed have been concerned with movements in the actual price index itself, and have confirmed reversals in trend after they have taken place. The concept of momentum helps to isolate subtle strength or weakness in a price index ahead of its ultimate trough or peak.

The concept of momentum can be understood through a simple example. When a ball is thrown into the air, it begins its trajectory at a very fast pace, i.e., it possesses strong momentum. Gradually the speed with which the ball travels upward becomes distinctly slower, until it finally comes to a temporary standstill before the force of gravity causes it to reverse its course. This slowing-down process, known as a loss of upward momentum, is also a phenomenon of the stock market. If the flight of a ball is equated to a price index of the stock market, the rate of advance in the index begins to slow down noticeably before the ultimate peak in prices is reached.

On the other hand, if a ball is thrown in a room and hits the ceiling while its momentum is still rising, the ball and the momentum will reverse at the same time. Unfortunately, momentum indexes in the stock market are not dissimilar, since sometimes momentum and price peak simultaneously as either a ceiling of selling resistance is met, or buying power is temporarily exhausted. In such instances momentum as a lead indicator is not a particularly useful concept, although under such conditions the level of momentum is often as helpful as its direction in assessing the quality of a price trend.

The idea of downward momentum may be better understood by comparing it to a car being pushed over the top of a hill. As the gradient of the hill steepens, the car begins to pick up speed, and finally at the bottom it hits maximum speed. Although its speed decreases, the car continues traveling until it finally comes to a halt. Stock prices in a declining trend act in a similar fashion, since the rate of decline (or loss of momentum) often slows ahead of the final low in stock prices. This is not always the case, since momentum and price sometimes turn together (as at peaks) as prices meet a major level of support. Nevertheless, this concept of momentum leading price occurs sufficiently often to be useful in warning of a potential trend reversal in the indicator or market average which is being monitored.

TABLE 7-2*

Date	*DJIA (1)*	*DJIA 10 weeks ago (2)*	*10-week rate of change (col. 1 + col. 2) (3)*
Jan. 1	985		
8	980		
15	972		
22	975		
29	965		
Feb. 5	967		
12	972		
19	965		
26	974		
Mar. 5	980		
12	965	985	98.0
19	960	980	98.0
26	950	972	97.7
Apr. 2	960	975	98.5
9	965	965	100.0
16	970	967	100.3
23	974	972	100.2
30	980	965	101.6
May 7	985	974	101.1

* From *Technical Analysis Explained* by Martin J. Pring. Copyright © 1980 by McGraw-Hill, Inc. Used with the permission of McGraw-Hill Book Company.

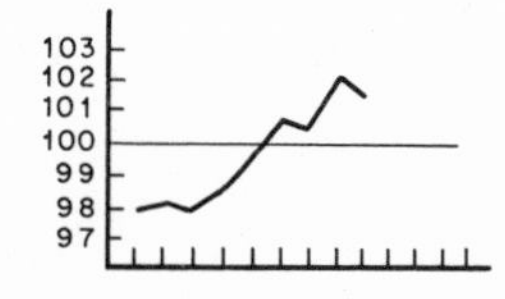

FIGURE 7-9
From *Technical Analysis Explained* by Martin J. Pring. Copyright © 1980 by McGraw-Hill, Inc. Used with the permission of the McGraw-Hill Book Company.

The simplest method of measuring momentum is to calculate the rate at which a market average, or other financial series, changes price over a given period of time. To construct an index measuring a 10-week rate of change, for example, the current price is divided by the price 10 weeks ago. If the latest price is 965 and the price 10 weeks ago was 985, the rate of change or momentum index will read 98.0, that is, 965 ÷ 985. The subsequent reading in the index would be calculated by dividing next week's price by the price 9 weeks ago from today (see Table 7-2). The result is an index that oscillates around a central reference point that marks the level at which the price is unchanged from its reading 10 weeks ago (Figure 7-9). Consequently, if a calculation were being made of the momentum of a market average that did not change price, its momentum index would be represented as a straight line.

When a momentum index is above the reference line, the market average which it is measuring is higher than its level 10 weeks ago.

If the momentum index is also rising, it is evident that the difference between the current reading of the market average and its level 10 weeks ago is growing. If the momentum index is above the central line but is declining, the market average is still above its level 10 weeks ago but the difference between the two readings is shrinking.

When the momentum index is below its central line and falling, this indicates that the market average is below its level 10 weeks ago, and the difference between the two is growing. When it is below its central line but rising, the market average is still below its level 10 weeks ago, but its rate of decline is slowing.

In short, a rising rate-of-change index implies a growth in momentum, and a falling index a loss of momentum. Rising momentum should be interpreted as a bullish factor and declining momentum as a bearish one.

There are two methods of scaling a rate-of-change chart. Since the choice does not affect the trend or level of the index, the method used is not important; but in view of the fact that the two alternatives are often found to be confusing, a brief explanation is in order.

The first method is the one described above and shown in Figure 7-9,

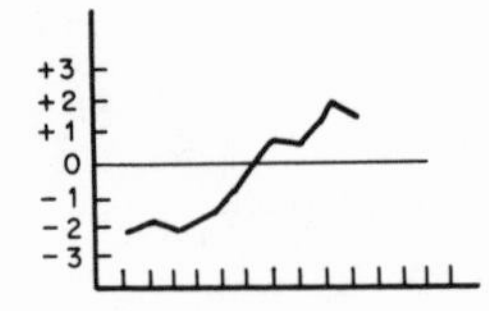

FIGURE 7-10
From *Technical Analysis Explained* by Martin J. Pring. Copyright © 1980 by McGraw-Hill, Inc. Used with the permission of the McGraw-Hill Book Company.

where 100 becomes the central reference point. In the example, 100 (this week's observation) divided by 99 (the observation 10 weeks ago) is plotted as 101, 100 divided by 98 as 102, 100 divided by 102 as 98, and so on.

The alternative is to take the difference between the index and the 100 level and plot the result as a positive or a negative number, using a reference line of 0. In this case, 101 would be plotted as $^+1$, 102 as $^+2$, 98 as -2, and so on (see Figure 7-10).

The momentum index is usually plotted below the indicator it is measuring, as shown in Figure 7-11. The example of the ball used earlier showed that maximum momentum was obtained fairly close to the point when the ball leaves the hand. In a similar fashion, stock prices usually reach their maximum level of momentum reasonably close to the bear market bottom.

In Figure 7-11 this is shown as point *A*. If the stock index makes a new high which is confirmed by the momentum index, no indication of technical weakness arises. On the other hand, should the momentum index fail to confirm (point *B*), a negative divergence is set up between the two indexes, and a warning of a weakening technical structure is given. Usually, such discrepancies indicate that prices are likely to undergo a corrective process, which can either be sideways or (more likely) downward. However, an index will sometimes continue upward to a third top accompanied by even greater weakness in the momentum index. Alter-

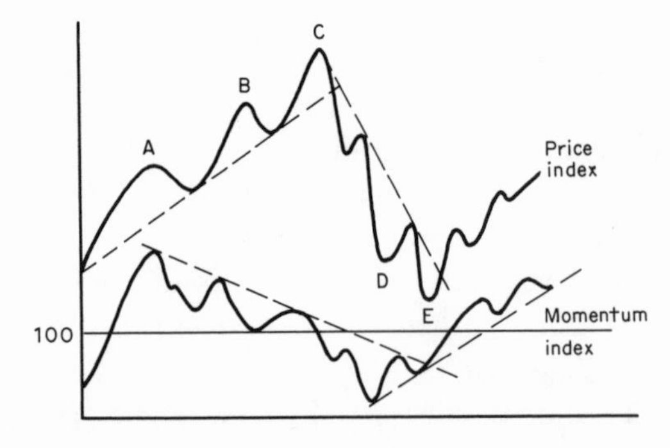

FIGURE 7-11
From *Technical Analysis Explained* by Martin J. Pring. Copyright © 1980 by McGraw-Hill, Inc. Used with the permission of the McGraw-Hill Book Company.

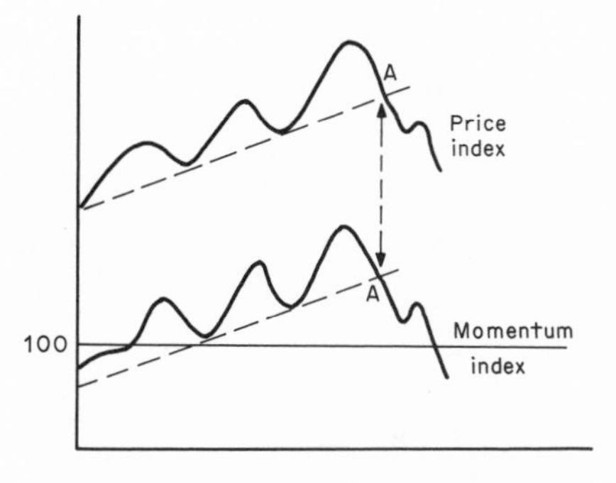

FIGURE 7-12
From *Technical Analysis Explained* by Martin J. Pring. Copyright © 1980 by McGraw-Hill, Inc. Used with the permission of the McGraw-Hill Book Company.

natively, the third peak in the momentum peak may be higher than the second but still lower than the first. Under either circumstance extreme caution is called for, since this characteristic is a distinct warning that a sharp reversal in price or a long corrective period may soon get under way.

Whenever any divergence between momentum and price occurs, it is essential to wait for confirmation from the price index that its trend has also been reversed. This confirmation can be achieved by (1) violation of a simple trendline, as shown in Figure 7-11; (2) crossover of a moving average; or (3) completion of a price pattern. This form of insurance is well worth taking, since during a long cyclical advance (such as the 1962–1966 U.S. equity bull market) it is not unknown for an index to continually lose and regain momentum without suffering a break in trend.

The same principles of divergence are also applicable following price declines. In Figure 7-11 the index makes a new low at point *E,* but the momentum index does not. This evidence of technical strength was later confirmed when the price index rose above its bear market trendline.

At times when the momentum index peaks simultaneously with price (as shown in Figure 7-12), no advance warning is given that a price decline is imminent. Nevertheless, a clue indicating technical weakness is given when a trendline joining the troughs of the momentum index is penetrated on the downside.

As with any trendline construction, judgment is still required to decide the significance of the break based on the principles outlined earlier. Moreover, the break in momentum should be regarded as an alert, and action should be taken only when it is confirmed by a break in the price trend itself (indicated by line *AA* in Figure 7-12).

Momentum indexes are also capable of tracing out price patterns. Usually these are of the accumulation type, although distribution forma-

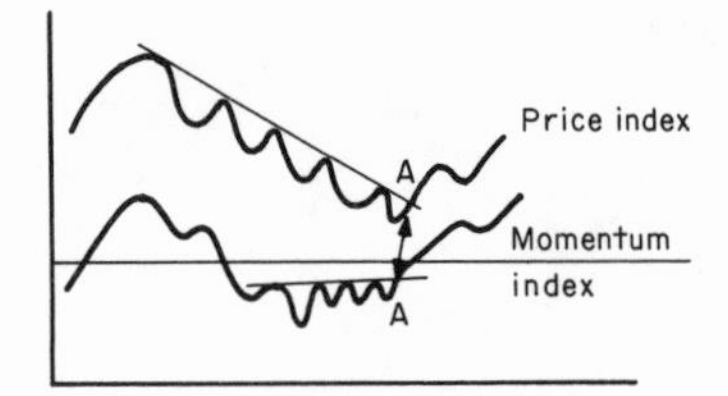

FIGURE 7-13
From *Technical Analysis Explained* by Martin J. Pring. Copyright © 1980 by McGraw-Hill, Inc. Used with the permission of the McGraw-Hill Book Company.

tions are not uncommon. Due to the shorter lead times normally associated with reversals of falling momentum, a breakout from an accumulation pattern when accompanied by a reversal in the downward trend of the index itself is usually a highly reliable indication that a worthwhile move has just begun. Such an example is shown in Figure 7-13.

There is another way in which momentum indexes may be useful, and that is with regard to their level. Since this type of index is an oscillator fluctuating backward and forward across its 0 or 100 reference line, there are clearly definable limits beyond which it rarely goes (see Figure 7-14).

The actual boundaries will depend on the volatility of the index being monitored and the time period on which the rate-of-change period is based, since the rate of change of an index has a tendency to vary more over a longer period than a shorter one.

In view of these two variables, there is no hard and fast rule as to what constitutes an unduly high (known as overbought) or low (known as oversold) level. This can be achieved only with reference to the history of the index being monitored and the maturity of the cycle. For example, when a bull market has just begun there is a far greater tendency for an index to move quickly into "overbought" territory and remain at very high readings for a considerable period of time. At such points the "overbought" readings tend to give premature warnings of declines. Consequently, during the early phases of the bull cycle when the market possesses strong momentum, reactions to the "oversold" level are much more responsive to price reversals, and such readings therefore offer

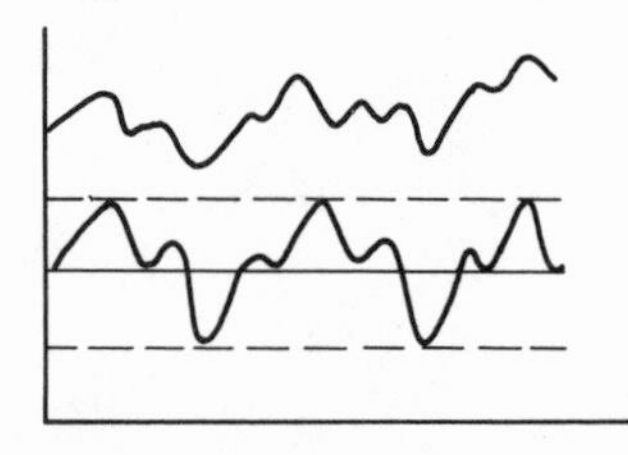

FIGURE 7-14
From *Technical Analysis Explained* by Martin J. Pring. Copyright © 1980 by McGraw-Hill, Inc. Used with the permission of the McGraw-Hill Book Company.

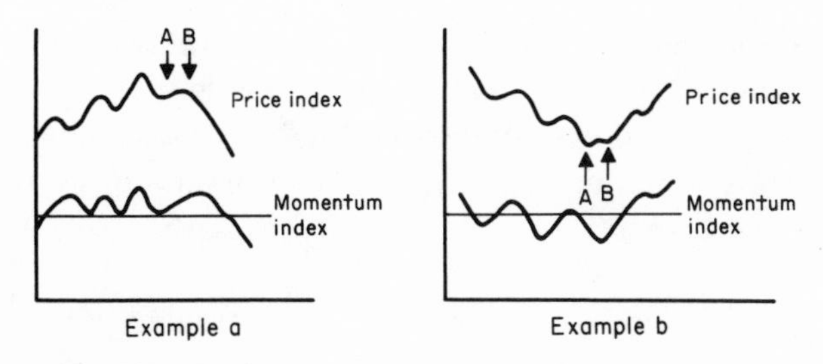

FIGURE 7-15
From *Technical Analysis Explained* by Martin J. Pring. Copyright © 1980 by McGraw-Hill, Inc. Used with the permission of the McGraw-Hill Book Company.

more reliable signals. It is only when the bull market is maturing or during bear phases that "overbought" levels indicate that a rally is shortly to be aborted. The fact that an index is unable to remain at such high readings for long periods is itself a signal that the bull market is losing momentum.

A further indication of the maturity of a trend is given when the momentum index moves strongly in one direction but the accompanying move in the price index is a much smaller one. Such a development suggests that the price index is tired of moving in the direction of the prevailing trend, for despite a strong push of energy from the momentum index, prices are unable to respond. This phenomenon is illustrated in Figure 7-15.

RELATIVE STRENGTH

This chapter has discussed many techniques used for identifying reversals in trend. The concept of "relative strength" also falls within the scope of this chapter and is important for determining *which* markets to buy and sell.

Relative strength (RS) is obtained by dividing the price of one index by another. Usually the divisor is a measurement of "the market." In the case of a particular American stock, the divisor would be the S&P 500, or the Dow Jones Industrial Average, etc. In the case of the stock market of a particular country, the divisor would be a global equity index such as The IBCA (International Bank Credit Analyst) World Stock Index, The Capital International World Index, or the Amro Pierson World Index.

The RS concept can be used to relate the price action of any two financial markets, such as the American stock market to the British stock market, gold bullion to gold shares, Japanese bonds to the American dollar, etc. The essential point to understand is that just as financial markets move in trends which have the habit of perpetuating, so the relationship between markets, i.e., their relative strength, also moves in trends.

A relative strength index will obviously have greater potential for wide swings for some relationships than for others. For example, Australian and Canadian stock markets often move in similar directions, so their relative strength relationship would not normally be subject to wide fluctuations. From a practical point of view, such relationships would not be particularly useful except in a few isolated circumstances where the magnitude of price movement would greatly differ. On the other hand, an RS index constructed from the movement of financial markets that are often moving in different directions, such as gold and specific equity markets, or bond and gold markets, would be very useful in determining when to switch from one market to another.

The analysis of RS trends is undertaken in the same way as that of the price indexes which the RS relationship is measuring. In other words, the principles of price patterns, trendlines, moving averages, and momentum can as validly be applied to RS indexes as the price indexes themselves.

Relative strength indexes of some relationships will be found to be erratic since they consistently offer whipsaw signals. Such relationships are best avoided in favor of those that are less violent and therefore more predictable.

A relative strength line is constructed by dividing one market by another, and by plotting this relationship weekly or monthly under one of the price indexes used in its construction. For example, Chart 1-3 in Chapter 1 shows the RS of the Dow Jones Industrials against the IBCA World Stock Index. A rising RS line indicates that the DJIA is outperforming the rest of the world, and a falling line the opposite.

Quite often a price index will make a series of ascending peaks in a bull market, but its relative strength line, whether measured against a composite index such as the World Stock Index or another market, will not confirm the last peak. This is known as nonconfirmation, and is shown by the dashed lines in Figure 7-16. At this point there may even be a break in the trend of the relative strength. Consequently, when the trend of the price index itself is broken, this represents an opportune time to either liquidate positions entirely, or switch to the financial mar-

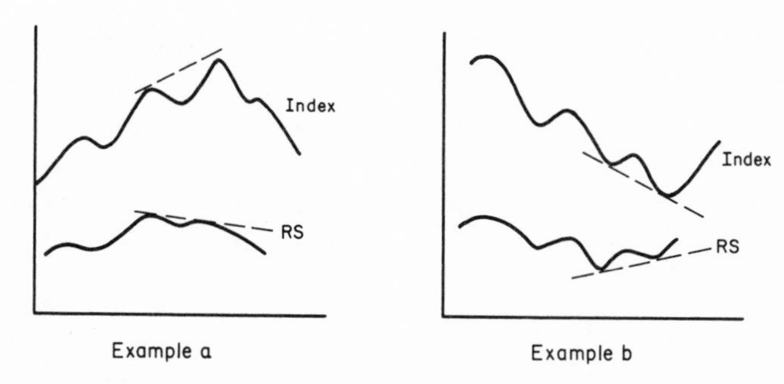

FIGURE 7-16
From *Technical Analysis Explained* by Martin J. Pring. Copyright © 1980 by McGraw-Hill, Inc. Used with the permission of the McGraw-Hill Book Company.

ket used in construction of the RS line. The decision will depend on whether the latter price index itself is in the early stages of a positive trend. This is because the declining RS line only indicates that the first market will be outperformed by the second. Both markets may in fact decline, with the drop in the second market being less than the first. Consequently, even though it is known that one market is likely to outperform another, it is still important to determine, from an analysis of the price trend itself, that the second index is in a positive trend.

Relative strength is also helpful in determining a buying point. In this connection a series of declining troughs in a price index which is not confirmed by the RS line (see Figure 7-16, Example *a*) is indicative of growing technical strength, so that when the trend of the price index in question is shown to be reversed, chances are this index will outperform the other index used in the relative strength construction. For example, if the German stock market was being compared to the World Stock Index, such a situation would strongly suggest that the German stock market, which had already been outperforming the World Stock Index, would continue to do so.

SUMMARY

The prices of assets trading in financial markets move in trends. Once a trend gets underway it perpetuates itself. Reversals in trend can be identified by certain price patterns, trendlines, moving average crossovers, and subtle changes in momentum. However imminent a trend reversal appears, it should always be assumed that the prevailing trend is in existence until the price action of the market itself concurs by decisively signaling an actual break.

The importance of the ensuing move will depend upon the magnitude and length of the previous trend. The knowledge that bull and bear markets have a tendency to evolve in three stages should also be used as background information to determine the significance of any trend reversal.

8

PUTTING TECHNIQUES INTO PRACTICE SOME EXAMPLES IN THE MARKETPLACE

This chapter will put the techniques discussed in Chapters 6 and 7 into practice by considering some actual examples in the marketplace. These examples will illustrate investment possibilities from the point of view of both major and intermediate trends, and will include examples of each type of financial market, e.g., equities, debt, gold, and currencies.

EQUITY MARKETS

The world's equity markets revolve around the global economic cycle. The magnitude of primary movements for each global cycle differs from country to country, depending on specific economic, monetary, and fiscal policies, the degree of equity market over- or undervaluation, and any institutional changes. These factors also affect the turning point of each market in relation to the theoretical peak and trough of the global stock market. Chart 8-1 shows the IBCA World Stock Index. The arrows above and below the index represent the approximate turning points of the 4-year global equity cycle. When deciding on a purchase or sale in a particular country's stock market, it is useful to understand the approximate position of the global stock cycle. If, for example, a specific stock market appears to be in an attractive technical position, the ensuing bull move may be less substantial if the global stock cycle is in its mature stage than if it has just begun.

From a technical point of view, analysis of a global equity index is a useful place at which to start. The most convenient to obtain is the Capital Internationl Index, which is published weekly in *Barron's*. It is not es-

CHART 8-1 World Stock Index and the 4-Year Cycle

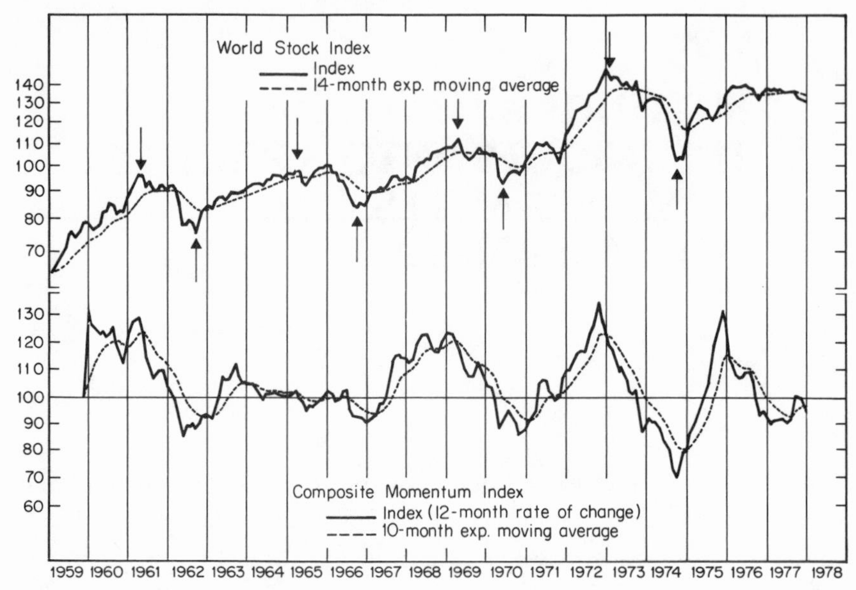

Courtesy of *The International Bank Credit Analyst.*

sential to follow the progress of a global composite index, but quite clearly if the position of the world's equity cycle is correctly appraised, chances of success in an individual stock market are greatly enhanced.

A general "feel" for the world cycle can also be obtained by simultaneously charting and analyzing the technical position of several countries. Most of them will usually look as if they are in the process of reversing their primary trends at the same time. If this proves to be the case, then the probability of a reversal in the global equity cycle will be increased. In the case of a new bull market, the best candidate for action can then be isolated through relative strength analysis. Given such a global turning point, the more pronounced a positive trend in relative strength has been for any particular market, the greater the upside potential is likely to be. For example, if the German market had deteriorated sharply in a relative sense over a 2-year period against the American market, and this poor RS trend was reversed at the same time that the world stock cycle was making a major reversal, it would normally be expected that in the ensuing bull cycle the German market would strongly outperform its American counterpart.

To chart the RS of various countries and markets against each other, even on a monthly basis, is quite a laborious task. Even though it is not essential, the effort will undoubtedly make the decision of which market to buy much easier. A simpler approach is to subscribe to Capital International, which publishes weekly charts of the world stock markets with the RS of each country every month (see Table 10-1).

Some actual examples of the application of trend-determining techniques are discussed below. In these and most of the other examples, trends in the rate of change index are used in conjunction with the price index itself.

GERMAN STOCK MARKET, 1955–1978

In order to clarify this technical description and avoid too much congestion on the charts, all bear market reversals are shown on Chart 8-2 and all bull market reversals on Chart 8-3.

Chart 8-2 shows the monthly average of the German stock market from 1955–1979. Below the stock index is its 12-month, or year-over-year, rate of change (momentum). A 12-month rate of change (ROC)

CHART 8-2 German Stock Market 1955–1978 Showing Important Bear Market Trendlines

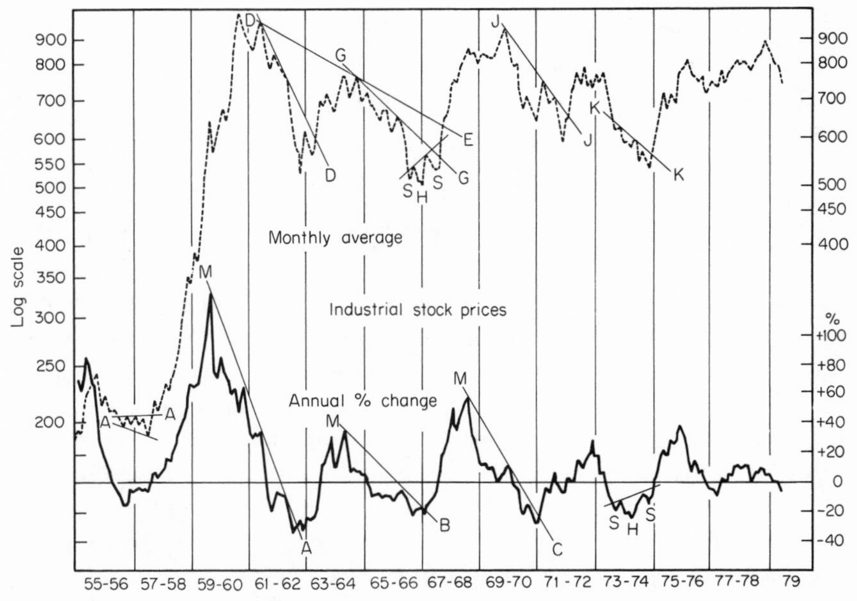

Courtesy of *The International Bank Credit Analyst.*

CHART 8-3 German Stock Market 1955–1978 Showing Important Bull Market Trendlines

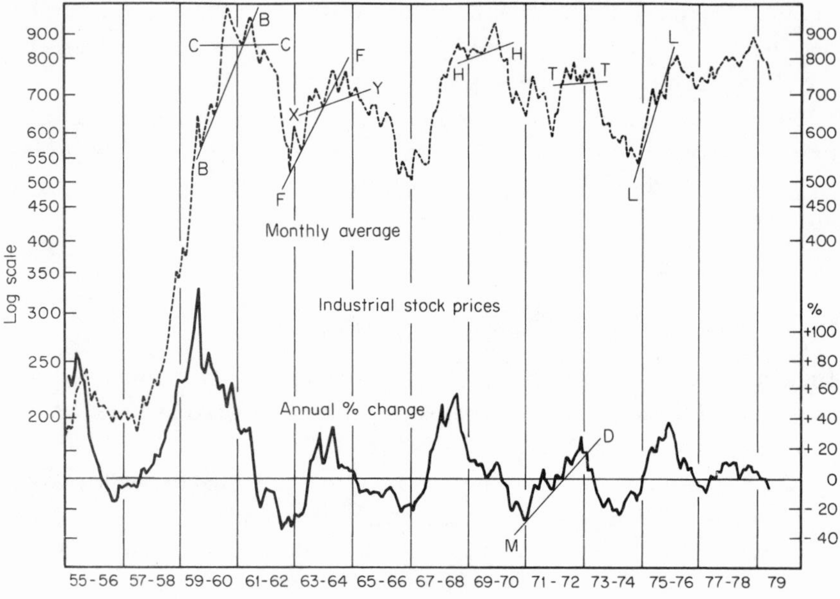

Courtesy of *The International Bank Credit Analyst.*

has been employed since it is useful for identifying cyclical or primary movements. Since a 12-month momentum compares the prices of the same month in succeeding years, seasonal tendencies are also eliminated. For example, during the past 50 years or so, January has typically been a strong month on average for stock prices in most countries, while May and October have a somewhat weaker record. Such discrepancies are therefore eliminated by using a 12-month rate of change.

The enormous 1957–1960 German bull market, during which prices more than quadrupled, began from a small broadening formation with a flat top. The flat top can be identified in Chart 8-2 by the line *AA* which joins the peaks at the end of 1956 and the beginning of 1957. Since there was no clearly definable trendline that could be drawn to usefully portray the 1956–1957 bear market, a break above trendline *AA* would have been used to signal a new bull market. Unfortunately, the 12-month ROC index also fell sharply and consistently during the bear phase so that no series of declining peaks, from which a useful trendline could be constructed, developed there either. What was significant during this period, however, was the fact that the ROC index made its low in late 1956, while the price index reached its trough in mid-1957. This indicated that downward momentum had begun to dissipate in late 1956 and therefore created a very positive divergence. This divergence could only be treated as a bullish *characteristic*, however, not as an outright indication of a basic trend reversal. The actual *signal* can only occur when a reversal in momentum is confirmed by a reversal in the trend of the price index itself. The positive divergence is therefore pointing up the fact that when the price reversal does take place, the ensuing move will be that much stronger. A clue to the ultimate strength of the move is given to some extent by the time period over which the divergence takes place. In this case the divergence extended for approximately 1 year, and suggested a very worthwhile move, but by no means to the extent of the bull market that actually evolved.

The bull market signal was given when the price index rose above line *AA*, as seen in Chart 8-2. During a bull market, prices normally begin a correction at about the one-third to the halfway mark of the ultimate peak. Once the intermediate decline has been completed it is possible to construct a trendline from the bear market low to the reaction low. This line then becomes the bull market trendline, the downward violation of which very often signals the termination of the primary advance. Whether it does or not depends largely on its steepness. The 1957–1960 bull market in German equities offered no such reference point since its momentum was far too great.

This type of explosive rally extending over a 3-year period is extremely unusual. However, an investor following the technical approach would have been well advised, if he had acted on the 1957 buy signal, to *follow the trend until it was shown to have been reversed*.

As discussed earlier, there is no known way to predict how far a trend will perpetuate once it has been set in motion. All investors can do, once a reversal has been identified, is to take advantage of a trend until there is sufficient technical evidence to indicate that it has been reversed.

In the case of the 1957–1960 German bull market there were two juncture points at which this conclusion could have been drawn. First, it was possible to join the bottoms of the two reactions in 1959 and early 1960 (line *BB* in Chart 8-3), and sell when this line was violated on the downside. Secondly, the two final rallies in 1960 and 1961 actually constituted double tops. Downward violation of line *CC*, which marked the level of the valley between them, combined with the fact that the momentum index was in a free-fall, would also have suggested that it was time to take profits.

Even though there was no strong indication of the almost 50 percent price decline that was to develop, whenever prices have risen fourfold over such a short period, it is usually wise not to be greedy and to take profits, given such a clear technical warning.

The ensuing bear market ended at the close of 1962, but it was not until early 1963 that a bull market signal was given. First the clearly definable declining trendline in the momentum index (MA) was violated on the upside during late 1962. Then in early 1963 the bear market trendline (line *DD* in Chart 8-2) was bettered, and a little later the index, having reacted in the opening months of 1963, rose above its January peak. In the process it successfully completed a double bottom and thereby indicated a reversal of the sharp bear trend.

The early 1963 reaction also served as a reference point for the construction of a bull market trendline (line *FF* in Chart 8-3) which was violated in early 1964. At this point it would have been wiser to take a small profit, and look around for a financial market in a better technical position.

In retrospect, the late 1963 and 1964 period proved to be one of distribution, and by the end of 1964 it was apparent that momentum was falling rapidly, especially when the index broke below the neckline of a head and shoulders distribution pattern (line *XY* in Chart 8-2). Even more serious was the fact that a long-term trendline joining the 1957 and 1962 bottoms had also been violated on the downside. This is shown in Chart 8-4.

During the ensuing bear market it was possible to construct two trendlines for the price index, one joining the 1961 and 1964 tops (line *DE* in Chart 8-2), and another joining the 1964 and 1965 peaks (line *GG* in Chart 8-2). The momentum index made a small top in 1964 which also served as a useful reference point for a bear market trendline (*MB*).

At the end of 1967 it was also posible to conclude that the 3-year bear market had been terminated, for not only were these three trendlines successfully penetrated but the price index itself had also traced out and completed an inverse head and shoulders pattern.

The following bull market proved to be very powerful, so it was not possible to construct a bull market trendline, either for the price index or for its momentum. It was not until after the penultimate peak was reached in 1969 that a trendline could be drawn, joining the December 1968 low to the trough of the late 1969 reaction (line *HH* in Chart 8-3). The break in this trendline in late 1969 combined with the obvious weakness in the momentum index, which had failed by a wide margin to confirm its 1968 high, would have served as a sufficient condition to liqui-

CHART 8-4 German Stock Market 1955–1978 Showing Secular Trendlines

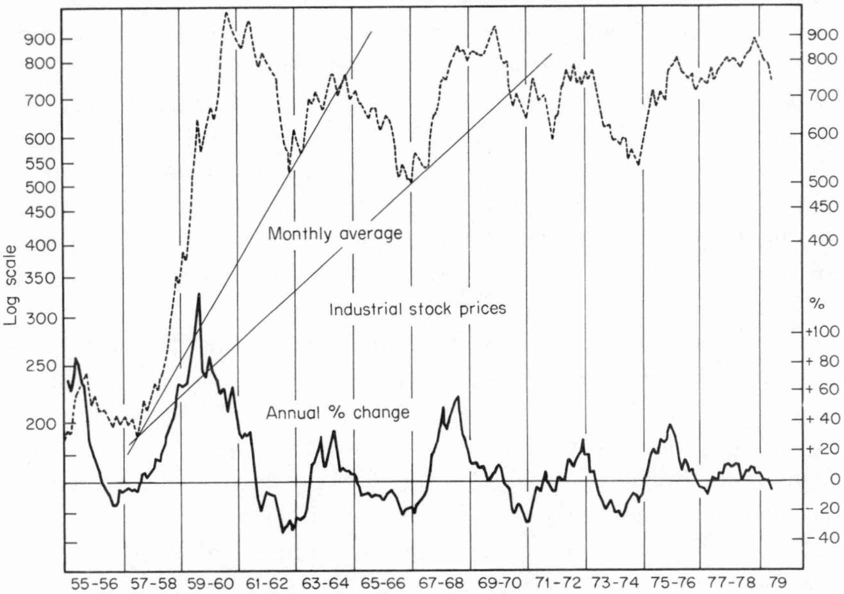

Courtesy of *The International Bank Credit Analyst.*

date positions, especially as it was evident at this time that most of the world's stock markets had already peaked out.

The German market fell for about 1 year, and then put on a rally at the beginning of 1971. Although the momentum index had reversed its declining trend by January 1971 (line *MC*, Chart 8-2), there was no reference point for the construction of a bear market trendline for the index itself from which a valid bull market signal could be obtained. In any event the major trendline joining the 1957, 1966, and 1967 bottoms (Chart 8-4) had been decisively violated on the downside, suggesting that the performance of the German stock market would most likely be constrained for a considerable time. This indeed proved to be the case, since prices had not surpassed their 1969 peaks even by the middle of 1979, 10 years later.

When a major 12-year trend such as this has been violated, it is always better to go in search of a more promising opportunity, for when it is possible to invest in so many different situations, it is clearly more prudent to search out the most viable.

For those who preferred to concentrate on the German market, the next major buying opportunity occurred in early 1972 when the bear market trendline joining the 1969 and 1971 peaks was successfully violated (line *JJ* in Chart 8-2). There was also a positive divergence between the momentum index, which made its low at the end of 1970, and the price index itself, which bottomed out late in 1971. The bull market which followed was very short, due not only to the warning given by the 12-year trendline violation, but also because of the maturity of the global equity cycle, which ended in January 1973. The termination of this short German bull market was signaled by the break in the positive trend in momentum in February 1963 (line *MD* in Chart 8-3) and the completion of the double top formation in the index itself later in the spring of 1973.

The bear market reference trendline could not be drawn from the peak in 1973 since the decline was too steep. However, a series of two small rally peaks in 1974 (line *KK* in Chart 8-2) isolated a more gently declining trend. The upward penetration of this line was sufficient to signal a new bull market. The bullishness of the signal was enhanced by a positive divergence in the momentum index, which made its low in mid-1974, and the breakout of this index from an upward-sloping inverted head and shoulders pattern in the December–January period of 1974 to 1975. The following rally was very powerful. A sharp upward trend in the index and its momentum were violated in early 1976 (line *LL* in Chart 8-3). Although the index subsequently went on to make a new cyclical high, no decisive signal to this effect was given. It could be argued that this second leg was indicated by a small inverted head and shoulders pattern formed in the fall of 1976 and spring of 1977, and confirmed by a positive break in the declining trend in momentum. However, these were not powerful signals, so that during this period an investor would have done better to turn to a more technically attractive situation.

In reviewing this example of the German stock market, it would appear that it was possible to identify all the major cyclical movements in that stock market in the period between 1955 and 1979. There were only three really outstanding buying opportunities, however, in 1957, 1967, and 1974. Each had strong technical characteristics and was accompanied by a positive divergence between the price and momentum indexes. In the case of 1967 there was not only a small 5-month divergence, but also a major 5-year one. All three buying opportunities corresponded with a cyclical trough in the global equity market, and two were associated with a breakout from a price pattern. In the case of 1967 this was also accompanied by the successful penetration of a 6-year bear market trendline. The 1974 buy signal was followed by a substantial 4-year advance, but the dynamics of the bull market were such that it would probably have been wiser, using the approach discussed above, to liquidate positions in early 1976.

The essential point is that it is relatively easy to identify cyclical buying opportunities, but a little extra care can isolate those markets that have the best potential and the investor can therefore achieve a greater return on capital employed. It is best, therefore, to look for as many favorable technical aspects as possible, and compare them to any other markets that may also appear to be good buying candidates at the same time. Look for price pattern breakouts accompanied by a trendline break in a long, clearly definable downtrend. The momentum index should either be extremely overextended on the downside, i.e. - 40 percent, or better still should have created a positive divergence with the price index over as long a period as possible.

Finally, it appears that cyclical buy signals are not nearly as profitable if they occur after the violation of long-term or secular trendlines joining two or more cyclical bottoms. By the same token, the upward violation of a secular bear market trendline will usually signal a cyclical bull market of greater than average magnitude.

GOLD

The gold market essentially can be divided into bullion and shares, although it is possible to invest in gold coins such as American double eagles, British sovereigns, etc. As discussed earlier, gold shares usually lead gold bullion. Chart 8-5 shows the American dollar price of gold and the Toronto and South African Gold Share Indexes between 1970 and 1979.

The price of gold bullion made a cyclical top in December 1974, but this peak was never confirmed by either of the share indexes. The Toronto index had made its high in the spring of 1974, and the South African in the summer of that year. This negative divergence between the shares and the metal was the first major sign of technical weakness during the whole cyclical move dating from 1971. The next came at the beginning of 1975, as the South African Index formed and broke down from a head and shoulders distribution pattern. Later that year the Toronto index completed a similar pattern, and the gold price also broke below its bull market trendline (labeled *AA* on chart). From the downside breakout of this trendline at $160, gold bullion was to fall for just over one year to an ultimate bear market low of $100.

While gold shares normally lead the bullion price, the actual price

CHART 8-5 Gold and Gold Shares

[1] Weekly high/low of fixings.

[2] Monthly average, January 1970–November 1973; weekly average from December 1973.

[3] Monthly close, 1970; weekly close, 1971–1976; weekly average from January 1976.

Courtesy of *The Bank Credit Analyst.*

level of the shares and bullion should only be compared over a 1- to 2-year period. In time the costs of mining an ounce of gold rise, so that at any given price of gold bullion the profits of a gold mining company are going to be less, other things being equal. Consequently, during a bull market in gold and gold-related assets, it is reasonable to expect successive peaks in the gold price to be confirmed by the gold shares, but it is not essential that a new secular high in the price of gold will also be achieved by the shares.

Divergences between these various gold assets can also be used to forecast intermediate as well as primary moves, but in this case the divergences are usually much smaller in time, lasting over a period of several weeks, compared to the 9-month divergence between the Toronto Gold Share Index and the price of gold bullion that occurred at the cyclical peak in 1974.

Approaching the trading of gold bullion from a secondary or intermediate point of view, Chart 8-6 shows an interesting and profitable technique. At the top of the chart is the weekly London closing price of gold bullion, below which is plotted its 13-week rate of change (momentum). The dashed trendlines indicate bullish movements and the solid lines are bearish trends. Whenever a definable trendline can be drawn for both indexes and both are jointly violated, valuable buy or sell signals are given. These are indicated by the arrows which connect both series.

Worth noting is the fact that the sharp bull move in mid-1974 was preceded by the completion of an inverse head and shoulders pattern for both indexes. The strong 1973 move was also preceded by a similar pattern in the momentum index, but not in the bullion price index itself. However, the move was signaled by a successful upward penetration of a significant trendline which not only possessed a gentle slope, but was also touched no less than four times before its violation. Another important favorable technical sign at this time was the strongly positive divergence between the momentum index, which made its low of - 20 percent well ahead of the low in the price of bullion itself. Subject to the provisos discussed in Chapter 3 concerning the changing relationships between far-out contracts and spot prices, this method could be successfully applied to the trading or investing of gold futures contracts.

CHART 8-6 Gold Bullion versus 13-Week Momentum

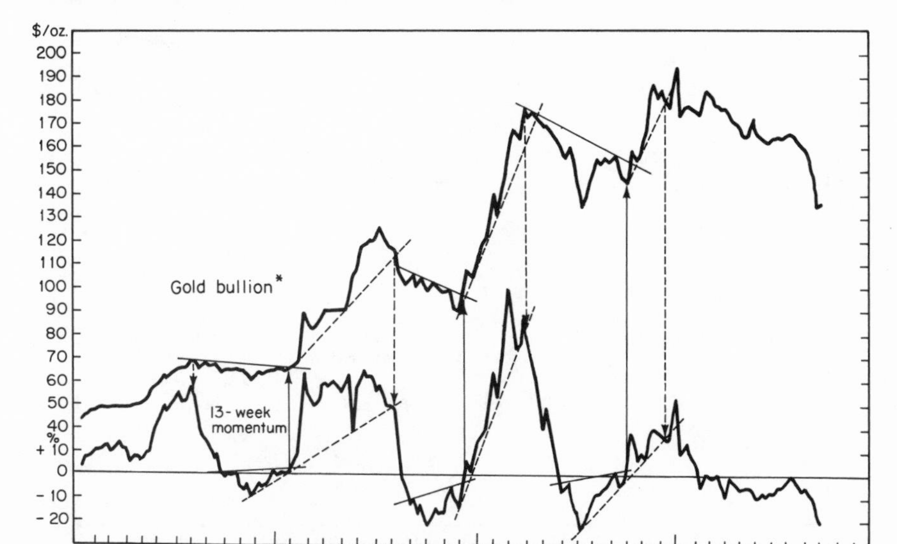

* Weekly close.

Courtesy of *The Bank Credit Analyst.*

BONDS

So far opportunities to invest in financial markets have been based upon monthly or weekly statistics. It is also possible to participate in worthwhile moves through the charting of daily data, but this of course is more time-consuming and is normally useful only in those markets that are relatively less volatile on a day-to-day basis, such as interest rate futures or bonds themselves. The example discussed below is one based on daily figures, but of course charts based on monthly or weekly figures can and should be used as a basis for making investment decisions on debt markets.

Chart 8-7 illustrates the daily closing bid price of a Government National Mortgage 8 percent Pass-Through Certificate and its 30-day rate of change (momentum). Price trends in these government-guaranteed debt instruments are a good proxy for the government bond market as a whole. More specifically, it is useful to follow the course of this bond, since it is the "spot" or cash market for the Government National Mortgage Association (GNMA) futures contract.

For charts based on daily data the 30-day period, whether in moving average or rate of change form, seems to be the most useful from the

CHART 8-7 GNMA Pass-Through Certificates versus 30-Day Momentum

Courtesy of *The Bank Credit Analyst Interest Rate Forecast.*

point of view of trend determination in virtually all the financial markets. Two lines have been drawn in Chart 8-7 so that it is possible to appreciate when the price move of the Ginnie Mae certificate is over- or underextended (overbought or oversold). Sometimes the momentum index exceeds these artificial boundaries. In such cases it is always worthwhile waiting for their return through the boundary and making sure that this is also confirmed by a breakout in the price of the bond itself above or below a definable trendline. Such an example developed in January 1977; in this case the trendline was an important one since it was long, possessed a gentle slope, and had been touched at least four times.

When the violation of a trendline as significant as this one takes place, it is an important signal to liquidate all trading positions. This particular violation signaled the end of the 1974–1977 bull market and heralded one of the worst postwar bear markets in bonds.

Another daily bond chart, Chart 8-8, incorporates the idea of confirming the trend breaks in momentum and the price discussed above.

CHART 8-8 Dow Jones Treasury Average versus 30-Day Momentum

Courtesy of *The Bank Credit Analyst Interest Rate Forecast.*

The approach is identical to that used in identifying intermediate trends in the price of gold bullion in Chart 8-6. In the example, the Dow Jones Treasury Average has been used. Due to weaknesses in its construction, it is not an index recommended for following movements in the Treasury market. Recording the price of a specific Treasury bond is far more useful. This index is therefore being used here for the purpose of illustrating possibilities of combining momentum and price trend breaks for trading in bonds or interest rate futures.

While the examples discussed above are concerned with the American debt market, the principles can equally well be applied to foreign markets, too. The problem in this case is the availability of data on a daily basis. For Canada and Britain this does not present a problem if a subscription to the appropriate publication is taken out, as discussed at the beginning of Chapter 10.

For the other well-developed foreign debt markets, Germany and Japan, such information can only be obtained through an appropriate local broker. For this reason it is far better to take a longer-term view of these markets, extending commitments over a 6-month to 2-year period, depending, of course, on the technical position as pointed up by the indicators.

CURRENCIES

The analysis of price trends in currencies should ideally be approached in two stages. The first stage would involve the charting of a trade-weighted currency, and the second a specific currency relationship, such as the American dollar in Swiss franc terms. The trade-weighted index is in a sense the "Dow Jones Industrial Average" for a particular currency, since it is a rough proxy of the performance of a specific currency against all other important currencies in the world. This composite index is constructed by taking the movement of a basket of currencies against the currency which is being measured, and weighting each according to the amount of trade that country does with the country for which the trade-weighted index is being calculated.

If a trade-weighted index was being constructed for the pound sterling, for example, the price of the pound against a number of different currencies would be recorded as of a certain date, which would be used as a starting point. The index would at that time be expressed as 100, and subsequent movements would take the index above or below 100, depending on whether the currency appreciated or depreciated. Movements in the index would be calculated by taking the percentage price change of individual currencies. Thus, in the first month the pound may have gained 5 percent on the Japanese yen, lost 3 percent against the American dollar, and gained 20 percent against the Swedish kroner. Instead of taking a simple average by adding up the total changes and dividing by the number of currencies used, each currency is weighted by the share of trade that the particular country does with Britain. Consequently, the 20 percent appreciation of the pound against the Swedish currency would not have a very great influence on the trade-weighted index since Sweden does not have a very high share of British trade.

Trade-weighted averages are calculated from several sources. The two most easily accessible are those published by the Morgan Guaranty Trust and the Bank of England. Bank of England figures for all the major currencies are published daily in the *Financial Times* of London, while Morgan Guaranty figures for the American dollar appear daily in *The Wall Street Journal*.

The movement of a trade-weighted index indicates whether a currency is *generally* strong or weak. The word "generally" has been emphasized since the trade-weighted measure is far from perfect in this respect. For example, America's biggest trading partner is Canada, so the Canadian dollar has a very high weighting in calculations of the trade-weighted U.S. dollar. At the end of 1976 the American dollar was weakening against virtually every currency in the world, except the Canadian dollar. Since the Canadian dollar fell sharply against its American counterpart, the U.S. trade-weighted index did not fall and therefore gave a misleading picture of American dollar strength. Such situations do not occur often, but investors should nevertheless be aware that they can and do develop.

The most profitable trading opportunities arise when a technically strong trade-weighted currency can be isolated against a technically weak one. A classic example occurred in mid-1976 between the American dollar and the Japanese yen. The monthly trade-weighted indexes of both countries and their 12-month rates of change are shown in Charts 8-9 and 8-10. Chart 8-9 shows that the uptrend in both the trade-weighted dollar and its 12-month rate of change were violated in early 1976. Although the trade-weighted index went on to make a new high later in the year, the dollar declined over this period in relation to virtually every other currency.

In the Japanese case exactly the opposite situation developed as the

CHART 8-9 United States Trade-Weighted Dollar versus 12-Month Rate of Change

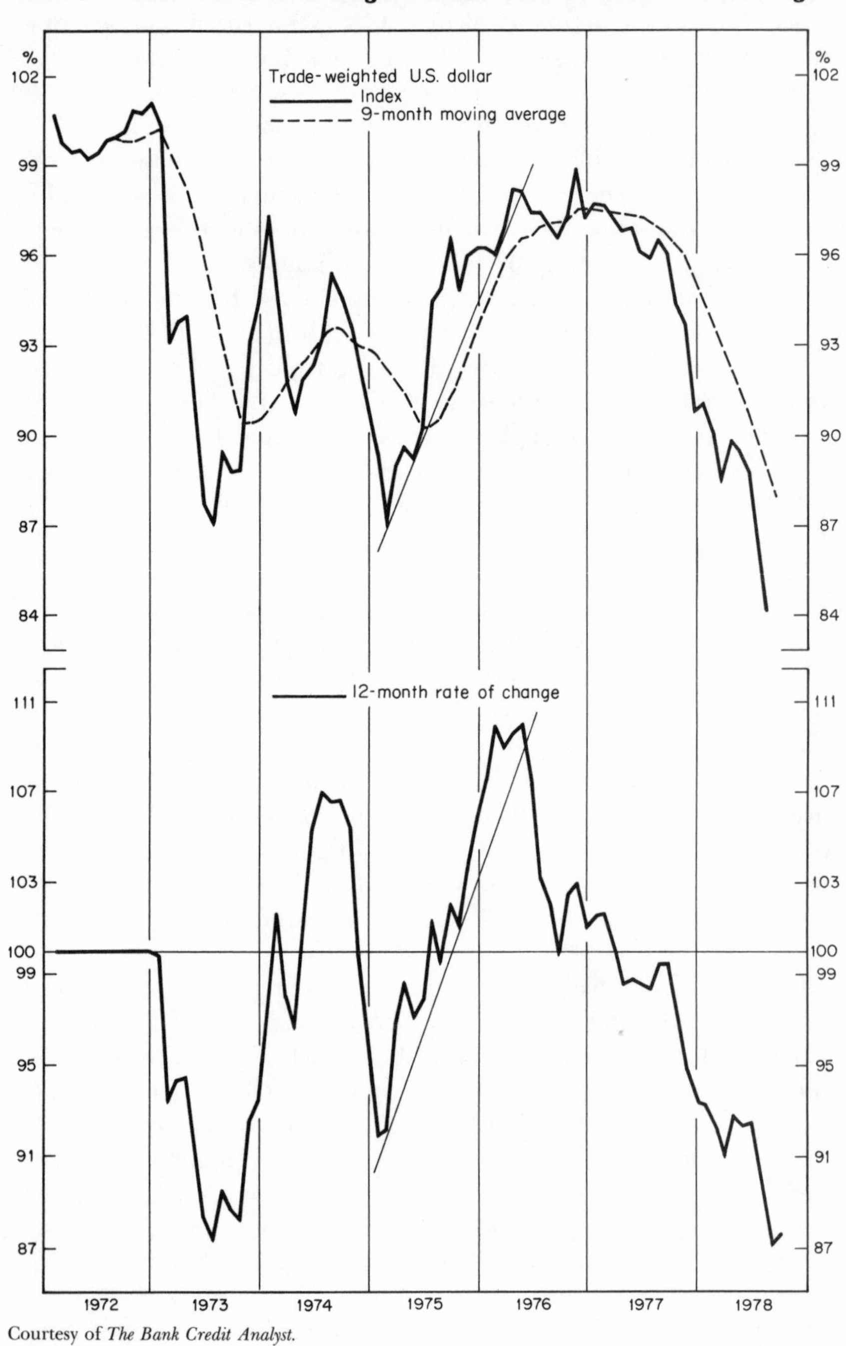

Courtesy of *The Bank Credit Analyst.*

CHART 8-10 Japanese Trade-Weighted Yen versus 12-Month Rate of Change

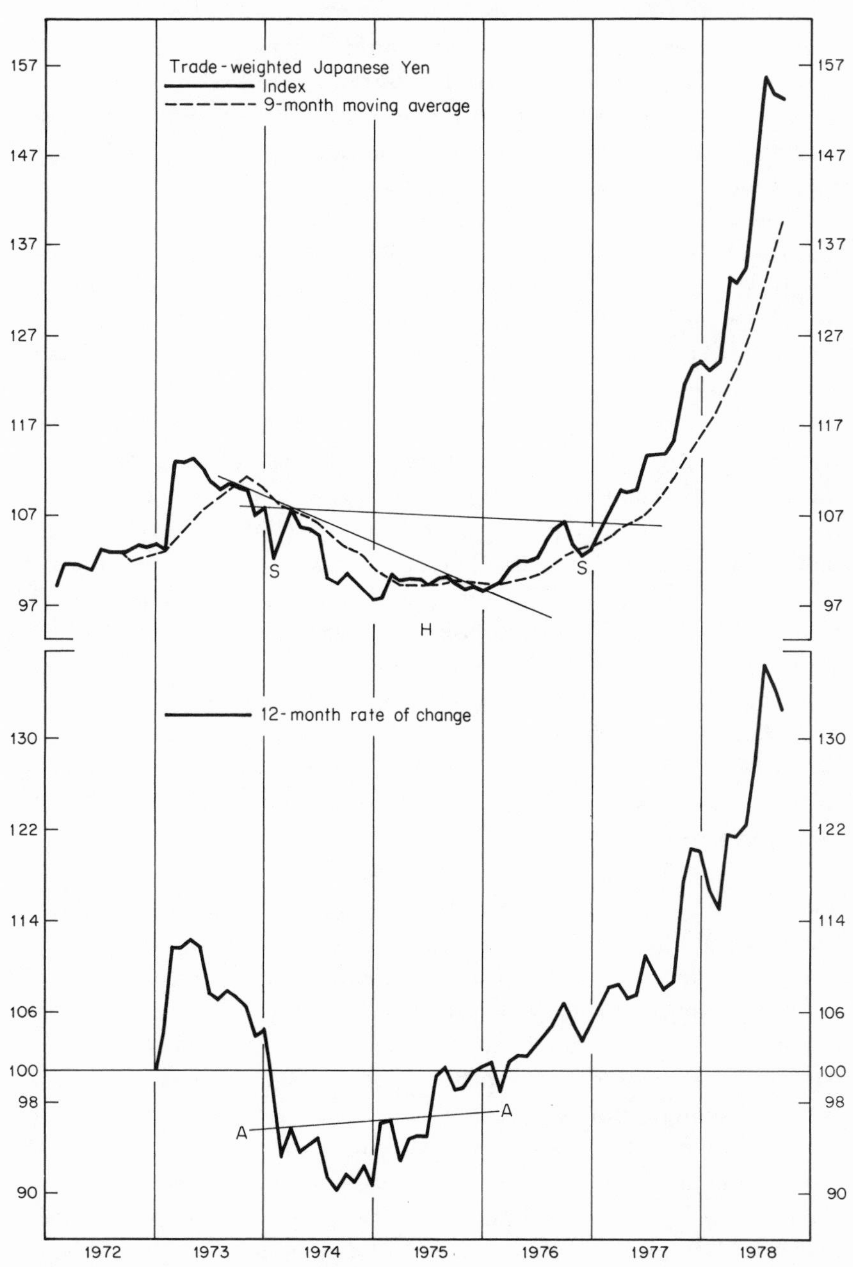

Courtesy of *The Bank Credit Analyst.*

yen began to move out of a 2-year trade-weighted decline at the beginning of 1976. In the case of the yen this represented a breakout from a shallow 2¼-year inverse head and shoulders pattern which developed between 1974 and 1976. Moreover, this was confirmed by a very buoyant trend in the 12-month rate of change of the trade-weighted yen. The analysis of the technical positon of these trade-weighted indexes therefore indicated that the dollar should be sold and the yen bought.

The second stage was to chart the specific yen/dollar rate to ensure that the broad picture indicated by analysis of the trends of the trade-weighted indexes was being confirmed by the specific relationship between the yen and the dollar.

Chart 8-11 shows the Japanese yen versus the American dollar, with a 13-week rate of change of this relationship. Although this line really represents a relative strength line of the yen versus the dollar, it will be referred to in the text as the yen price, since a rising index indicates an increasing value for the yen versus the dollar, and vice versa. The yen made its peak in the beginning of 1973, at which time it entered a bear market lasting almost 3 years. The bear market trendline could be constructed by joining the 1973 spring and summer peaks (line *BB*). This trendline was not successfully violated on the upside until the spring of 1976. Reference to the 13-week ROC indicates a massive 2-year positive divergence, since the yen itself made successive lows in early and mid-1974 and late 1975, but this series of lower troughs was unaccompanied by one of successively lower lows in the momentum index. The breakout of the 13-week ROC index above the accumulation trendline *AA* in late 1975 was therefore a very bullish development.

By mid-1976 it was obvious that the yen had formed an inverse head and shoulders pattern, the late 1976 rally representing the beginning of the breakout move. The ensuing reaction took the yen index itself back toward the neckline of this pattern. Careful observation of Chart 8-10 shows that between late 1973 and early 1977, the yen had been tracing out an even larger inverse head and shoulders pattern. This 3¼-year accumulation proved to be the platform for a huge rise in the index, far beyond the minimum objective set by the pattern, and extremely profitable for any investor who participated in the move.

Charting and analyzing the trade-weighted indexes are not essential for successful currency trading or investment, but quite clearly inclusion of this analysis greatly reduces the risk of making unprofitable decisions. The example discussed above is a classic one, since such clear technical signals do not often fall into place. Examination of other currency charts

CHART 8-11 Japanese Yen in Terms of U.S. Dollar

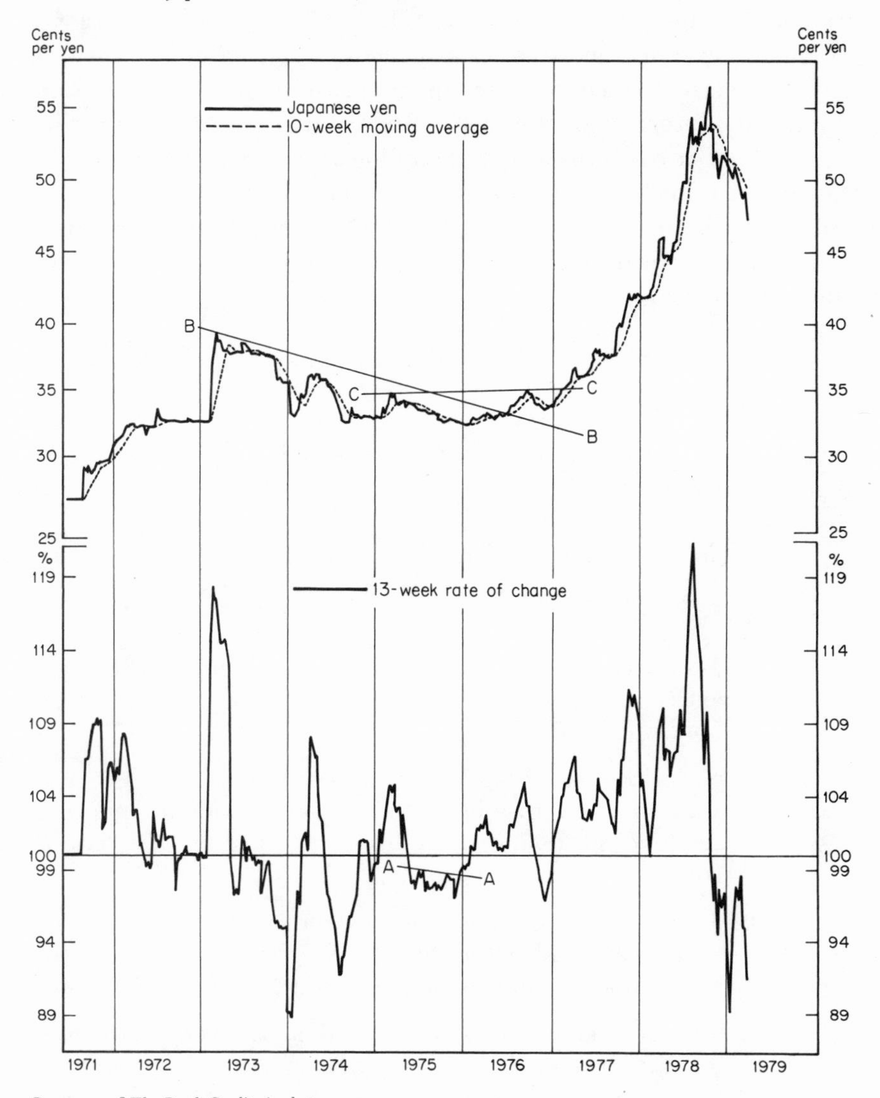

Courtesy of *The Bank Credit Analyst.*

illustrated elsewhere in this book will reveal that similar opportunities were not widely available at that time.

This fact more than any other demonstrates the advantage of following many different financial markets. For only by calling on a wide range of situations is it possible for the investor to consistently take positions, maybe only two or three times a year, and do so in the knowledge that technical conditions are almost perfect. It should be emphasized that the examples illustrated above were isolated from the charting of the spot rate. Since actual execution in the marketplace will most likely be done through the futures market in view of the leverage available, it is important to make sure that the technical position of the far-out contracts is in agreement with that of the spot, or, alternatively, investments should only be made in the nearby months. In this way potential distortions which will limit or even eliminate profits between the spot and far-out contracts will be greatly reduced.

SUMMARY

When looking for a major buying opportunity it is important to ask the following questions:

1. How important is the trend that has just been reversed? Has a long, important trendline been violated or is it just a short one?
2. Has a trendline violation been associated with a divergence between the low in the price index and that of a longterm momentum index?
3. If a price pattern has been completed, how large is it? Can you combine a price break in the pattern with an important trendline violation, thereby improving the odds of an important reversal?
4. Has a secular trendline (one extending over many cycles) been violated? If so, the chances of a greatly prolonged move in the opposite direction are significantly enhanced.
5. Are you making an investment decision based on the *possibility* of a trend reversal? If so, *don't*. Always wait and pay a higher price (or sell at a lower one) when the signal is unequivocal. This will increase the likelihood of success.

9

SOME SYSTEMS DESIGNED TO BEAT THE MARKET

The buying and selling signals discussed in Chapter 8 were all essentially based on judgment. This chapter will introduce some mechanical fail-safe systems which have historically proved to be useful techniques. Although all the systems described in this chapter would have been extremely profitable if they had been incorporated into an investment program, they are introduced here with some reluctance, because there is absolutely no guarantee whatsoever that any of them will continue to perform as well in the future.

The systems described here are basically mechanical devices that trigger buy and sell signals at infrequent intervals. The signals do not give any indication of either the magnitude or extent of a potential move, they merely point out the probability that a previous trend has been reversed. Buy signals imply that commitments are likely to be profitable, and sell signals that liquidation of a position will prove more beneficial than its retention. In some cases where a long bull trend is evident, some of the systems will prove less profitable than a buy-hold approach. In any event, the objective in using a system is to make profitable commitments, either on the long or the short side of the market. If a system consistently obtains that objective and gives a good return on the equity invested, little more can be asked of it.

A mechanical system designed to identify intermediate moves is not concerned with the primary or major direction of a financial market although secondary reactions, which develop contrary to the major trend, very often result in loss or almost no profit at all.

The systems introduced in this chapter have all been chosen because they offer signals at relatively infrequent intervals so commission costs can be kept to a bare minimum. It is mandatory when using a system to act immediately whenever a signal is given. Quite often it will appear to the investor at the time that a particular signal is going to be wrong, but if this approach is to be successful, investors must have the discipline to act faithfully on the indicated signal. By the same token investors may, for no good reason, feel that a signal is about to be given. Again, no action should be taken, for the signal may never materialize. Under such circumstances the investor could "lose his position" and be unable to reacquire it, thereby missing the important part of a move.

It is important in designing a system first of all to assess the characteristics of the financial market under consideration. Clearly, it must be subject to substantial price swings. However, since systems are mechanical devices triggered, for example, by a moving average crossover or a rate of change index reaching a specific point, it is very important that price movements within these major swings are not overly volatile or else many unprofitable and misleading whipsaws will develop. Such misleading signals can never be entirely avoided but judicious market selection, combined with the incorporation of a device to filter out as many of these whipsaws as possible, will greatly improve the profit potential of any system.

Despite the use of filtering devices, a system will quite often give three or four poor or even loss-producing signals due to the interim volatility of a market. Just as the investor is beginning to lose patience, a really worthwhile and highly profitable move develops. Such are the characteristics of financial markets, and it is as well to remember this point whenever such a frustrating period is occurring, for there is then a very high degree of probability that the next signal will be followed by a long and important move. From a technical viewpoint, this concept of several misleading signals followed by a substantial move is actually indicative of a major distribution, accumulation, or consolidation succeeded by a significant breakout.

PRIMARY MOVEMENTS IN THE CANADIAN STOCK MARKET

The following system was developed by Leon Tuey, a capable technical analyst at Pitfield, Mackay, Ross, a Canadian investment dealer, and is one for which the author can therefore take no credit whatsoever.

It involves the use of a 12-month rate of change combined with a

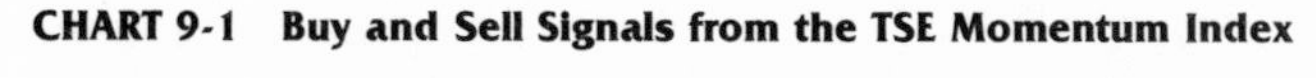

CHART 9-1 Buy and Sell Signals from the TSE Momentum Index

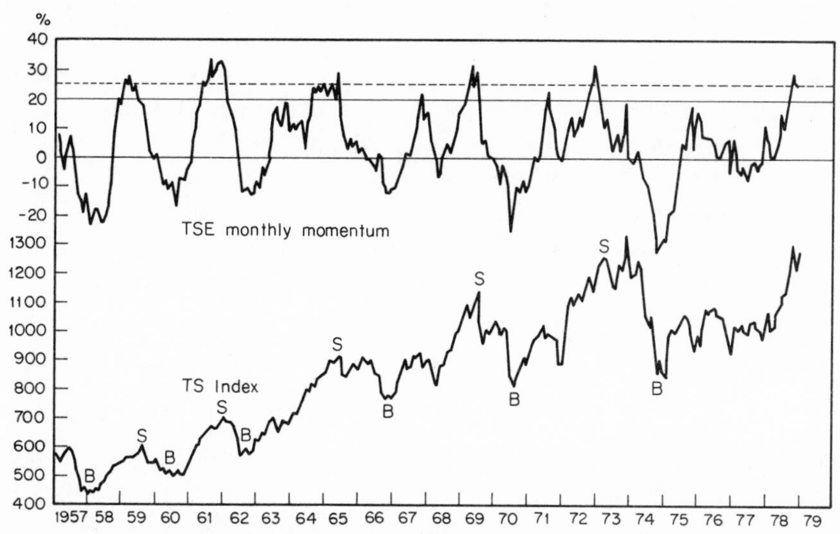

monthly average of the Toronto Stock Exchange 300 Composite Index. Buy signals are triggered 2 months after the rate of change index falls below the −10 percent level. Sell signals occur when the rate of change index rises above the +25 percent level and then falls below the +19 percent mark. These buy and sell signals have been indicated by the letters on the chart above and below the Toronto Stock Index. Reference to Chart 9-1 shows that this method has worked very well in the 1957–1979 period. These rules also called every major market top and bottom from 1945 to 1976 for the old Toronto Stock Exchange Industrial Index. Mr. Tuey is quick to point out that such an approach may not continue to operate so successfully in the future.

This type of system relying solely on rate of change data suffers from two important drawbacks. The first is that in some cycles the index may not move to the +25 percent or the −10 percent extremes. Thus, the investor, having been committed to a substantial position as a result of a crossing of the rate of change index through the −10 percent reference level, may be stuck with his position if the rate of change index rises to only −5 percent, for instance, in the next cycle since no sell signal will be given under such circumstances. The second drawback is that a system which relies on a wide swing in prices more or less assumes that stock prices will continue to operate around the 4-year business cycle. However, there is no reason why the business cycle cannot extend beyond 4 years, as indeed it has in the past. From 1924–1929, for example, stock prices rose almost uninterruptedly and would undoubtedly have resulted in a premature sell signal. Similarly, between 1929 and 1932 prices fell, but were interrupted by some important rallies in 1930 and 1931 which would have resulted in some extremely premature and costly buy signals.

These remarks are not intended to discredit this system, which is a very good one, but merely to point out to investors that a method relying totally on a rate of change index works extremely well over a typical or normal cycle, but can result in considerable loss given an unusual one.

A MOVING AVERAGE SYSTEM FOR BRITISH AND GERMAN STOCK MARKETS

An alternative method to the rate of change approach is one that uses a moving average. For primary movements, crossovers above and below a 40-week moving average have proved useful buy and sell points for many financial markets. Signals triggered by this mechanism often miss quite a large part of the initial stages of a move, but since misleading signals are relatively rare, this approach permits investors to participate in the major part of long moves. The fact that the signals often come quite late is not important as long as they are not triggered unnecessarily closely and the system is making relatively consistent profits. In any event, investors incorporating an approach involving a 40-week moving average crossover and who are also following several financial markets at the same time, would probably be better advised when taking an initial position to ignore signals that are unduly late and concentrate on those situations where a price index is only marginally up from its low at the time of the crossover, so that the chances of participating in the largest part of the move are enhanced. Clearly, it would not be possible to know whether the sell signal would be just as timely, but at least investors would have entered commitments knowing that purchases had been made close to the bottom.

Charts 9-2 and 9-3 show the Financial Times 500 Index and the Commerzbank Index for the German stock market with their 40-week moving averages, in the 1966–1978 period. At first glance it would appear to be profitable to buy and sell each of these markets whenever the index crossed above or below its moving average, as indeed it would if profits and losses were netted out over the whole period. On closer examination

CHART 9-2 Financial Times 500 Index 1966–1978 and 40-Week Moving Average

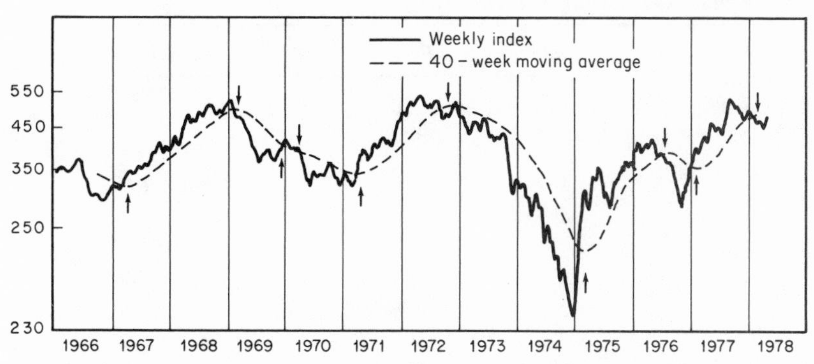

From *Technical Analysis Explained,* by Martin J. Pring. Copyright © 1980 by McGraw-Hill, Inc. Used with the permission of the McGraw-Hill Book Company.

Courtesy of *The Bank Credit Analyst.*

it becomes apparent that both markets are subject to whipsaws when using this approach. This is especially true of the German market. When it is considered that commission costs for equity markets normally amount to 4 percent for a round trip (buy and sell), it clearly becomes important to try and filter out some of these signals without unduly losing out on the genuine ones.

The approach suggested is to divide the weekly closing price by the 40-week moving average, and then wait until the index moves above or below the moving average by more than 2 percent in the case of the British market, and 2.5 percent in that of its more volatile German counter-

CHART 9-3 German Stock Market 1966–1978 and 40-Week Moving Average

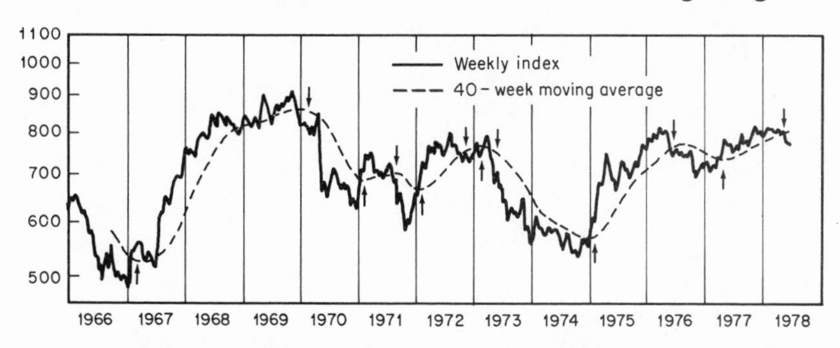

From *Technical Analysis Explained,* by Martin J. Pring. Copyright © 1980 by McGraw-Hill, Inc. Used with the permission of the McGraw-Hill Book Company.

Courtesy of *The Bank Credit Analyst.*

TABLE 9-1 Financial Times 500 Share Index vs. 2% Crossover of 40-Week Moving Average

Signal	*Date*	*Price*	*Profit*	*Loss*
Buy	3/17/67	329		
Sell	2/21/69	470	141	
Buy	1/2/70	412		
Sell	4/24/70	381		31
Buy	4/9/71	349		
Sell	9/22/72	475	126	
Buy	1/31/75	237		
Sell	7/23/76	378	141	
Buy	1/7/77	365		
Sell	2/3/78	459	94	
Total			502	31

SUMMARY	
Gross profit	471
Buy-hold profit	130
Gain over buy-hold	341

TABLE 9-2 German Stock Index vs. 2½% Crossover of 40-Week Moving Average

Signal	*Date*	*Price*	*Profit*	*Loss*
Buy	2/3/67	543		
Sell	1/16/70	807	264	
Buy	1/29/71	710		
Sell	9/3/71	672		38
Buy	1/28/72	678		
Sell	10/20/72	726	48	
Buy	1/19/73	775		
Sell	5/4/73	722		53
Buy	1/3/75	587		
Sell	7/9/76	741	154	
Buy	4/7/77	760		
Sell	4/28/78	769	9	
Total			475	91

SUMMARY	
Gross profit	384
Buy-hold profit	226
Gain over buy-hold	158

part. The actual trading results of these two systems are shown in Tables 9-1 and 9-2. Table 9-1 shows that the net profit from the 10 signals was 471 points compared to a 130 point appreciation for the "buy hold" approach between early 1967 and early 1978 for the British market. Moreover, if it had been possible to "short" the British market, an additional 341 points would have been gained.

In the case of the German stock market, the system still proved to be profitable but did not give such good results as for the United Kingdom. In this case the net profit was 384 points (see Table 9-2), against a 226 gain for a buy-hold approach. Signals resulting from the percentage filtering approach are shown by the arrows above and below the two indexes.

A SYSTEM USING RATES OF CHANGE OF BOND YIELD AND STOCK PRICES

Before leaving systems designed to identify reversals in price trends of cyclical or primary importance, it is worth introducing another approach which attempts to forecast stock price movements with the aid of changes in the level of interest rates. It is a well-documented fact that primary movements in interest rates lead those in stock prices. For example, every American stock market bottom and peak in the century has been preceded by a like move in either the long or short ends of the debt markets, and usually by both.

The approach used here is one that combines the 12-month rate of change of the London Financial Times 500 Share Index with the 12-month rate of change of the Financial Times Government Yield Index. The aim of this system is to forecast British equity prices.

The bond yield/stock price momentum index is calculated by adding the 12-month rate of change of stock prices to the inverse 12-month rate of change of the Government Yield Index. If, for example, the monthly stock index in January 1978 is 20 percent above the corresponding month in 1977 and government yields are 10 percent below (i.e., −10 percent) the same period, the index would be calculated by adding +20 percent and +10 percent to give a total of +30 percent. In order to maintain a manageable scale for plotting, the combined bond yield/stock yield index is then divided by two to give a reading of +15 percent. On the other hand, if stocks were down by 10 percent (−10 percent) and yields down by 10 percent (−10 percent), the index would be zero, i.e.,

CHART 9-4 Financial Times Industrial Ordinary Index versus Bond/Stock Momentum Index

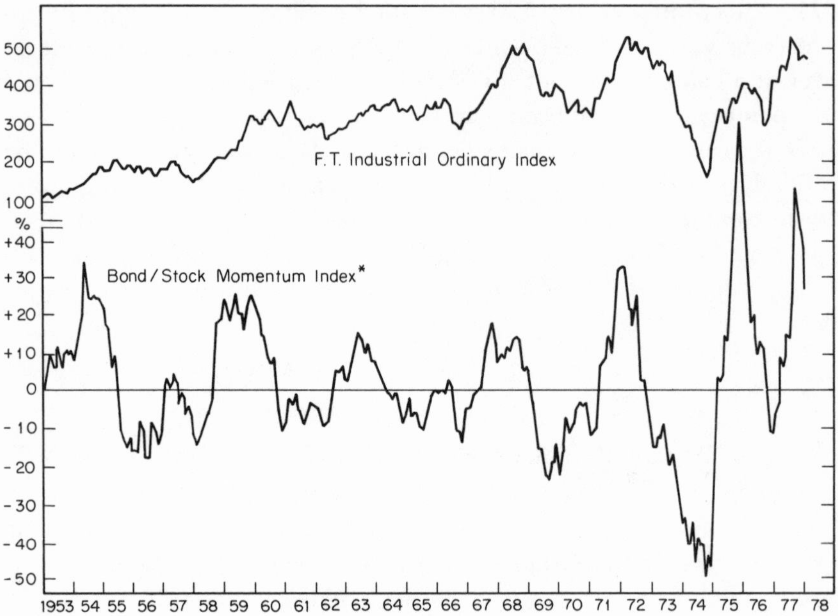

* One-half the sum of the 12-month rate of change of stock prices and the inverted 12-month rate of change of bond yields.

Courtesy of *The Bank Credit Analyst.*

+10 percent added to −10 percent. In other words, the sign on the rate of change for yields is always reversed since falling yields are favorable for stock prices and rising yields unfavorable.

Signals are given whenever the combined Stock Yield Index crosses its zero reference line. A rise above zero results in a buy signal, and a decline below zero gives a sell signal. Chart 9-4 shows this debt momentum index with the stock index itself. The results of the system are shown in Table 9-3.

This approach suffers from the drawback that whenever the stock market moves to an extreme and quickly reverses, then the zero crossing signals can be frustratingly late. This problem can be solved by adding two additional rules.

The first is concerned with the termination of bull markets, and states that if the stock yield index falls below +15 percent, having previously risen above +25 percent, this constitutes a valid sell signal. Consequently, if the index rises to +19 percent and then falls, a sell signal is not triggered until the index falls below its zero reference level. On the other hand, if the index rises to +32 percent and then declines, a move below +15 percent is sufficient to trigger a signal.

The second rule, which is concerned with market bottoms, states that if the index falls below −15 percent, the −5 percent level substitutes for the zero reference level as far as buying signals are concerned, until the index actually rises above the real zero reference line. Thus, if the index falls to −18 percent (as it did in 1956) and rises to −4 percent, a buy signal is given. If the index then rises above zero, the −5 percent level is then forgotten until the index falls below −15 percent again (in this case not until 1969). On the other hand, as a protection against a false signal, if the yield index falls to −20 percent, rises to between −4 percent and

TABLE 9-3 United Kingdom Market Using the Debt/Equity Momentum System (Using zero crossings)

Signal	*Date*	*Price*	*Profit*	*Loss*
Buy	Jan. 1953	117.5		
Sell	Aug. 1955	201.9	84.4	
Buy	Feb. 1957	185.9		
Sell	July 1957	204.5	18.6	
Buy	Sept. 1958	193.0		
Sell	Oct. 1960	325.9	132.9	
Buy	Aug. 1962	276.0		
Sell	May 1964	343.2	67.2	
Buy	Jan. 1966	345.4		
Sell	Feb. 1966	355.0	9.6	
Buy	May 1966	363.3		
Sell	Aug. 1966	308.0		55.3
Buy	July 1967	352.7		
Sell	Feb. 1969	485.4	132.7	
Buy	May 1971	389.1		
Sell	Mar. 1973	491.6	102.5	
Buy	Mar. 1975	292.7		
Sell	Oct. 1976	293.6	.9	
Buy	Mar. 1977	418.2		
Sell	Sept. 1978	515.9	97.7	
Total			646.5	55.3

SUMMARY	
Gross profit	591.2
Buy-hold profit	398.4
Gain over buy-hold	192.8

−0.1 percent but does not cross the zero reference line, a return to the −5.1 percent level or below immediately triggers a sell signal as it did in November 1970. In this case, the subsequent buy signal was given in April 1971 at −2.8 percent.

Using this filtering technique increases the net profit of the system from 591.2 points to 668.2 points.

A SYSTEM FOR U.S. SHORT-TERM INTEREST RATES

It is important to know the future course of the trend of short-term interest rates for two reasons. First, reversals in the trend of short-term interest rates *usually* lead or coincide with those at the long end. Secondly, as a result of the development in interest rate futures contracts, it is now possible to actually profit from swings in short-term interest rates. As discussed in Chapter 3, movements in futures markets are usually similar to the cash or spot market. However, at certain points in the cycle, the far-out or distant contracts (i.e., those due for delivering 6 to 18 months), are quite often less sensitive to movements in the cash market, and occasionally move in an opposite direction for short periods of time. In order to minimize such distortions and to avoid the necessity of keeping track of these changing spreads, investment in nearby contract months (where the distortions are considerably less) is recommended, and assumed in the following examples of interest rate and currency markets.

There are two relatively liquid types of futures contracts for short-term interest rates: 3-month T-bills and 90-day commercial paper.

Chart 9-5 shows the weekly average of 4- to 6-month commercial paper, its 13-week moving average, and its 13-week rate of change. This cash interest rate is a useful guide for investors wishing to participate in the 90-day commercial paper futures market. Sell signals are given whenever the 4- to 6-month commercial paper crosses above its 13-week MA, and this is confirmed by the 13-week rate of change also moving above its 100 reference line. The negative signal remains in force until the index moves below its 13-week MA, and this in turn is confirmed by the 13-week rate of change returning to a position below its 100 reference line. Note that a signal can be generated only when *both* indexes confirm the action of the other.

The combination of a momentum and a moving average system helps to filter out many unprofitable and misleading signals without unduly

CHART 9-5 Weekly 4–6 Month Commercial Paper Rate versus 13-Week Rate-of-Change Index

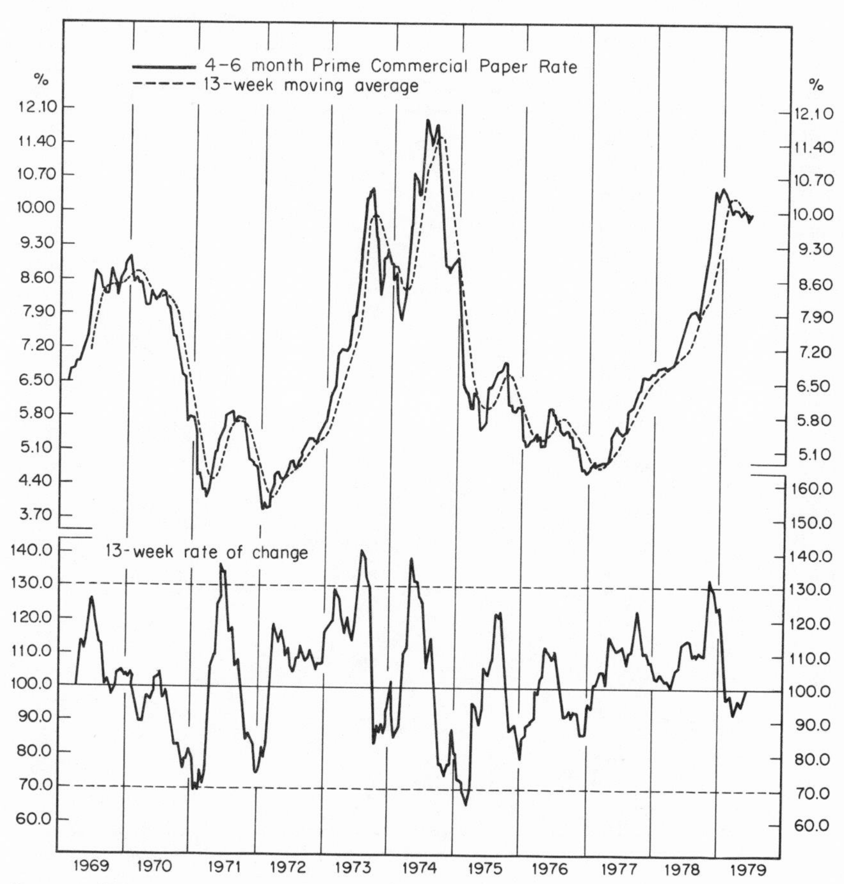

Courtesy of *The Bank Credit Analyst Interest Rate Forecast.*

delaying their timeliness. While this type of system is relatively sensitive, it is unable to catch the major part of the sharp reversal such as the one which took place at the end of 1973 and the beginning of 1974. However, if an additional rule is inserted that permits a valid signal (even though unconfirmed by the momentum index) to be given by a moving average crossover of more than 5 percent, then an additional .35 basis points are saved on the late 1973 sell signal. Earlier signals are also given in April 1971 and April 1972, but in no way are the signals from the unamended system affected adversely.

Table 9-4 shows how the unamended system would have performed

TABLE 9-4 Commercial Paper Trading System

			Basis points			
			Long position		*Short position*	
Signal	*Date*	*Yield*	*Profit*	*Loss*	*Profit*	*Loss*
Sell	1/24/69	650				
Buy	10/10/69	873			223	
Sell	11/14/69	841	32			
Buy	2/20/70	855			14	
Sell	6/26/70	825	30			
Buy	8/7/70	800				25
Sell	4/30/71	480	320			
Buy	10/15/71	563			83	
Sell	4/7/72	450	113			
Buy	10/19/73	903			453	
Sell	3/29/74	910		7		
Buy	10/27/74	1058			148	
Sell	6/27/75	618	440			
Buy	10/24/75	623			5	
Sell	4/30/76	515	108			
Buy	8/20/76	550			35	
Sell	3/4/77	485	65			
Buy	2/16/79	1002			517	
Total			1108	7	1478	25

SUMMARY	
Total profitable positions	2586
Less total unprofitable positions	32
Net profit	2554

in the 1969–1979 period. A total of 18 signals were given, of which 16 proved profitable and two were unprofitable. The total net gain from taking positions on the long and short side was 2554 basis points. Such results would not necessarily have been identical from trading a nearby futures contract, but even so the indicated profit leaves a considerable margin for any difference.

CURRENCIES

THE DEUTSCHEMARK VERSUS THE DOLLAR

Chart 9-6 shows the spot exchange rate (weekly close) of the deutschemark against the American dollar with its 13-week rate of change. A rising index indicates that the deutschemark is appreciating against the American dollar, and vice versa. The deutschemark is a very liquid currency relative to Swiss or French francs, for example, so that while the deutschemark/dollar relationship experiences volatile swings, its daily price changes are rarely dramatic and are subject to limit moves on the currency futures markets. For this reason the deutschemark/dollar relationship lends itself well to mechanical trading systems.

The system suggested is similar to that for 4- to 6-month commercial paper, except that the moving average of the currency is reduced to 10 weeks, and the 13-week rate of change is smoothed by a 3-week moving

CHART 9-6 Deutschemark in Terms of U.S. Dollar versus Momentum Index

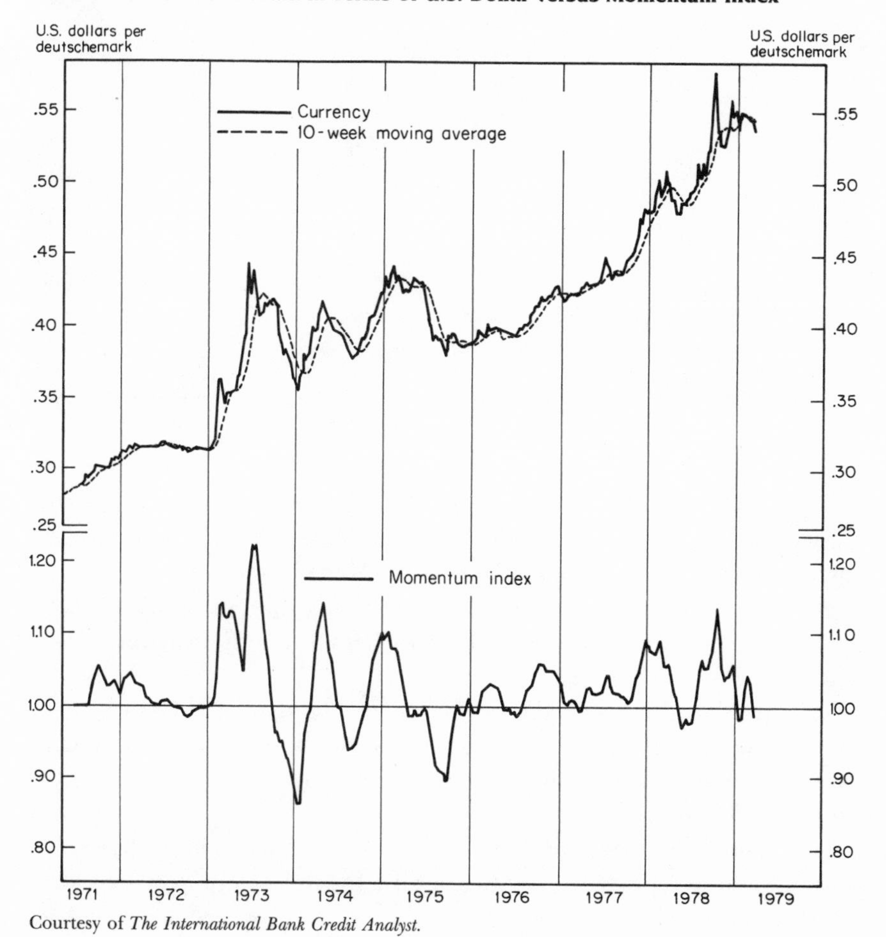

Courtesy of *The International Bank Credit Analyst.*

TABLE 9-5 Deutsche mark vs. U.S. Dollar Trading System

			Long position		*Short position*	
Signal	*Date*	*Value (U.S. cents)*	*Profit*	*Loss*	*Profit*	*Loss*
Buy	6/4/71	28.35				
Sell	8/25/72	31.32	2.97			
Buy	1/26/73	31.41				.09
Sell	9/21/73	41.40	9.99			
Buy	3/22/74	38.81			2.59	
Sell	7/12/74	39.18	.37			
Buy	11/8/74	39.20				.02
Sell	4/25/75	41.92	2.72			
Buy	12/26/75	38.21			3.71	
Sell	5/28/76	38.60	.39			
Buy	8/13/76	39.48				.88
Sell	2/11/77	41.64	2.16			
Buy	3/4/77	41.80				.16
Sell	3/25/77	41.84	.04			
Buy	4/22/77	42.17				.33
Sell	5/19/78	47.13	4.96			
Buy	7/28/78	48.91				1.78
Sell	3/30/79	53.58	4.67			
Total			28.27		6.30	3.26

SUMMARY

Total profit from long and short positions	34.57c
Less total losses from long and short positions	3.26
Net profit	31.31c

average. Smoothing the momentum index filters out several unwelcome whipsaw signals where the 13-week ROC index would otherwise anemically cross its 100 reference line and then return below it after a 2- to 3-week period. On the other hand, the smoothing does not unduly delay any of the remaining signals. The record for this system from 1971–1978 is shown in Table 9-5.

Reference to this table shows the net profit that could have been earned by judiciously following this system would have been 31.31c. When it is considered that the value of a 1c move in a deutschemark futures contract is $1250, it can readily be seen that the almost $40,000 profit derived from the trading of one contract would have been well worthwhile, assuming, of course, that the nearby future did not diverge significantly from the value of the spot.

THE POUND STERLING VERSUS THE AMERICAN DOLLAR

The final system deals with the sterling/dollar relationship, shown in Chart 9-7. Like the deutschemark, the pound is an actively traded currency subject to long-term volatile swings but sufficiently docile on a week-to-week basis to warrant profitable intermediate trading possibilities.

The system developed for the pound involves a 10-week moving aver-

CHART 9-7 Pound Sterling in Terms of U.S. Dollar versus Two Momentum Indexes

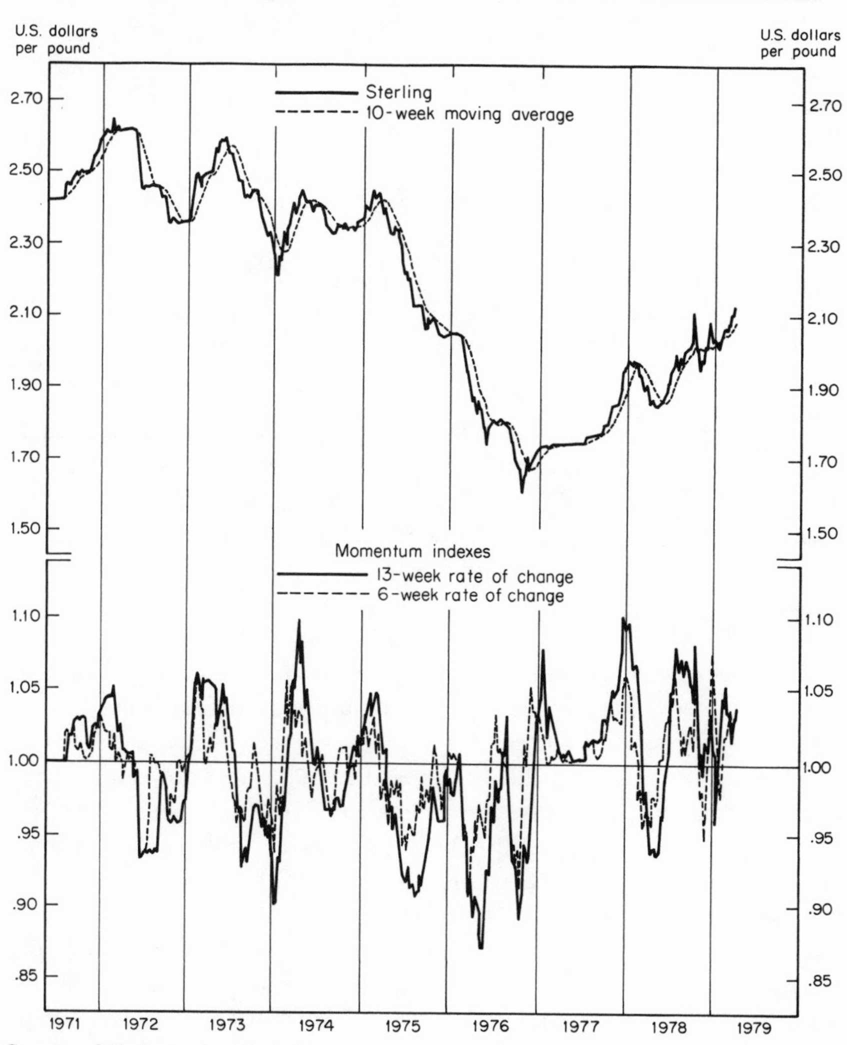

Courtesy of *The International Bank Credit Analyst.*

TABLE 9-6 Pound Sterling vs. U.S. Dollar Trading System

			Long position		*Short position*	
Signal	*Date*	*Value U.S. $*	*Profit*	*Loss*	*Profit*	*Loss*
Buy	6/4/71	241.90				
Sell	6/16/72	259.40	17.50			
Buy	1/26/73	236.10			23.30	
Sell	8/10/73	247.80	11.70			
Buy	3/15/74	233.30			14.50	
Sell	6/28/74	239.10	5.80			
Buy	12/27/74	234.60			4.50	
Sell	4/25/75	235.20	.60			
Buy	12/31/76	170.26			64.94	
Sell	3/13/78	186.50	16.24			
Buy	7/7/78	187.70				1.20
Sell	11/17/78	193.10	5.40			
Total			57.24c		107.24	1.20

SUMMARY

Total profit from long and short position	164.48
Less total losses from long and short position	1.20
Net profit	163.28

age of the currency itself with a 6- and 13-week rate of change. Signals are given when the pound crosses above or below its 10-week MA, and this is confirmed by both rates of change crossing above their 100 reference lines in the same direction. Normally the 6-week ROC will lead its 13-week counterpart both up and down, but quite often during potential whipsaw moves the 6-week ROC will return to its previous position vis-á-vis the 100 reference line before the 13-week index can confirm what would otherwise be a whipsaw signal. For example, during the middle of 1976 the 6-week ROC rose sharply above its 100 reference line at a time when the currency had crossed above its 10-week MA. The 13-week ROC lagged behind and did not cross the 100 line until some weeks after. By this time, however, the 6-week ROC had fallen below the 100 line and the price index was just about to undertake a sharp decline to its ultimate bear market low. Because of the severity of the decline and the fact that the 13-week ROC works on a longer cycle than the 6-week one, the inclusion of this shorter-term ROC index would have kept the 1975 sell signal in force, thereby permitting investors to maximize profits on "long" dollar positions and minimize commission costs. Reference to Chart 9-7 shows that this filtering technique was also useful in early 1976.

Table 9-6 shows that the adoption of this system would have resulted in 11 buy and sell signals during the 1972–1978 period. Ten of the signals would have been profitable and only one unprofitable. If an investor had adopted this system using 10 percent margin on a futures contract (3 to 4 percent is normally all that is required), and assuming that the movement in the nearby contract months did not differ appreciably on a net basis from the spot, then by reinvesting the profits from each signal an initial investment of $10,000 in 1971 would have grown to over $1 million by the end of 1978. Even though hypothetical transactions ignore commission costs and capital gains taxes, the results would still be staggering. The calculations are shown in Table 9-7.

It should be noted that this system in no way guarantees such a successful performance in the future. However, the fact that it has worked profitably for several other currencies with excellent, though less spectacular, results shows that it has been a consistent money-maker. The example discussed here is clearly an extreme one, and is used to demonstrate the potential of a reasonably reliable mechanical system combined with the power of leverage that can be obtained in the futures markets. Nevertheless, leverage works both ways, and can work against as well as for the investor. Consequently, a position should never be undertaken in the futures market until some experience has been gained in the cash markets which are considerably less risky.

TABLE 9-7 Profit from a $10,000 Investment Using the £ Trading System (Based on 10% margin)

Signal	*Date*	*Percentage profit (loss)*	*Percentage increase (decrease) adjusted for leverage*	*Cumulative profit*
Buy	6/4/71			$10,000
Sell	6/16/72	7.2	72	$17,200
Buy	1/26/73	9.0	90	$32,680
Sell	8/10/73	5.0	50	$49,020
Buy	3/15/74	5.9	59	$77,942
Sell	6/28/74	2.5	25	$97,428
Buy	12/27/74	1.9	19	$115,939
Sell	4/25/75	.3	3	$119.418
Buy	12/31/76	27.6	276	$449,011
Sell	3/31/78	9.5	95	$875,572
Buy	7/7/78	(.6)	(6)	$823,038
Sell	11/17/78	2.8	28	$1,053,489

PART THREE

SOURCES OF INFORMATION

10
INFORMATION SOURCES FOR EQUITY AND BOND MARKETS

With the explanation of trading techniques completed it is appropriate to review sources which will provide data or charts which can be used as a basis for formulating investment decisions. This chapter also will provide names, addresses, and other relevant information on institutions offering suitable vehicles for trading the various financial markets.

DATA SOURCES

Several sources of financial data have been referred to in the preceding chapters. It is not necessary to subscribe to a large number of publications, but it is more or less essential to receive either *The Wall Street Journal* or *The New York Times, Barron's,* and the *Financial Times* of London.[1] The combinantion of the *Financial Times* of London and one or more of the American publications will provide data on the world's gold asset, currency stock markets, and international interest rates.

Unfortunately, no indexes of foreign interest rates or bond prices (except for the United Kingdom) are published in these newspapers. However, the *Finanaical Times* of London has started publishing a selection of Eurobonds denominated in foreign currencies as well as American dollars which, if so desired, can be individually plotted to follow the bond markets of these currencies more closely. Quotations on futures contracts are available in *The Wall Street Journal* and *Barron's*.

[1] *Financial Times*, of London, Bracken House, Cannon St., London, U.K. Mail subscription approximately $365.

These publications also carry quotes of many American and foreign mutual funds. The international coverage of mutual funds is extremely comprehensive in the *Financial Times* of London, the only truly international financial newspaper. The *International Herald Tribune*[2] publishes American stock and Eurodollar bond prices and also international mutual funds.

For information on specific countries, the following English-language publications are recommended.

AUSTRALIA	*Australian Financial Review* (daily). Broadway, Sydney, Australia. 1501 Broadway, New York, N.Y., 10036.
	The Daily Telegraph, 168 Castelreigh, Sydney, Australia.
	Sydney Morning Herald, 235 Jones Street, Broadway, Sydney, Australia.
BRITAIN	*Investor's Chronicle,* 30 Finsbury Square, London, U.K.
CANADA	*The Toronto Globe and Mail* Business Reports (daily). 444 Front Street West, Toronto, Ontario, Canada.
	Financial Post (weekly). 481 University Avenue, Toronto, Ontario, Canada.
	Financial Times (weekly). 1885 Leslie Street, Don Mills, Ontario, Canada.
ITALY	*Daily American,* Due Macelli, 23 Rome, Italy.
JAPAN	*The Japan Economic Journal* (weekly). 9-5 Otemachi, 1-chome Chiyoda-KV Tokyo, Japan.
	The Japan Stock Journal (weekly). CPO Box 702, Tokyo, Japan.

Historical data on individual stock indexes can usually be obtained by writing to the particular stock exchange concerned. In this connection, a list of foreign stock exchanges, stock brokers, and local non-English financial publications are listed in Appendix 4.

Back data on futures markets can be purchased from the Commodity Research Bureau[3] for a relatively nominal charge. For investors wishing to follow the American debt markets in greater detail, a subscription to *The Money Manager*[4] is recommended.

In order to obtain a wider number of financial markets to trade with-

[2] *International Herald Tribune,* 21 Rue de Berri, Paris, France.

[3] Commodity Research Bureau, 1 Liberty Plaza, New York, N.Y., 10006.

[4] *The Money Manager,* 1 State Street Plaza, New York, N.Y.

out the drudgery of charting them all, it is possible to subscribe to several chart services. These services usually plot only the price action of a market. Sometimes volume, relative strength, or a proprietary momentum index is published, but very rarely is a simple 12-month or 13-week rate of change offered which the investor can update for himself (see Table 10-1).

A WORD ON TAXES

Most foreign governments withhold taxes on interest rates and dividends from securities held by nonresidents. The percentage amount depends upon both local tax law and whether or not the country has a tax treaty with the United States. Any tax paid to a foreign government in this way can be used to offset American taxes, subject to certain limitations. Capital gains taxes are not generally levied by foreign governments on American residents, but are taxable by American authorities in the same way as a domestically earned capital gain. One of the few cases where foreign governments tax nonresidents on capital gains occurs indirectly through the purchase of an investment trust. It would appear that American residents are unable to offset such taxes when filing American tax returns.

One of the advantages of investing in any of the offshore mutual funds based in a tax haven discussed below or listed in Appendix 3 is that there are no withholding taxes on interest and dividend disbursements. Eurobond issues are not subject to withholding taxes either.

One word of caution is in order, for while every effort has been made to ensure the reliability of information described here, tax laws are always in a state of flux. Consequently, investors are advised to always check out the facts through a tax or financial adviser.

INVESTMENT VEHICLES: EQUITY MARKETS

Equity markets can of course be purchased (at least in part) by acquisition of individual stocks. From the point of view of the international investor, it is easier, and in most cases cheaper, to buy mutual funds geared to a particular country's stock market. Unless the portfolio of a fund is weighted precisely the same way as the stock index, its performance will not correspond exactly with that of the index. However, the relationship is usually close enough to the stock average concerned, as reference to some of the charts included in this chapter will show. In any event, it is possible to obtain a prospectus of any fund intended for purchase from

TABLE 10-1 International Chart Services

Company name	*Address*	*Market*	*Published**
Investment Research	28 Panton St. Cambridge, CB2 1Drl U.K.	Currencies	Weekly
Investment Research	28 Panton St. Cambridge, CB2 1Drl U.K.	Gold and gold assets	Weekly
Chart Analysis	37–39 St. Andrews Hill London EC45DD, U.K.	Currencies	Weekly
Chart Analysis	37–39 St. Andrews Hill London EC45DD, U.K.	Currencies and commodities	Weekly
Chart Analysis	37–39 St. Andrews Hill London EC4 5DD. U.K.	International stock markets and individual stocks	Weekly
Commodity Research Bureau, Inc.	1 Liberty Plaza New York, N.Y., 10006	Commodity futures including gold, currencies, and interest rates	Weekly
Capital International SA	51 Rue de Cendrier Geneva	International stock markets	Monthly
Interest Rate Review	11 Regency Place London SWIP2EA, U.K.	International interest rates, charts, and data	Biweekly
Trendline	345 Hudson St. New York, N.Y., 10014 Tel. 212-924-6400	U.S. stock indexes, currencies, and individual U.S. stocks	Weekly
Independent Survey Co.	P.O. Box 6000 Vancouver, B.C., Canada	Canadian industrial stocks, mining, and oil stocks	Monthly
Graphascope	32 Front Street Toronto, Ont., Canada	Canadian industrial resource stocks and selected Canadian mutual funds	Monthly
Securities Research	Boston, Mass.	U.S. stock indexes Industry indexes and individual stocks (2-year history)	Monthly
Securities Research	Boston, Mass.	U.S. stock indexes Industry indexes and individual stocks (10-year history)	Quarterly

* A complimentary sample copy or inexpensive trial can usually be obtained from most organizations on request.

which a clear knowledge of its performance and investment policy can be gained. Moreover, many fund managers will provide a historical chart comparing the performance of their fund to that of the stock index to which the portfolio of the fund is geared.

AMERICAN STOCK MARKET

There are basically two types of open-ended mutual funds[5] in the United States, those that have an acquisition or loading fee, and those, known as "no-load funds," that do not. The investment performance of both sets of funds has differed very little so that in recent years the tendency has been for the industry to move more toward the no-load concept, which of course has been to the advantage of the investor, since the acquisition charge of up to 8 percent typically went to agents as a commission and did not directly benefit the investor. Fund managers usually obtain their reward from a nominal annual fee of ½ to ¾ percent of the fund's net asset value. A comprehensive list of no-load funds, with their investment objectives, etc., is given in Appendix 2. Most funds are valued daily and are quoted in *The Wall Street Journal* and most of the other American financial publications.

The largest mutual fund group in America, Fidelity Management, has recently changed to the no-load system. Moreover, the company permits switching between its various funds at no charge, either by wire or other form of written communication, or by telephone. The group consists of a wide variety of funds including equity, U.S. corporate, government, tax-exempt, and money market vehicles.

It is now possible to buy mutual funds in the United States that are almost perfectly indexed to the S&P 500. One such fund is the First Index Investment Trust.[6] This particular fund is mentioned because there is no purchase or redemption charge and also because investors holding stocks included in the S&P 500 who wish to purchase the fund can do so by trading in their components at the prevailing market value without any additional cost. The fund obtains its income from a modest management fee. It is also part of the Vanguard Group of funds which allows switching between its individual funds at no charge in a similar manner to the Fidelity Group, except that as a general rule written re-

[5] For a description of open-ended versus closed-end funds, see the Glossary.

[6] The Vanguard Group Inc., Drummer's Lane, Box 1100, Valley Forge, Pa., 19482, tel. 800-523-7910.

quests are required for switching. Other funds included in the group are a money market fund (with check-writing privileges), a corporate bond fund, three tax-exempt bond funds (short, medium, and long maturity), as well as an equity fund oriented toward emerging growth companies.

There are many advantages of dealing with a diverse family of funds with no acquisition or redemption charge. For example, a trading system based on the S&P 500 would require periodic entry and exit from the market. At times when the technical approach indicated that investors should be out of the market, positions could be transferred almost immediately to a money market fund, which calculates interest on a daily basis, until the stock market environment appeared more encouraging.

FOREIGN STOCK MARKETS

In continental Europe stocks and bonds are usually purchased through a bank rather than a broker as is the case in most of the rest of the world. A list of major banks and brokers for each country is given in Appendix 4.

Many institutions offer mutual funds based on specific foreign stock markets, but unfortunately few of them can be obtained in the United States, since they have not been registered with the SEC. It is not illegal for Americans to own these funds, but it is against the law for the funds themselves to solicit American clients directly. Consequently, it is necessary for an American investor to purchase these overseas funds by contacting the companies on his own initiative.

The countries for which mutual funds are readily available are Australia, Britain, Canada, Germany, and Japan. A list of funds in these and other countries, with other relevant information, is given in Appendix 3. It should be noted that this is only a partial list; resourceful readers will be able to find many other funds.

Since the object is to purchase a mutual fund that reflects an actual stock market index as closely as possible, it is not really necessary to become involved with more than one fund for any particular country. Almost all the funds listed in Appendix 3 are the open-ended variety and can be obtained from the sponsoring manager as indicated.

An open-ended fund is one that can issue and redeem its own shares.[7] The legal form of open-ended funds varies from country to country. In Britain, for example, there are "trusts" in the strict sense that the assets

[7] For a detailed definition of closed-end and open-ended funds, see the Glossary.

are held by a trustee on behalf of the unit holders, and are managed under the terms of a management contract by a management company. The precise legal form is not important from an investment point of view. However, where a fund has been established in a country with very loose or even nonexistent laws, and where government supervision is clearly suspect, the investor should assure himself that in addition to the manager there is an independent trustee or custodian who will look after the interests of unit holders. Although no guarantee is given, the funds listed in Appendix 3 are managed by reputable investment groups with a reasonably long track record of fair and ethical conduct.

The purchase of most foreign funds involves the payment of a load-

CHART 10-1 European Growth Fund versus Eurosyndicat Index*

This chart shows how it is possible to gear a mutual fund portfolio to a selection of different countries. In this case the European Growth Fund is shown to correlate very closely with the Eurosyndicat Index as compiled by Capital International and published in several newspapers, including *The Wall Street Journal.* As is often the case, the individual fund outperforms the index against which it is measured.

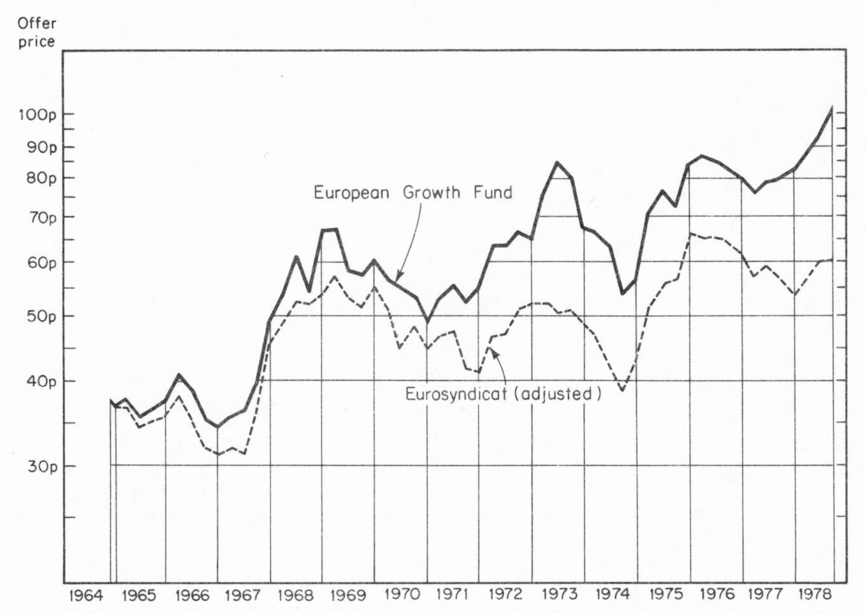

SOURCE: Baring Brothers & Co., Limited.

* European Growth Fund is an authorized U.K. unit trust, part of the Save and Prosper Group. It is invested in Continental securities, has been managed by Barings since its inception in November 1964, and is currently £8.5 million in size. It is financed by both premium and loans, and the Eurosyndicat Index is adjusted in proportion.

ing charge. This is usually a commission payable to a distributor or agent, and normally varies from 1½ to 8 percent of the net asset value, depending on the particular fund and the size of the purchase. Typically, there is a small management fee between ½ to ¾ percent per annum of the total net asset value of the fund. Redemptions are usually free of charge and are based on the net asset value. Redemption procedures vary from fund to fund. Most of the funds form part of a larger group and in many cases switching privileges are available, usually for a nominal fee well below the initial acquisition charge. In addition, most funds have automatic investment and systematic withdrawal plans. There is usually no charge for reinvesting dividends or interest. A substantial number of these groups of funds are quoted in the *Financial Times* of London under the heading of Authorised Unit Trusts, or under the Offshore and Overseas Fund sections.

There are about 400 unit trusts in Britain managed by about 100 different management groups. Managers include brokers, merchant banks, independent management companies, clearing banks, and insurance companies. Units in the trusts can be obtained either from the manager or an authorized distributor. Unit trusts generally invest in British securities, international bonds, or international equities. However, many also specialize in equities of specific countries such as Japan, Canada, Austrailia, Germany, etc. The M&G Fund is the largest British unit trust organization. Unit trusts provide a wealth of information on their funds, including an annual yearbook showing the performance of the funds against the appropriate share index. The yearbook also includes other useful information for investors.

Offshore and overseas funds quoted in the *Financial Times* of London are usually located in tax havens such as Luxembourg, the Channel Islands, Bermuda, etc.

The term "offshore" is given to any mutual fund established in a specific location to reduce or defer tax obligations, and complete freedom in the movement of funds is retained. These funds are therefore completely free to invest and disburse money in any part of the world. They are rarely managed in the country of their legal seat. Because of the higher costs involved and the greater advantage to investors, such funds usually charge higher initial sales charges and management fees than their domestic counterparts.

One tremendous advantage in purchasing any foreign mutual fund, as opposed to individual shares, is that the administrative chore of choosing shares, obtaining and transferring certificates, etc., which can

CHART 10-2 Stratton Trust versus Financial Times Actuaries 500 Index

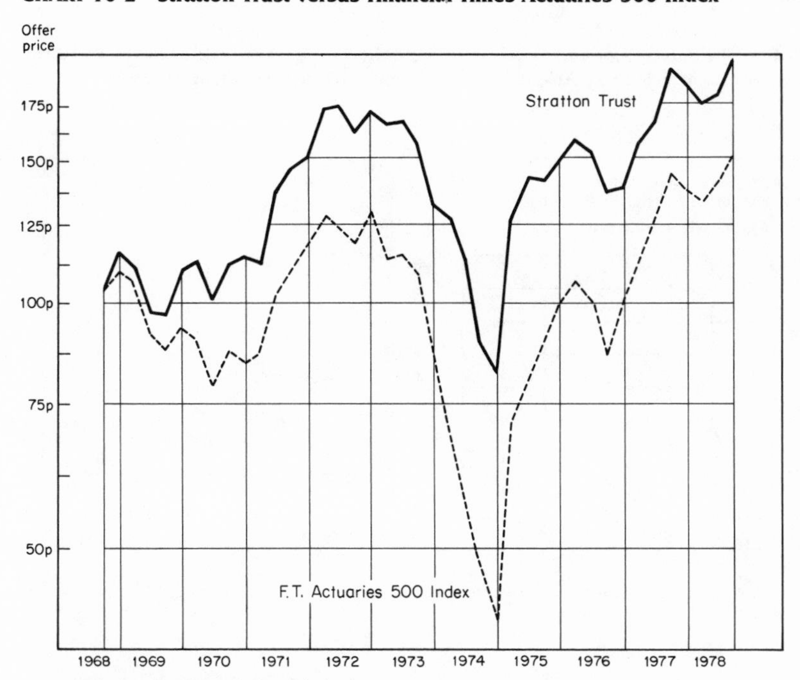

SOURCE: Baring Brothers & Co., Limited.

Information concerning the Stratton Trust is presented in Appendix 3.

CHART 10-3 Henderson-Baring Japan Fund versus Tokyo Stock Exchange Index

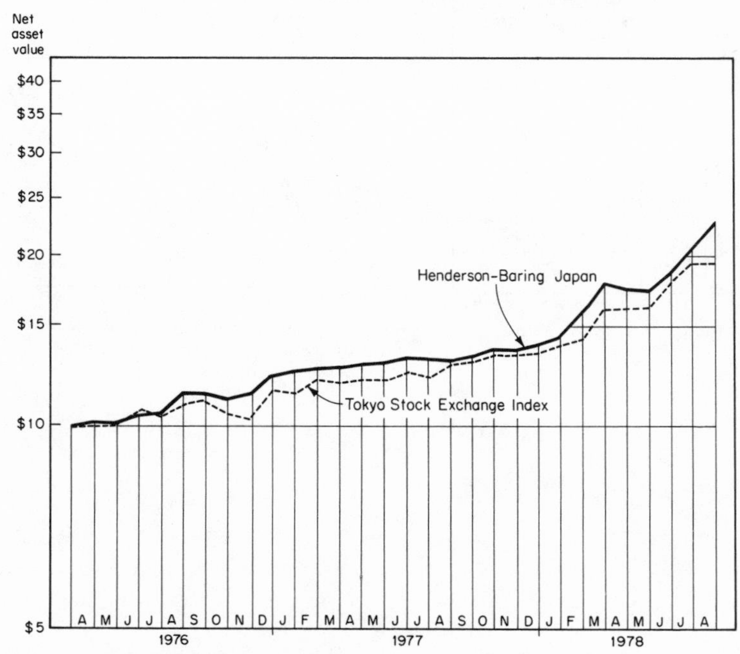

SOURCE: Baring Brothers & Co., Limited.

Information concerning the Henderson-Baring Japan Fund is presented in Appendix 3.

CHART 10-4*a* The Australian and General Exempt Fund versus the Sydney All-Share Index

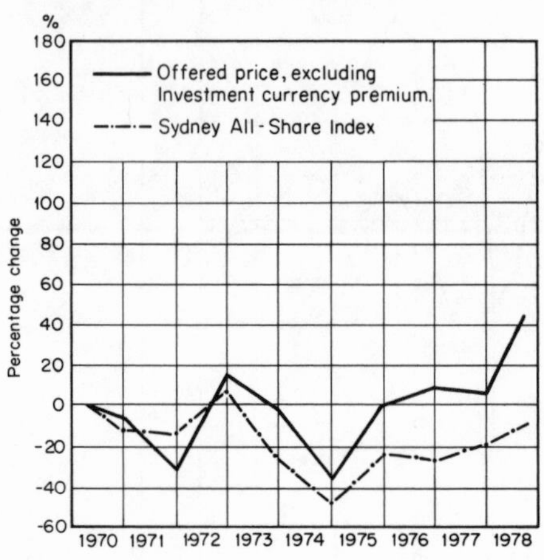

Information concerning this fund is presented in Appendix 3.

CHART 10-4*b* The M&G European Fund versus the Eurosyndicat Index

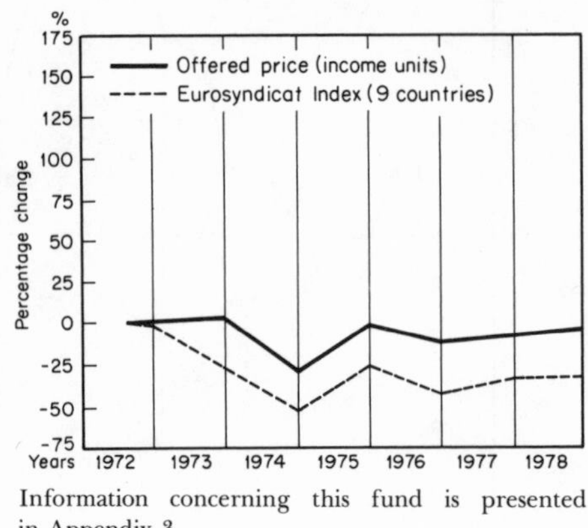

Information concerning this fund is presented in Appendix 3.

CHART 10-5 The M&G Australasian and General Fund versus the Sydney All-Share Index

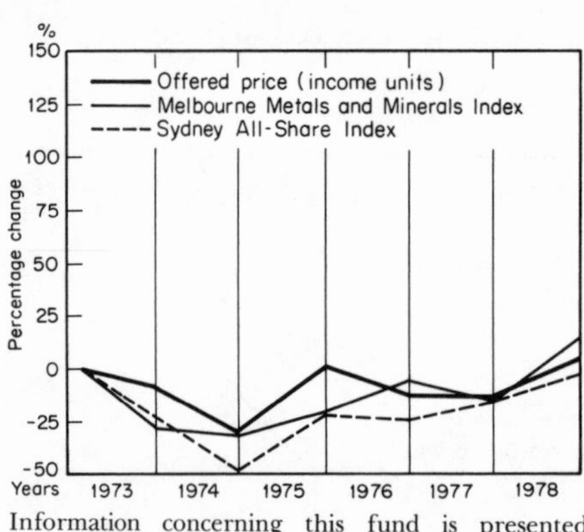

Information concerning this fund is presented in Appendix 3.

CHART 10-6 The M&G Japan Fund versus the New Tokyo Stock Exchange Indexes

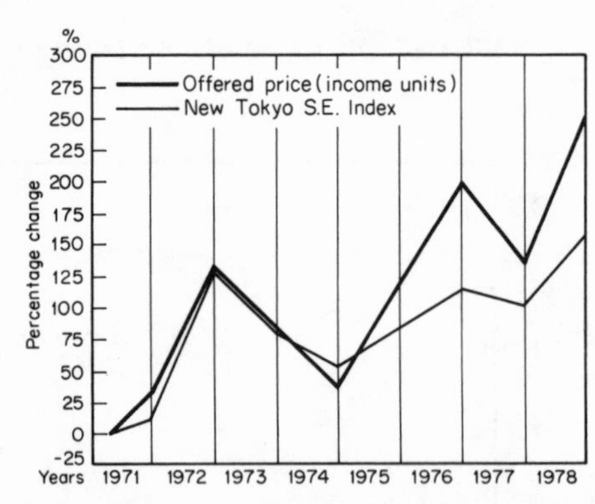

Information concerning this fund is presented in Appendix 3.

CHART 10-7 The M&G Far Eastern Fund versus the Hang Sen and Straits Times Indexes

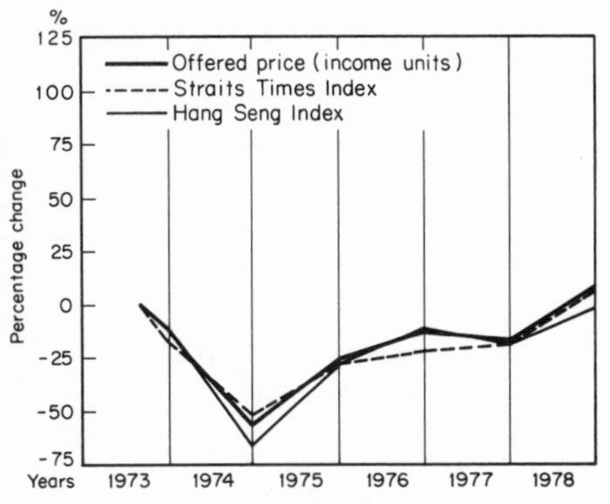

Information concerning this fund is presented in Appendix 3.

CHART 10-8 The M&G Recovery Fund versus the Financial Times Ordinary Index

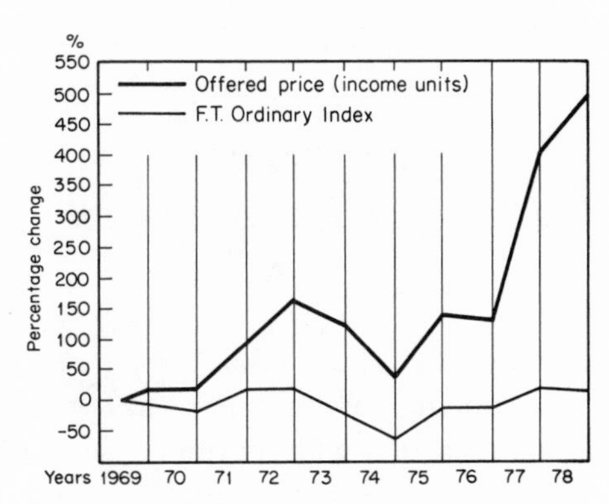

Information concerning this fund is presented in Appendix 3.

be very complicated when dealing with foreign governments, is significantly reduced.

The Union Bank of Switzerland offers the largest number of funds geared to specific stock markets. These are Australia, Canada, France, Germany, Italy, Japan, South Africa, and Switzerland. Acquisition costs are approximately 4 percent if purchased directly from the Union Bank. The shares can also be purchased on the Zurich stock exchange and it is well worth comparing the two sources, since listed prices are quite often well below the Union Bank's net issuing price. There is usually little or no redemption fee. Unlike the larger fund groups in the United States, it is not possible to make a commission-free switch from one fund to another.

The main drawback to incorporating this family of funds into an investment program is that most of them are not quoted in the English-language financial press, and can therefore only be obtained from the Bank itself or from a newspaper that quotes prices on the Zurich stock exchange. Since the net asset values of these funds reflect general market action, the inability to obtain quotes on a regular basis should not necessarily be viewed as a significant drawback since the investor will presumably be following the market index of the particular country concerned. If regular quotations are required, a subscription to one of the Swiss financial newspapers listed in Appendix 4 should prove worthwhile.

DEBT MARKETS

THE UNITED STATES

There are a variety of investment vehicles that can be used to participate in fluctuations of American bond prices. Bonds can be purchased on a cash basis or with margin, either individually or through a mutual fund. Greater leverage can of course be obtained from the purchase or sale of interest rate futures contracts. Individual bonds can be bought through any reputable investment banker or stockbroker.

Cash Markets The daily price action of government bonds can easily be monitored through the major financial publications such as *The Wall Street Journal, The New York Times,* or weekly through *Barron's.* Prices are published in thirty-seconds of a point. For the purposes of charting and calculating moving averages, etc., it is usually better to convert these quoted fractions into decimals. Thus, 95 $^{16}/_{32}$ becomes 95.5, 96 $^{24}/_{32}$ becomes 96.75, etc. Data quoted in the financial press are the closing bid (price you will be paid in selling), the closing offered (price at which the bond can be purchased), and the yield to maturity. For charting purposes the bid price is the one normally used. Although this data is published on a daily basis, investments intended to be maintained for 3 months or more do not require such frequent recording. In such cases a weekly average or a Friday close presents a sufficient data base from which to proceed.

Although discrepancies between prices of individual U.S. Treasury bonds can occur from time to time due to temporary aberrations in their supply and demand relationships, these are only of minor significance, so that the long end of the bond market can easily be followed by recording and charting one bond. In any event, it is possible to follow the course of the American government bond market through weekly yields published by Moody's, S&P, or the Federal Reserve Board, each of which has a yield index for long-term U.S. government bonds. Such data is not readily available in the financial press but yield indexes are published in the St. Louis Federal Reserve Bank's *Weekly Monetary Statistics,* which is normally available on request.[8] *The New York Times* also publishes a government and corporate yield index, based on data compiled by Salomon Bros., a major investment house.

As discussed in Chapter 3, U.S. Treasury obligations can be purchased with as little as 10 percent margin. Given this amount of leverage, a 1 percent movement in the prices of these bonds will result in a 10 percent movement in the value of the equity put up. Margin can be arranged through most banks and stockbrokers.

Quotations for individual corporate and tax-exempt obligations are not so readily available. The monitoring of these markets is therefore better accomplished by recording and charting widely followed bond yield indexes such as Moody's AAA or S&P's AAA.

Such yields can be charted on a weekly basis. Unfortunately, they are not quoted in *The Wall Street Journal* or *Barron's.* This is probably because their publisher (Dow Jones and Company) has its own bond index. The Dow Jones Corporate Bond Indexes are based on prices of bonds traded on the NYSE. Since by far the greater number of bond transactions are done on the over-the-counter market, the Dow Jones Index has a tendency to lag the bond market. Monitoring this index is therefore not recommended.

A good alternative to purchasing individual bonds is the acquisition of a no-load mutual fund. This enables investors to obtain a portfolio of debt obligations without the necessity of paying commissions.

The purchase and sale of such vehicles should be based on the trend in the yield index to which their investment policy orients them. Investment decisions on a corporate bond fund should therefore be based on the performance of Moody's or S&P AAA yields, a government fund on a long-term government yield index, and so on.

Price movements will never correspond exactly to those in the respective yield index, since many mutual funds include funds of differing quality, or in the case of government funds, different maturities. For this reason it is often a good idea to review the portfolio of a fund which is intended for purchase from the prospectus, and also to chart its price from data published in the financial press. Back data on a particular fund can usually be obtained on request so that its performance can be compared to a yield index such as Moody's AAA, etc. A list of no-load U.S. bond mutual funds is shown in Appendix 2.

[8] Federal Reserve Board of St. Louis, 411 Locust, St. Louis, Mo., 63166.

Since tax-exempt bonds can and often do diverge from the performance of taxable obligations, it is important to chart an appropriate index such as the Money Manager Twenty Bond Index (published weekly in *The Money Manager* and the Federal Reserve Bank of St. Louis' weekly financial data) as well as the fund itself from which investment decisions can be made.

One important advantage of purchasing a no-load mutual bond fund, apart from the initial nonexistent transaction cost, is the fact that it is often possible to switch from a bond or tax-exempt fund to a money market fund at no cost. It is also possible to purchase a tax-exempt money market fund. The Warwick Municipal Fund offers a portfolio with a short-term maturity. This fund is part of the huge Vanguard Group which permits switching at no charge into any of its other bond equity or money market funds. The Fidelity Group has also recently introduced a tax-exempt money market fund.

United States Interest Rate Futures For investors who wish to obtain maximum leverage from changes in interest rate trends, interest rate futures contracts represent the ideal trading or investment vehicle. These instruments have only been available since late 1976, but in the subsequent years both the volume of daily transactions and the number of contracts available have increased substantially. A list of these different contracts is summarized in Table 10-2. Reference to the table shows that contracts representing significant amounts of money can be purchased with very little margin.

Contracts for short-term interest rates have a substantially greater outstanding value than longer-term maturities. Treasury bond contracts, for example, are denominated in $100,000 amounts while the comparable amount for a 3-month Treasury bill is $1,000,000. This is because the price movement for short-term bonds is considerably less than longer-term bonds so that a given economic development will have a tendency to affect the movement in value of these contracts more or less equally, although in practice a specific development has a specific effect on each market.

The prices of contracts for short-term interest rates are expressed as follows. The futures contract for U.S. (90-day) Treasury bills calls for par (100) delivery of T-bills having a face value of $1,000,000 at maturity. The actual price of a contract is quoted in terms of an index devised by the exchange which represents the annualized interest yield subtracted from 100. Thus, an index number of 93.0 indicates an annual

TABLE 10-2

Contract	*Exchange traded*	*Size of contract*	*Approx. round trip commission cost*	*Approx. margin*	*Minimum fluctuations*	*Daily limit*	*Dollar value of 1-point move*	*Liquidity*
Treasury bills	International Money Market	$1,000,000	$75	$1,700	1 basis point	50 basis points $1,250	1 point = $25	Good
30-Day commercial paper	Chicago Board of Trade	$3,000,000	$75	$1,700	1 basis point	25 points = $625	1 point = $25	Very poor
90-Day commercial paper	Chicago Board of Trade	$1,000,000	$75	$1,700	1 basis point	25 pts. = $625	1 point = $25	Poor
1 year T-bills		$250,000	$75	$600	1 basis point	50 points = $1,250	1 point = $25	Very poor
GNMA	Chicago Board of Trade Amex Commodity Exchange	$100,000 Principal	$75	$2,000	$\frac{1}{32}$ pt. = $31.25	2 points $2,000	1 point = $1,000	Good
Treasury bonds	Chicago Board of Trade	Face Value of $100,000 (coupon rate 8%)	$75	$2,250	$\frac{1}{32}$ pt. = $31.25	2 points $2,000	1 point = $1,000	Good

CHART 10-9 Ninety-Day Commercial Paper Futures Contract, December 1979

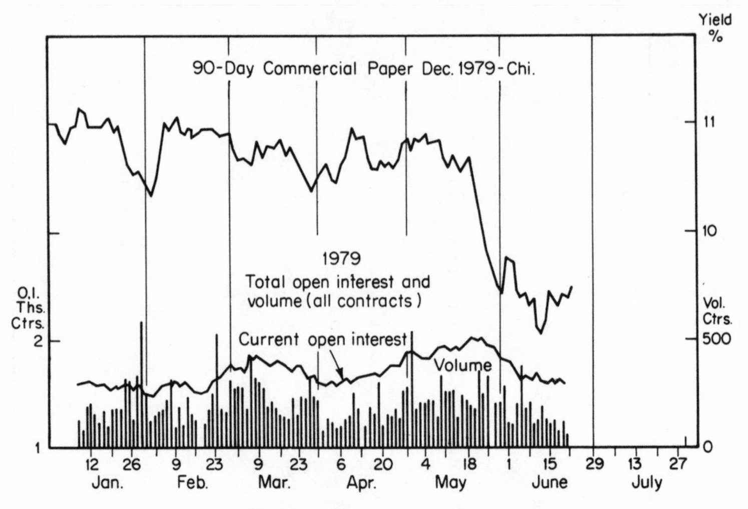

SOURCE: Commodity Research Bureau, Inc.

CHART 10-10 Ginnie Mae June 1979 Futures Contract versus Cash GNMA, 8%

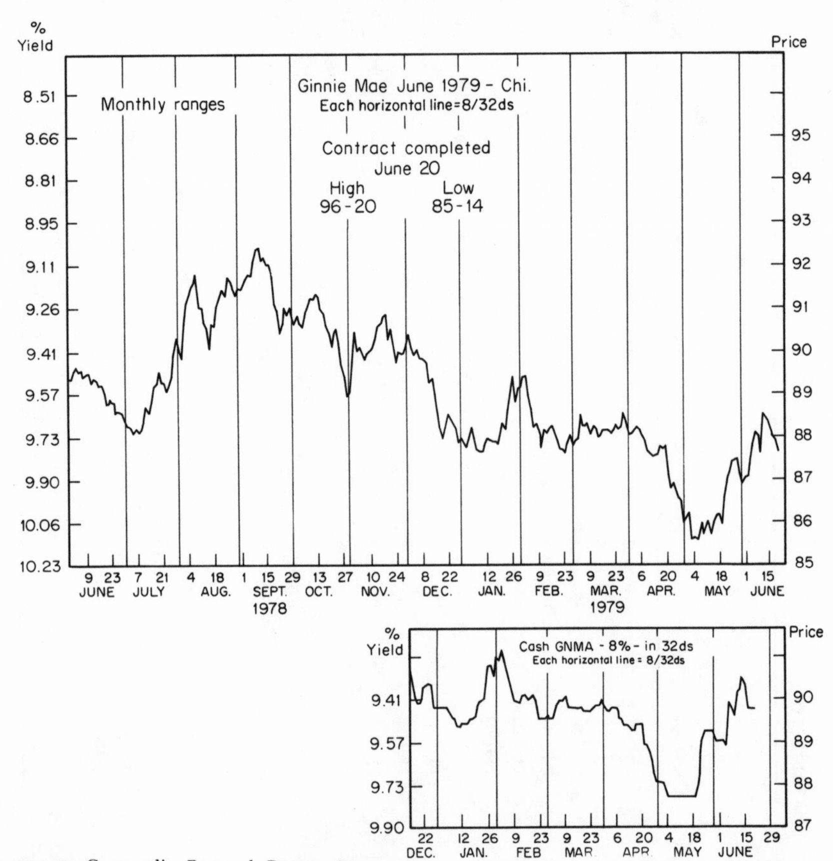

SOURCE: Commodity Research Bureau, Inc.

yield of 7 percent, 92.6 a yield of 7.4 percent, etc. The contract gains in value as the price goes up (i.e., the interest rate falls) and vice versa. Ninety-day commercial paper contracts are expressed in a similar manner.

GNMA and long-term government bonds are priced in thirty-seconds of a point. A movement of a whole point alters the value of the contract by $1000. A change of 16/32 of a point represents a half-point move, which results in a $500 change in value, etc. GNMAs (or Ginnie Maes as they are normally referred to) are government-guaranteed mortgage certificates. The trading unit of $100,000 has a stated interest rate of 8 percent and a maturity of 12 years. Price movements of Ginnie Mae futures correspond to long-term government bonds rather than corporate bonds. Treasury bonds are also traded in units of $100,000 and have a stated interest rate of 8 percent but a maturity of 20 years. Interest rate futures can be purchased through any reputable commodity dealer.

CHART 10-11 United States Treasury Bond September 1979 Futures Contract versus Cash U.S. Treasury Bond 7⅝ of 2002-7

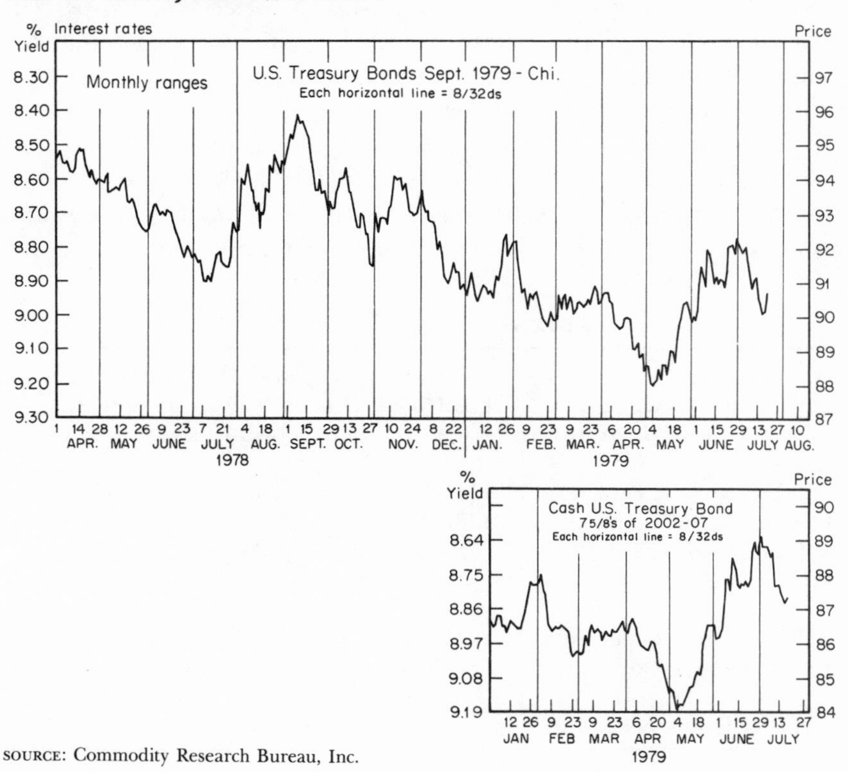

SOURCE: Commodity Research Bureau, Inc.

FOREIGN INTEREST RATES

British Bonds The United Kingdom has a well-developed market for British government securities but not for the corporate sector. These debt instruments are known as government stock gilt-edge securities, or more simply as "gilts." Gilts may be purchased through most British brokers in the United Kingdom, a few of which have a U.S. branch.

The names and addresses of several British brokers are listed in Table 10-3 below.

British debt obligations can also be obtained through the acquisition of a British debt-oriented mutual fund or a unit trust; a unit trust is the approximate British equivalent of a mutual fund.

The British debt market can be followed from quotations published in the *Financial Times* of London. In addition to listing prices of individual bonds, this newspaper also publishes several government security indexes based on varying maturities. The interest on some British bonds is not subject to withholding tax. Such issues are indicated in the *Financial Times* of London by a special notation. In this respect, the 3½-percent War Loan is a popular investment vehicle for nonresidents, not only because of its advantageous tax treatment, but also because of its low coupon and subsequent price volatility.

The British government also has several other undated bonds outstanding, i.e., those with no set maturity date. The bellwether bond in this respect is the 2½-percent Consol, which is well worth charting since its low coupon enables it to undergo substantial price swings.

TABLE 10-3 British Bond Dealers

W. Greenwell	Bow Bells House, Bread Street, London, U.K.
Phillips and Drew	Lee House, London Wall, London, U.K.
Rowe & Pitman, Hurst Brown	City Gate House, 39–45 Finsbury Sq., London, U.K.
Affiliate: Rowe & Pitman Inc.	111 Pine St., San Francisco, Ca., 94111
Cazenove & Company	12 Tokenhouse Yard, London, U.K.
Affiliate: Cazenove Inc.	67 Wall Street, New York, N.Y., 10005
James Capel & Co.	Winchester House, 100 Old Broad St., London, U.K.
Affiliate: James Capel Inc.	20 Exchange Place, New York, N.Y., 10005
Joseph Sebag & Co.	Bucklersbury House, 3 Queen Victoria St., London, U.K.
Affiliate: Joseph Sebag Inc.	523 West 6th St., Los Angeles, Ca., 90014

In view of the basic weakness of the British financial structure, cyclical swings in bond prices have been particularly large since the 1960s. Although margin purchases are difficult to arrange in Britain, it has still been possible to make handsome profits, especially during those periods when the British currency has been strong as well. Under the British system, payment for purchases is made every 24 days, so that the settlement date can range from as long as 3 weeks to as little as 10 days. This payment date is known as the account. Commission charges for gilt purchases and sales are approximately 1 percent each way. Several British unit trusts specializing in British gilts are quoted in the *Financial Times* of London. The details of two of them appear in Appendix 4.

Canadian Bonds The Canadian debt market is also well developed. There are three basic categories of bonds: government of Canada, provincials, and corporates. The greatest liquidity is to be found in the government sector, and it is in this area that the investor is advised to concentrate. The best source for Canadian debt quotations is the business report of *The Toronto Globe and Mail,* which is mailed daily. The Bank of Canada also publishes weekly average yields of federal and provincial obligations. Canadian bonds can be purchased from any big American stockbrokers which have offices in Canada such as Merrill Lynch, etc., but better prices will normally be obtained from the New York branches of Canadian dealers. A partial list of Canadian dealers is shown in Table 10-4.

European and Japanese Bonds The price trends of European and Japanese bonds often diverge for significant periods from their North American counterparts, so it is useful to monitor their progress.

While there are many mutual funds that offer a diverse portfolio of international bonds, few specialize in the debt instruments of a particular currency. Two such funds, oriented to deutschemark and Swiss franc bonds, are listed in Appendix 3.

One major problem concerning international bond market investment is the availability of data in the American financial press. Local financial newspapers and brokers (such as those listed in Appendixes 4 and 5) do carry such information, but to take out subscriptions for each country becomes a costly and tedious business.

TABLE 10-4 Dealers and Brokers of Canadian Bonds

Canadian investment dealers with New York City branches	*American brokers with Canadian branches or affiliates*
A. E. Ames & Co., Inc. 2 Wall Street New York, NY 10005	Bache Halsey Stuart Canada 18 King Street Toronto, Ontario, Canada
Burns, Fry Inc. 100 Wall Street New York, NY 10005	Dominic K Corporation of Canada Ltd. P. O. Box 272 Royal Trust Tower Toronto Dominion Centre Toronto, Ontario, Canada
Dominion Securities 100 Wall Street New York, NY 10005	Merrill Lynch Royal Securities 20 King Street West Toronto, Ontario, Canada
Greenshields & Co. Inc. 70 Pine Street New York, NY 10005	Shearson Hayden Stone Canada Inc. Suite 3304 Stock Exchange Tower Montreal, Quebec, Canada
McLeod, Young & Weir Inc. 63 Wall Street New York, NY 10005	
Pitfield, Mackay Inc. 30 Broad Street New York, NY 10004	
Wood Gundy Inc. 100 Wall Street New York, NY 10005	

Eurobond Market An alternative to purchasing foreign domestic bonds (which normally involves the payment of withholding taxes) is the Eurobond market, for which quotes are available in the *Financial Times* of London. A Eurobond is a bond issued by an international syndicate and sold outside the country in which it is denominated. Thus, a bond denominated in deutschemarks might be offered in London, one in sterling issued in Zurich, etc. Eurobonds have a number of important characteristics:

1. There is no withholding tax on interest payments.
2. They are not generally subject to government regulations.
3. They often yield more than domestic bonds.
4. Interest is paid annually.

This compares to most domestic issues whose payment is made semi-annually, and means that for a given yield the real return on a Eurobond issue is less than a domestic issue.

Since Eurobonds are not registered with the SEC they cannot be offered in the United States. However, after a certain period has elapsed, about 90 days, American brokers will sell bonds to American residents. Eurobonds are normally issued in bearer form. The most widely used currencies for Eurobond issues (apart from the American dollar which dominates the market) are the pound sterling, deutschemark, Canadian dollar, Dutch guilder, French franc, and Japanese yen.

Issuers of Eurobonds are essentially the same as in domestic markets, ranging from sovereign governments to local authorities and corporations. The size of offerings can range from the equivalent of less than $10 million to over $500 million.

Many Eurobonds are listed on the Luxembourg or some other official exchange to make them eligible for portfolios of institutions that can only buy listed securities. However, the vast amount of trading is done on the over-the-counter markets.

Initially, trading in most issues was very thin but as the market has developed liquidity over the years this has improved, but not to the degree of most domestic markets. The Association of International Bond Dealers[9] publishes monthly market quotations and yields of Eurobond issues as well as a directory of its members. Unfortunately, it has yet to develop and publish indexes of Eurobonds other than those denominated in Eurodollars. Table 10-5 gives a brief list of a few of the major American Eurobond dealers.

The *Financial Times* of London quotes prices for Eurobonds denominated in major currencies, and this is probably the best source of data yet available.

[9] c/o Allgemeine Trevhand A.G. P.O. Box 1057, 8022 Zurich, Switzerland.

TABLE 10-5 Major American Eurobond Dealers

Dealer	Address
Arnhold & S. Bleichroeder Inc.	30 Broad St., New York, N.Y., 10004
Kidder, Peabody & Co. Inc.	10 Hanover Square, New York, N.Y., 10005
Merrill Lynch Pierce Fenner & Smith Inc.	1 Liberty Plaza, New York, N.Y., 10006
Salomon Bros.	1 New York Plaza, New York, N.Y., 10004
White, Weld & Co. Inc.	91 Liberty Street, New York, N.Y., 10006

Most of the time Eurobond yields and prices move in the same directions as those of the domestic market of the currency concerned. In other words, Euroyen yields might be expected to closely follow those of domestically oriented Japanese bonds. However, from time to time Eurobonds can move fairly independently from domestic bonds due to the fact that foreign ownership of Eurobonds is greater and is therefore more responsive to currency fluctuations as well as local bond market conditions. For example, if monetary conditions are moderately restrictive in Canada, forcing yields to rise gently, and if the currency is under considerable pressure, non-Canadian owners of Eurobonds denominated in Canadian dollars will have two reasons for selling their bonds and will push the yields of Canadian dollar Eurobonds much higher than domestic Canadian yields. At the same time, because of regulations and unfavorable tax treatment, most Canadian financial institutions will be unable to take advantage of the higher Euro-Canadian yields or switch out-of-debt issues denominated in Canadian dollars. At some point the difference will become arbitraged, but due to institutional factors such as these, the arbitrage lag for most Eurobond markets seems to be much greater (lasting for several weeks or more) than for other markets, where it is usually instantaneous.

11
INFORMATION SOURCES FOR GOLD AND CURRENCY MARKETS

CASH MARKET

Gold bullion can be purchased at most major banks. An alternate method of buying gold is to purchase it through an agent and have it stored in the vault of a bank under a special custody agreement. The purchaser is issued a Gold Certificate of Deposit so that if the certificate is lost the records will still show the true ownership of the gold. Storing of the gold bullion by the agent also makes it easier to sell, since he arranges for transportation to the buyer. Dealing through an agent also excludes the need for expensive assaying costs. Moreover, purchases and sales can often be made with a simple telephone call.

The greatest advantage of all is that bulk purchases by the agent enable considerable cost savings to be passed on to the individual investor. For example, Dreyfus Gold Deposits Inc.[1] charges only a 3 percent sales fee on initial bullion investments of $2500 and a small storage fee of 10 cents per ounce per month.

For investors who are not dealing in substantial amounts of money and wish to limit their investment program to the cash market, this alternative has considerable merit.[2]

[1] Dreyfus Gold Deposits Inc., 600 Madison Avenue, New York, N.Y., 10022.

[2] Citibank of New York also offers gold bullion certificates in relatively small denominations.

GOLD FUTURES

Gold futures can be purchased through any reputable dealer in commodities. A variety of contracts are available on the New York Comex and Mercantile Exchange, and the International Money Market Exchange in Chicago. Gold futures contracts range in size from 1 kilo to 400 ounces. The larger the contract, the greater the change in value for any given price change. For example, a $1 movement in the price of gold translates to a $30.38c change in the value of a 1-kilo contract and a $400 change in the value of a 400-ounce contract.

Prices of gold futures contracts are invariably higher than those in the

CHART 11-1 June 1979 Gold Futures Contract versus Spot Gold

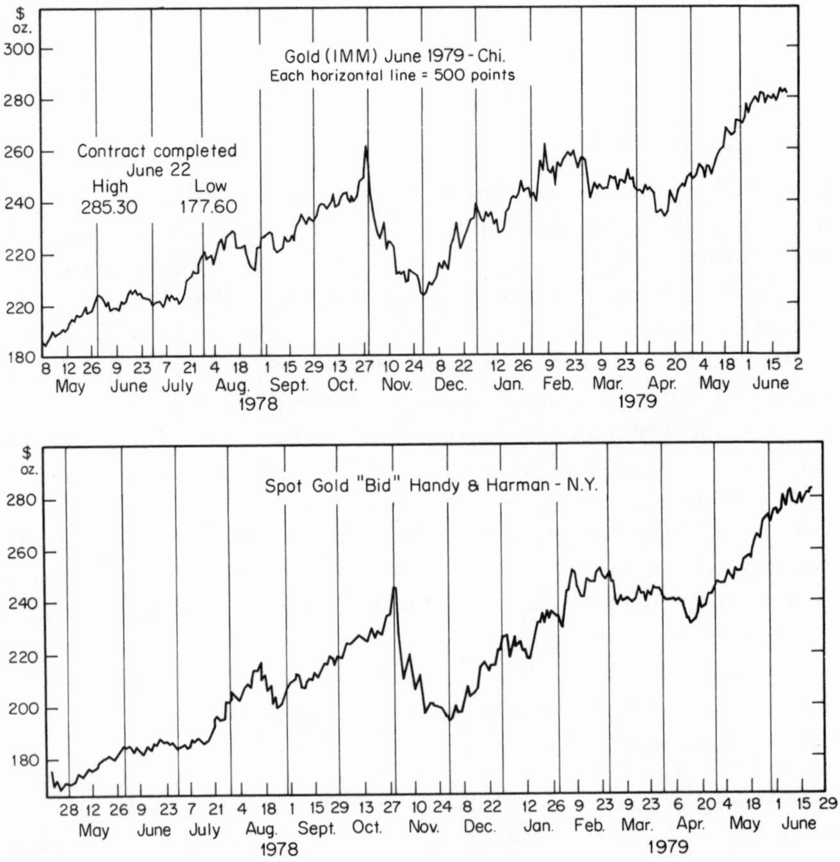

SOURCE: Commodity Research Bureau, Inc.

cash or spot markets because of an arbitrage against interest and storage costs. For example, if the prices of the spot and futures markets were the same, industrial users of gold could cut their gold inventories substantially since they would not have the cost of storing it or borrowing the money with which to finance their gold inventory. Given an identical price for cash gold and gold futures, investors would also prefer to own futures contracts because the very small margin required for futures contracts would release their surplus cash to be invested in interest-bearing assets. Consequently, the more distant a gold futures contract is, the higher its price tends to be in relation to that of the cash market. The actual spread (i.e., price difference) will depend on investor expectations of the future gold price as well as these arbitrage factors, storage, and interest rate levels. In some cases pessimistic expectations can be sufficiently extreme to create an inversion in prices, so that the distant futures actually sell at a discount to the spot price.

The relevant commission costs, contract size, etc., for gold futures contracts are illustrated in Table 11-1.

The margin requirements indicated are approximate amounts since each broker has different requirements and amounts can change dramatically over time given sharp price fluctuations. For example, in January 1979, the margin on a 100-ounce gold contract was $1000. By March 1980 it had risen to $20,000 per contract. The commission costs shown in Table 11-1 are also approximate. Quantity commission discounts are available from virtually all commodity dealers, while many even discount commission costs on single contracts.

GOLD SHARES

Gold shares can be purchased individually on the exchanges or the over-the-counter markets, or in the form of a mutual fund. Gold equities can be roughly thought of in three areas: Canadian, American, and South African. The latter are usually bought in the United States through the purchase of an American Deposit Receipt (ADR).

An ADR is issued by an American bank whenever there is sufficient investor interest in a stock. ADRs are issued for the shares of many different foreign companies other than South African gold mining shares, and may represent one underlying share or several. They can be registered either in the name of the broker (i.e., street name) or in that of the purchaser. The ADR bank collects dividends, and takes care of rights

TABLE 11-1 Gold Futures Contracts

Exchange traded	*Size of contract*	*Approximate round trip commission*	*Approximate margin*	*Minimum price fluctuation*	*Daily limit*	*Value of $1 move*	*Liquidity*
Comex	100 troy ozs	$75	$20,000	10c oz = $9.60	$25	$1 = $100	Poor
International Money Market	100 troy ozs	$75	$20,000	10c oz = $10	$25	$1 = $100	Good
New York Mercantile Exchange	1 kilo/32 troy ozs	$75	$6,000	20c oz = $6.40	$25	$1 = $32	Poor
	400 ozs	$250	$80,000	5c oz = $20	$25	$1 = $400	Poor

issues for which it charges a small fee. A small charge is also levied from their issue, transfer, and surrender. Investors will also suffer a small loss for currency conversions in connection with dividends. ADRs are traded on the over-the-counter market and are quoted in *The Wall Street Journal, The New York Times,* and *Barron's.* Their main advantage to American investors is that they can easily be bought or sold in American dollars through any major broker. In addition, time-consuming administrative problems of dividend collection, currency conversion, etc., are all taken care of for a nominal fee so that purchase and sale of an ADR becomes almost as simple as a transaction in a domestic stock.

South Africa is the free world's largest producer of gold and therefore offers a wide selection of shares. In view of the obvious political risks, South African gold equities have traditionally sold at much higher yields than their North American counterparts.

In contrast, Canadian gold shares offer significantly lower yields. Unfortunately, many of these companies have diversified away from being pure gold producers, as has the largest American producer, Homestake. For this reason the performance of specific stocks can often differ from that of gold equity markets as represented by the various indexes. Consequently, the investor is better advised to select a mutual fund that contains a wider range of stocks if he seeks to duplicate the performance of the indexes concerned.

One stock traded on the NYSE is a closed-end mutual fund specializing in South African gold stocks. The company is called ASA. Its price action during the 10 years from 1969 to 1979 is shown in Chart 11-2. A comparison between this chart and Chart 8-5 shows that the price movement of ASA fairly closely reflects those of the South African share index, although the magnitude of the movements differs due to the fact that the company's portfolio differs from the stocks included in the index, and also because trading in ASA is dominated by American investors, compared to the South African stocks themselves, which are influenced more by European interests. Moreover, since ASA is a closed end mutual fund, its price is continually moving between a discount and a premium over net asset or breakup value.

Another South African gold investment fund traded in America is AMGOLD (Anglo American Gold Investment Company). This ADR, which has an excellent portfolio of gold securities, usually sells at a discount to its net asset value.

Two open-ended, gold-related mutual funds that are available on a no-load basis are Golconda Investments and United Financial Services.

CHART 11-2 ASA 1967–1979

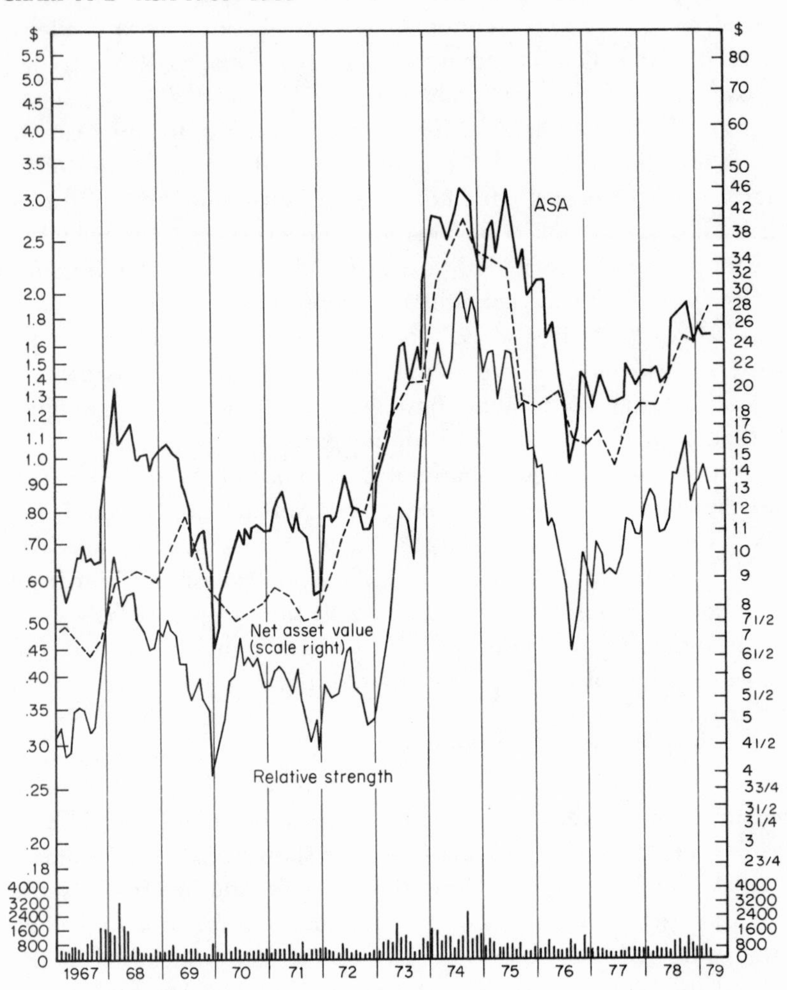

Courtesy of Securities Research.

Charts 11-3 and 11-4 show the price performance of these two funds in the 1976 to 1978 period. These charts should also be compared with Chart 8-5, which illustrates the South African Gold Share Index. One drawback to the United Services Fund is that there is a small redemption charge if investments are withdrawn within 6 months from the date of purchase. This fee is 2 percent if redeemed within 90 days, and 1 percent if redeemed between 91 days and 6 months. Its management and

CHART 11-3 Golconda Gold Fund

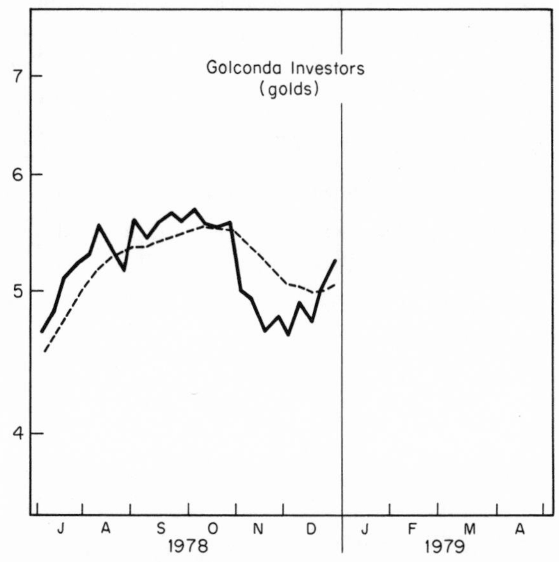

SOURCE: Switch Fund Advisory, 13024 Chestnut Oak Drive, Egithersbury, Md., 20760.

CHART 11-4 United Services Gold Fund

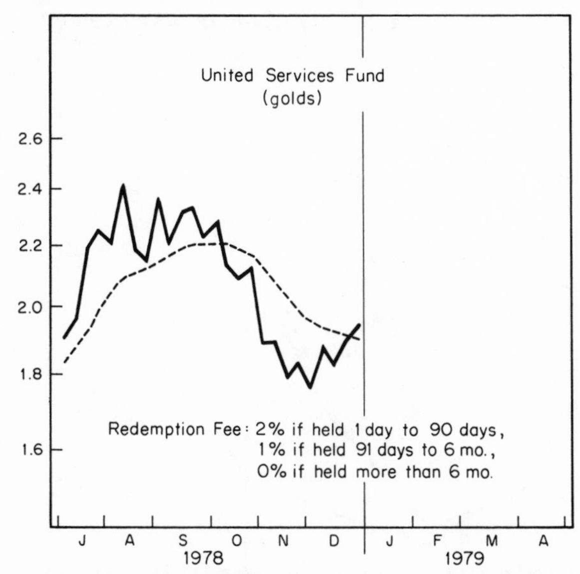

SOURCE: Switch Fund Advisory, 13024 Chestnut Oak Drive, Egithersbury, Md., 20760.

expense fees are also much higher than the industry average. Other relevant details of these two funds and the Gold Exempt Fund, which is managed by the M&G Group, are discussed below.

GOLCONDA INVESTORS LTD.

Golconda Investors Ltd. concentrates on equity securities of companies involved directly or indirectly in mining, processing, or dealing in gold. Assets under management were $2 million in 1978. There is no redemption charge. Shares may be exchanged for other members of the Bull and Bear Group at no charge.
Address:
111 Broadway, New York, New York, 10006.
Tel. 212-267-5100

UNITED SERVICES FUND

United Services Fund was incorporated February 28th, 1969, with the objective of investing in precious metals and mining shares. Approximate assets under management are $17 million. There is an annual management fee of 1 percent and an additional charge for promotional expenses that shall not exceed 1½ percent of the net asset value (NAV) per

CHART 11-5 The Gold Exempt Fund versus Gold Bullion and the Johannesburg Gold Index

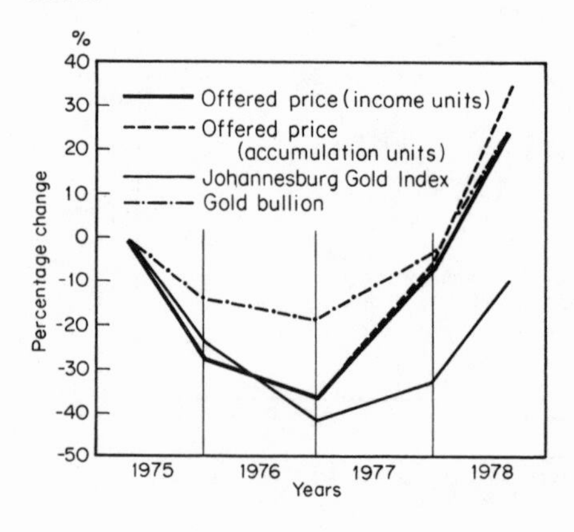

TABLE 11-2

*Currency**	*Exchange traded*	*Size of contract*	*Approximate round trip commission cost*	*Approximate margin (U.S.$)*	*Price quoted in*	*Minimum fluctuations*	*Daily limit*	*Value of 1c move*	*Liquidity*
British Pound (£)	International Money Market (IMM), Chicago	£25,000	$75	$1,500	c/£	$\frac{5}{100}$c = $12.50	5c = $1,250	1c = $250	Good
Canadian dollar (Cdn $)	IMM	100,000 Cdn $	$75	$1,500	c/Cdn$	$\frac{1}{100}$c = $10.00	$\frac{3}{4}$c = $750	1c = $1,000	Good
Dutch guilder (DG)	IMM	125,000 D flrs.	$75	$1,500	c/D flrs	$\frac{1}{1,000}$c = $12.50	1c = $1,250	1c = $1,250	Poor
French franc (Fr f)	IMM	250,000 Fr f	$75	$1,500	c/Fr.f	$\frac{5}{1,000}$c = $12.50	$\frac{1}{2}$c = $1,250	1c = $2,500	Poor
German Deutschemark (DM)	IMM	125,000 D-M	$75	$2,500	c/D-M	$\frac{1}{100}$c = $12.50	1c = $1,250	1c = $1,250	Good
Japanese yen	IMM	12,500,000 yen	$75	$2,500	c/Yen	$\frac{1}{100}$c = $12.50	1c = $1,250	1c = $1,250	Good
Mexican peso	IMM	1,000,000 pesos	$75	$2,500	c/peso	$\frac{1}{1,000}$c = $10	$\frac{15}{100}$c = $1,500	1c = $10,000	Poor
Swiss franc (Sf)	IMM	125,000 Sf	$75	$3,000	c/Sf	$\frac{1}{100}$c = $12.50	$1\frac{1}{2}$c = $1,875	1c = $1,250	Good

* All currencies traded on the International Money Market Exchange, Chicago.

annum. Minimum investment is $500. For performance see Chart 11-4.
Address:
110 E. Byrd Boulevard, Universal City, Texas 78148.
Tel. 658-3562 or 800-531-7510

THE GOLD EXEMPT FUND

The Gold Exempt Fund was designed to provide a means for investors to invest in a managed, diversified portfolio of gold bullion, coins, and shares. An acquisition fee not exceeding 5 percent of NAV is charged with an annual management fee of ½ percent. Minimum holding is 100 units. Prices are quoted in the Offshore Mutual Fund section of the *Financial Times* of London. For performance see Chart 11-5
Address:
M&G (Cayman) Ltd., P.O. Box 706, Cardinal Ave., Grand Cayman, B.W.I.

CURRENCIES

Currency future contracts can be bought and sold through any major American commodity dealer. A listing of available contracts and the relevant information useful for trading purposes is shown in Table 11-2.

The same principles for gold and interest rate futures contracts also apply to currencies. Prices of currency futures are quoted in the commodity section of most major financial newspapers. Trade-weighted currencies as calculated by the Bank of England with cross rates are quoted daily in the *Financial Times* of London. When dealing in currencies it is important to concentrate on the more liquid, less volatile contracts such as the pound sterling, the Canadian dollar, and the deutschemark.

Currency futures contracts, which are all priced in terms of American dollars, are traded at the International Money Market in Chicago. At the beginning of 1978 eight contracts were available: the pound sterling, deutschemark, Swiss franc, Dutch guilder, Japanese yen, French franc, Canadian dollar, and Mexican peso.

A FINAL WORD

12

PSYCHOLOGICAL ASPECTS TO TRADING

By now a sufficient number of financial market possibilities have been discussed from which it should be possible to discover at least two or three major investment opportunities each year.

The techniques discussed in Chapters 6 and 7 are useful but they are by no means infallible. Their adoption, however, will definitely enhance the odds of a successful international investment program. While the principles that have been outlined are fairly easy to follow, putting them into practice in the marketplace becomes much more difficult, since the moment money is committed or withdrawn from the marketplace a new factor—emotion—is brought into play, and what should be a relatively objective process turns into a far more subjective one. It is one thing to beat the market but quite another to beat yourself. For this reason it is worthwhile, as a final note, to discuss some of the psychological pitfalls and traps that all investors are exposed to but which the most successful investors normally avoid. The word "normally" has been carefully chosen, since all market participants make mistakes from time to time. The most important thing, therefore, is to learn as much as possible from those mistakes. These final thoughts are offered in an attempt to bypass this learning process as much as possible and to review some of the points discussed earlier. A more controlled and positive investment attitude will be gained by developing a set of rules investors can follow and refer to, especially when important decisions are being taken.

1. *First, do not commit more resources than you can afford to lose.* While this principle represents basic common sense, it is surprising how many people can fall into this trap. If an investor is continually trying to rise above his financial water he will in the first place become far more emotionally involved in his investment decisions, which will make them less objective and rational, and secondly he may not be able to ride out an unexpected setback. This overcommitment aspect is even more important when investments are made in the highly leveraged financial futures markets. In this respect it is vital to establish a downside risk based on a support level, trendline, etc., at which a stop-loss order is entered. There is no guarantee that this will represent the maximum loss, since markets often "gap" down on unexpected news, but at least the position is protected under most circumstances.

2. *If the market goes against you, liquidate your position and look for a better opportunity elsewhere.* If such a development takes place, chances are that your judgment was incorrect. Small losses have a habit of turning into big ones. Perhaps the hardest lesson in the investment process is learning to take a loss. The most successful traders are those who are able to appreciate this fact and discipline themselves to get out if a market fails to act correctly.

3. *Never answer margin calls.* This principle is an extension of the previous one, for if a margin call is received it undoubtedly means that developments have not gone according to plan.

4. *Make a point of diversifying.* It is always a good idea to diversify investments into at least two or three markets. If you put all your money into one venture and that venture fails, you are left with nothing. On the other hand, if the principles outlined above are carefully followed, the odds favor success so that one or two failures along the way, while discouraging, will not be the end of the world.

5. *Try to maintain some cash reserves at all times.* While in an absolute sense cash will not earn such a high return as properly invested money, in an indirect sense it is always a good idea to maintain some level of reserves, since an outstanding buying opportunity may arise at a time when it is inconvenient to liquidate other positions.

6. *Do not assume you have to be active all the time.* The important point to remember is that an investment should only be made when there is a good and obvious opportunity available. Too often people are forced into the situation of having to have an opinion on something, or feel defensive and uninformed. The best time to have an opinion is when a basic reversal in a particular market is obvious and clear-cut.

7. *Always wait for a near-perfect situation.* Given the number and diversity of international financial markets, there is no excuse for plunging into any of them unless the technical characteristics are perfect or near-perfect. The stronger the situation, the greater the possibility that a new major trend will be set in motion. This does not necessarily mean that the more perfect the technical structure, the greater will be the move, although this does often prove to be the case. The essential point to bear in mind is that there is always some element of risk in the investment process. Finding a strong technical structure reduces the level of risk and thereby increases the chances of making a profit.

8. *Do not overtrade.* This principle follows naturally from the previous paragraph. Many studies have shown that the most profitable moves are of an intermediate, i.e., 8 to 16 weeks, or primary nature, i.e., 1 to 2 years. Also, these types of price movement are often easier to spot than minor ones. In many markets commission costs, which can run up to 5 percent for a round trip, can eat into profits, so if an investor is constantly buying and selling he may pay his broker as much as he is making himself. Quite often an investor who is continually trading is so involved that he fails to see the big picture.

9. *As a general rule avoid counterreactions to the main trend.* It is very important for investors to establish the direction of the main or primary trend and make commitments accordingly. Rather than reversing positions and playing the counterreaction or secondary movement, it is normally far more profitable to await the completion of the correction or move into another market entirely. This is because corrections within a trend are extremely difficult to predict and by definition rarely extend in duration as far as intermediate movements in the main trend. A quick review of the losing transactions for the systems described in Chapter 9 will show that most of them were positioned against the primary trend.

10. *If you are using a system such as those described in Chapter 9, wait for the system to tell you when to get out, otherwise you may lose your position in the middle of a large move.* Using a system will quite often result in several consecutively unprofitable moves, because the market is in the accumulation or consolidation phase. In such situations the breakout will normally be followed by a substantial price move which can offer the potential for significant profits. Participation in such moves is often the "payoff" for faithfully following the system. Premature liquidation of positions based on gut feel therefore considerably reduces this potential.

11. *Do not let success go to your head.* If you find that successful application of the techniques described here leads to substantial profits, never be afraid to withdraw from the market for a while. Success generally breeds carelessness and encourages risk-taking that would not normally be considered. For this reason it is also unwise to pyramid or reinvest all profits, letting the money ride, because sooner or later a setback will occur.

12. *Listen to the opinions of others but always take action based on your interpretation of what the charts are saying.* If the charts disagree with what you consider to be the majority or establishment opinion, the odds of the charts being correct are greatly enhanced, since the opinion of the majority will already have been built into the market.

These 12 principles are offered as a guide in the practical application of the investment of money in the marketplace. If followed faithfully they will greatly increase your chances of success. They can basically be summed up as avoiding pride of opinion which, combined with greed, has been responsible for more financial downfalls than any other factors.

Before setting up an investment program or even an individual commitment, it is important to set a realistic objective which should be kept to as closely as possible. These goals can be changed in the right circumstances as warranted from time to time. Knowing where you want to go and when you want to get there is an important step in maintaining a positive mental attitude. It will also help to constrain any instincts of greed.

Today's world is an ever-changing one. Creativity and the thirst for profits by the many stock and commodity exchanges and financial institutions around the world are resulting in the development of more and more types of investment vehicles. The success of these new ventures has been guaranteed, both by investors who have become frustrated trying to make money in the stock market and who wish to remain ahead of the investment game, and by institutions who are looking for some hedge against growing volatility in the currency and interest rate areas. It is a fact that the greatest gains are made before opportunities are widely grasped. It is also true that the majority of American investors are still emotionally and financially committed to the traditional domestic stock and bond markets. An awareness of opportunities elsewhere is growing, but is still in its infancy. By the time these opportuntities are more fully realized, it will probably be time to look for another approach, since the majority is usually late and wrong. Until that point occurs, the possibilities of making substantial investment profits are open to anyone who adopts an international approach to investment.

APPENDIX 1

SUPPLEMENTARY CHARTS

CHART A1-1 Principal Stock Indexes versus 12-Month Rate of Change (For Japan, Germany, and United Kingdom)

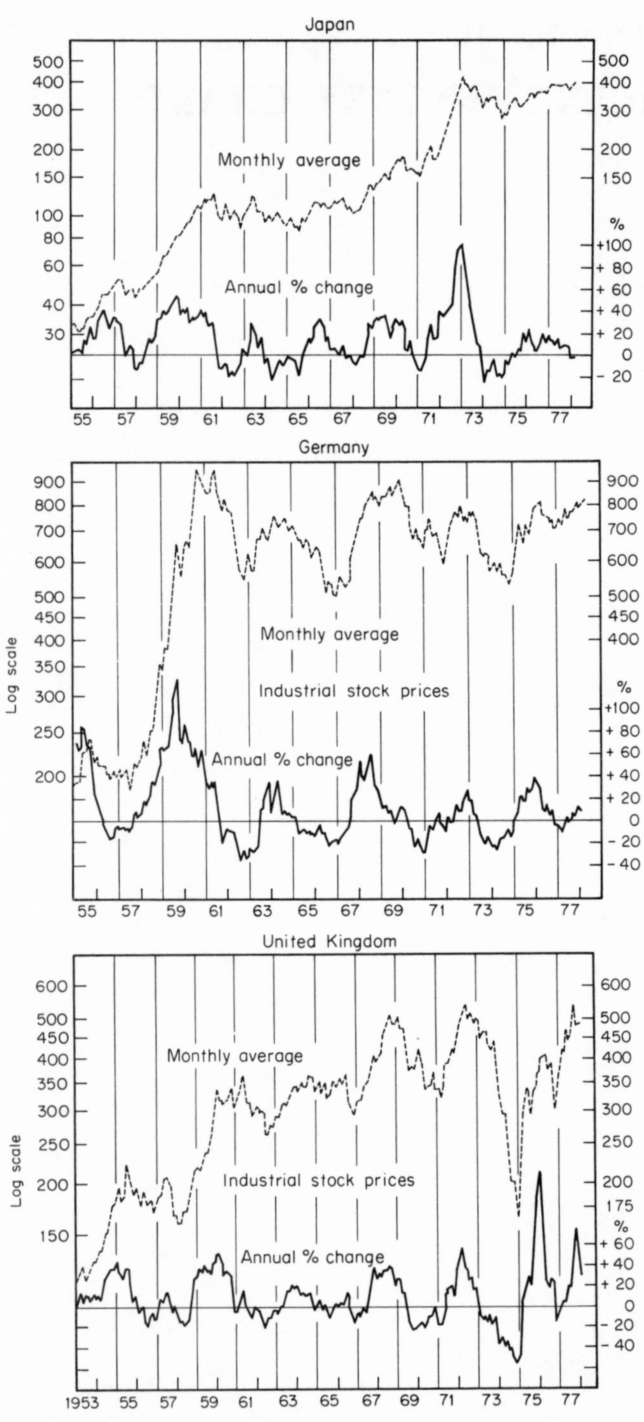

Courtesy of *The International Bank Credit Analyst.*

CHART A1-2 Principal Stock Indexes versus 12-Month Rate of Change (For South Africa, France, and Italy)

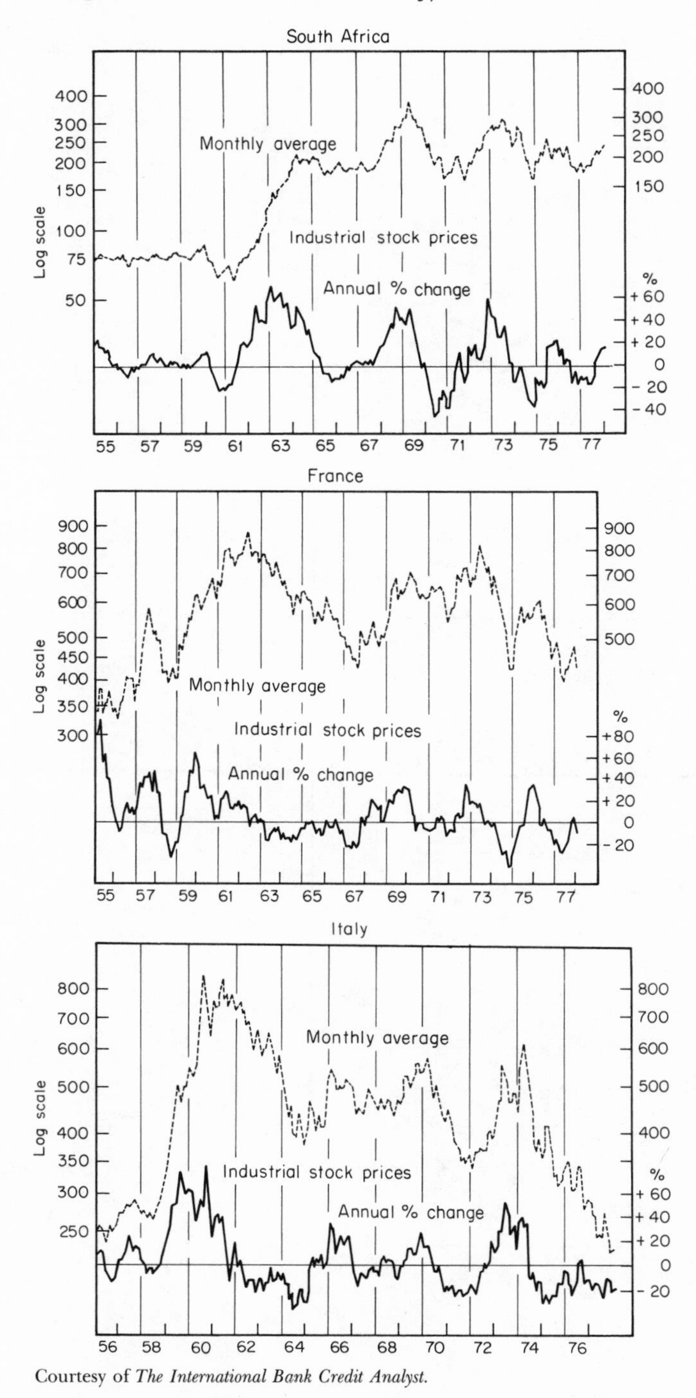

Courtesy of *The International Bank Credit Analyst.*

CHART A1-3 Principal Stock Indexes versus 12-Month Rate of Change (For Australia, Canada, Netherlands, and Spain)

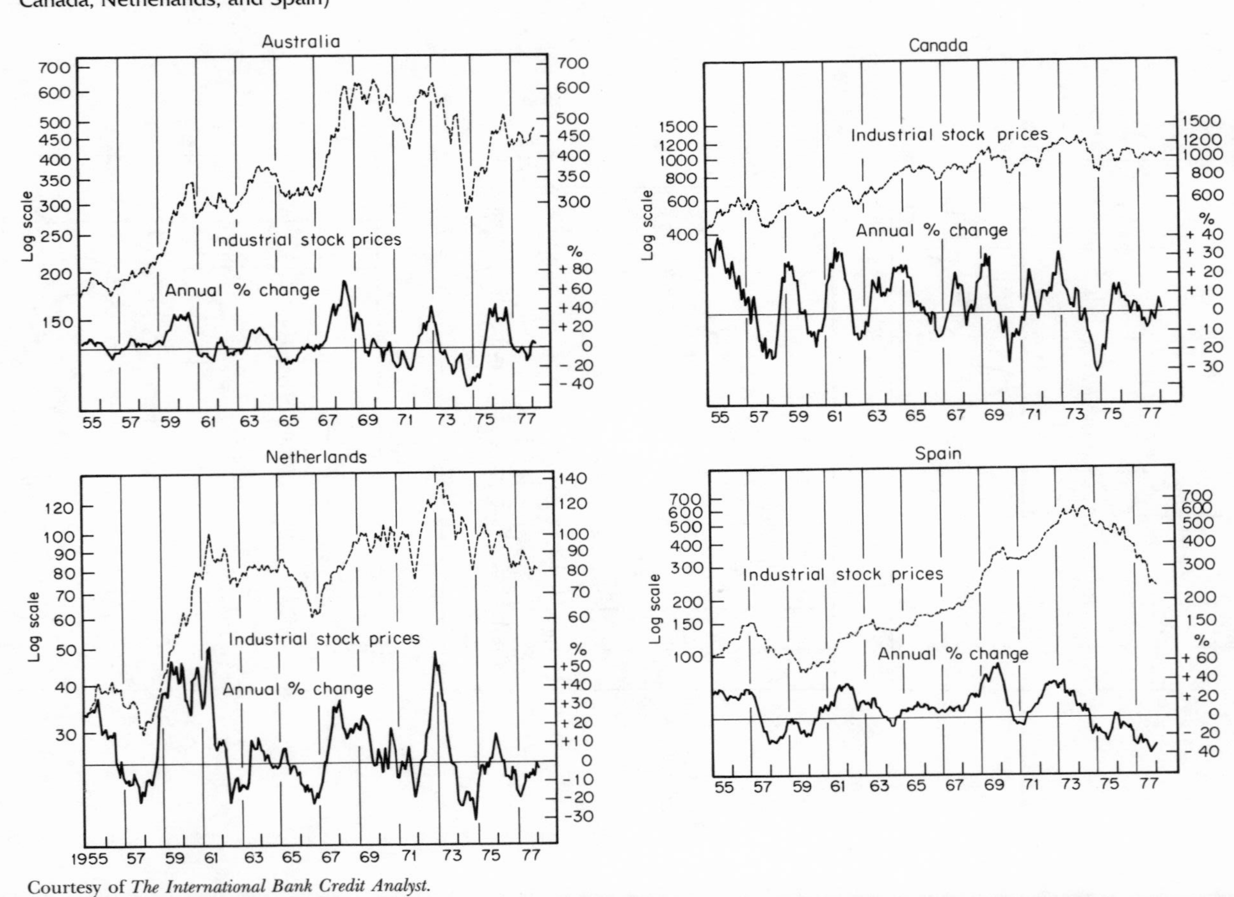

Courtesy of *The International Bank Credit Analyst.*

CHART A1-4 Principal Stock Exchanges and Relative Strength (Showing indexes for World, United States, Europe, Japan, United Kingdom, and Germany)

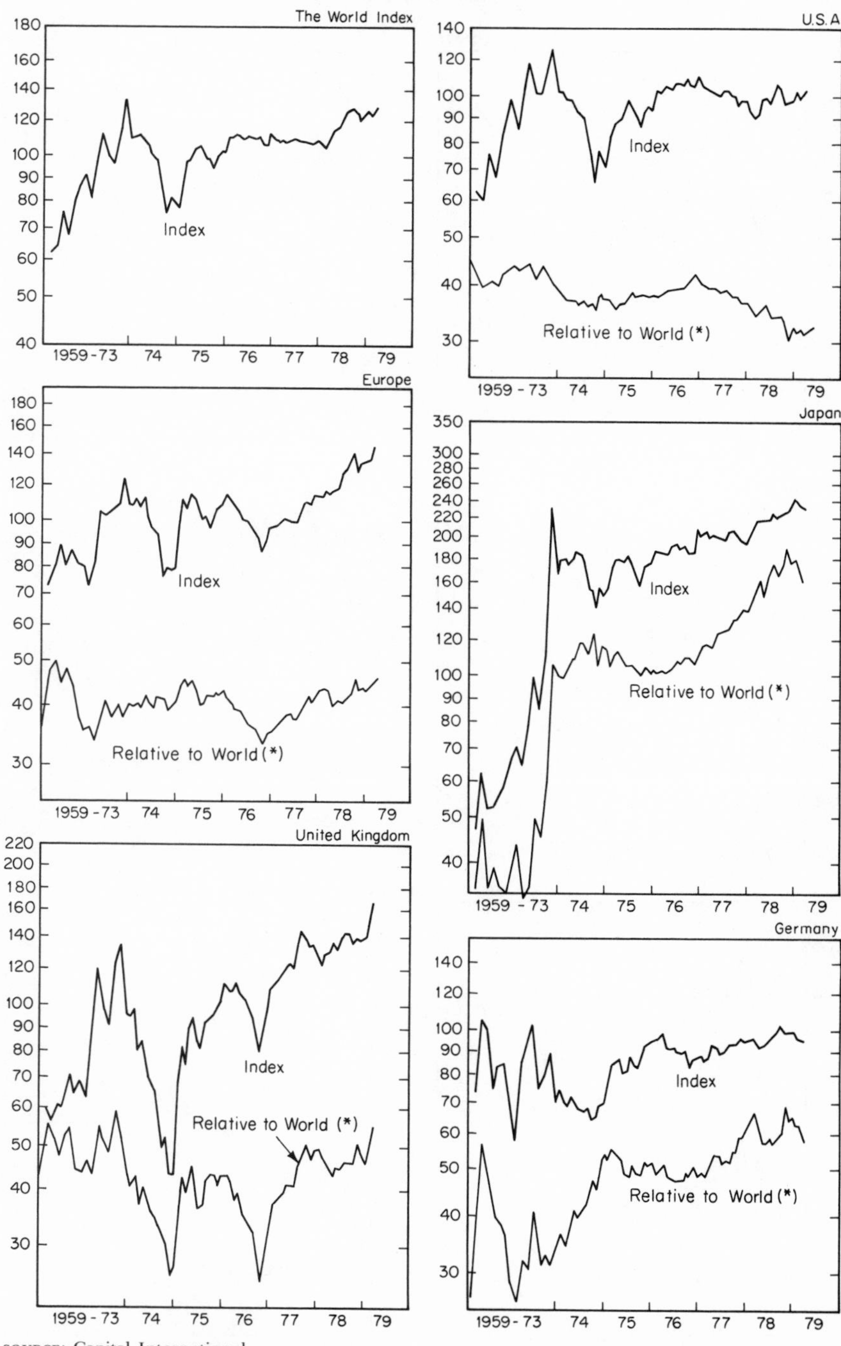

SOURCE: Capital International.

* All "Relative to World" curves take into account exchange gains and losses relative to the U.S. dollar. Courtesy of *The International Bank Credit Analyst.*

CHART A1-5 Principal Stock Exchanges and Relative Strength (Showing indexes for Canada, France, Switzerland, Netherlands, Australia, and Spain)

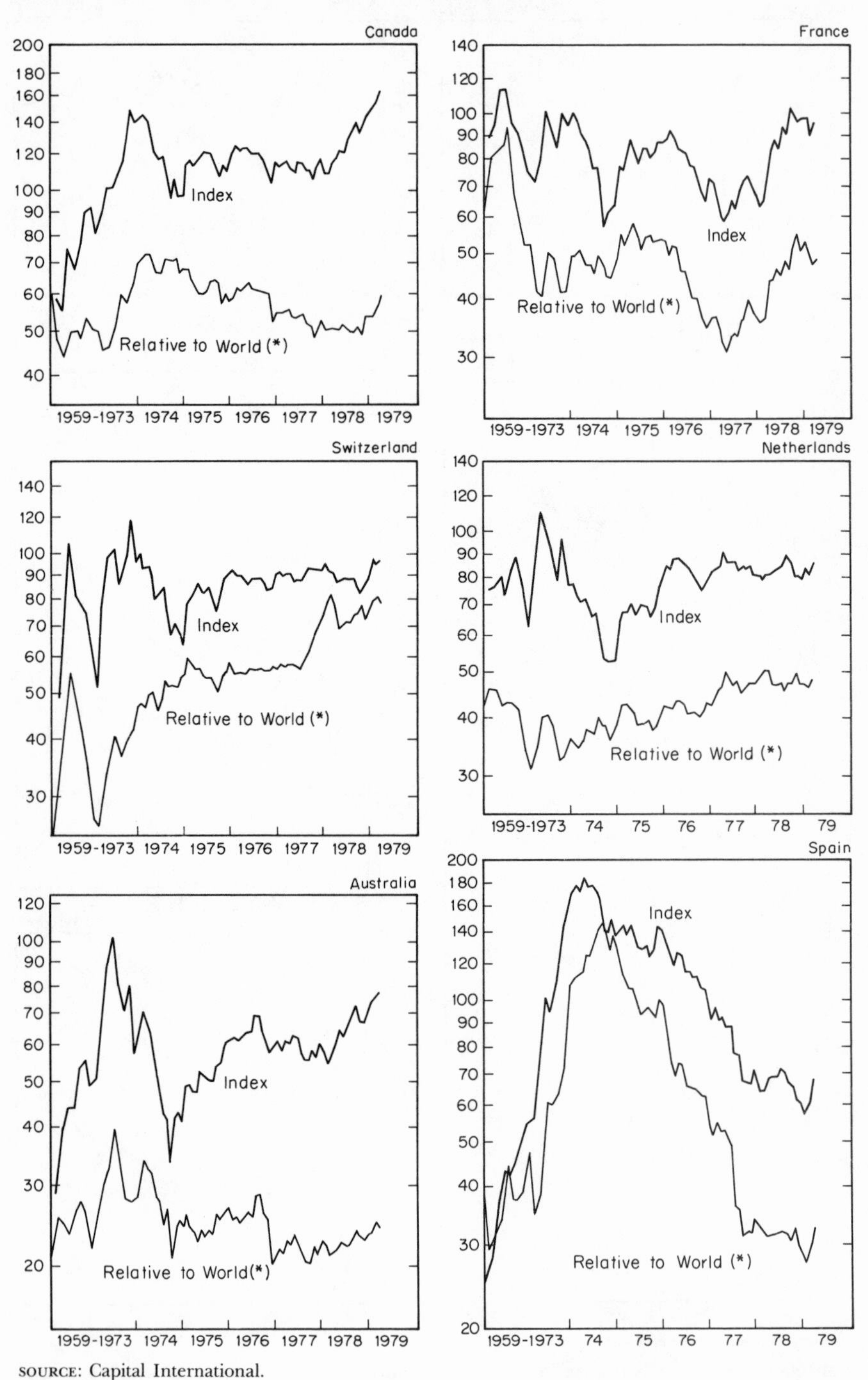

SOURCE: Capital International.

* All "Relative to World" curves take into account exchange gains and losses relative to the U.S. dollar.

CHART A1-6 Principal Stock Exchanges and Relative Strength (Showing indexes for Hong Kong, Belgium, Singapore, Italy, and Sweden)

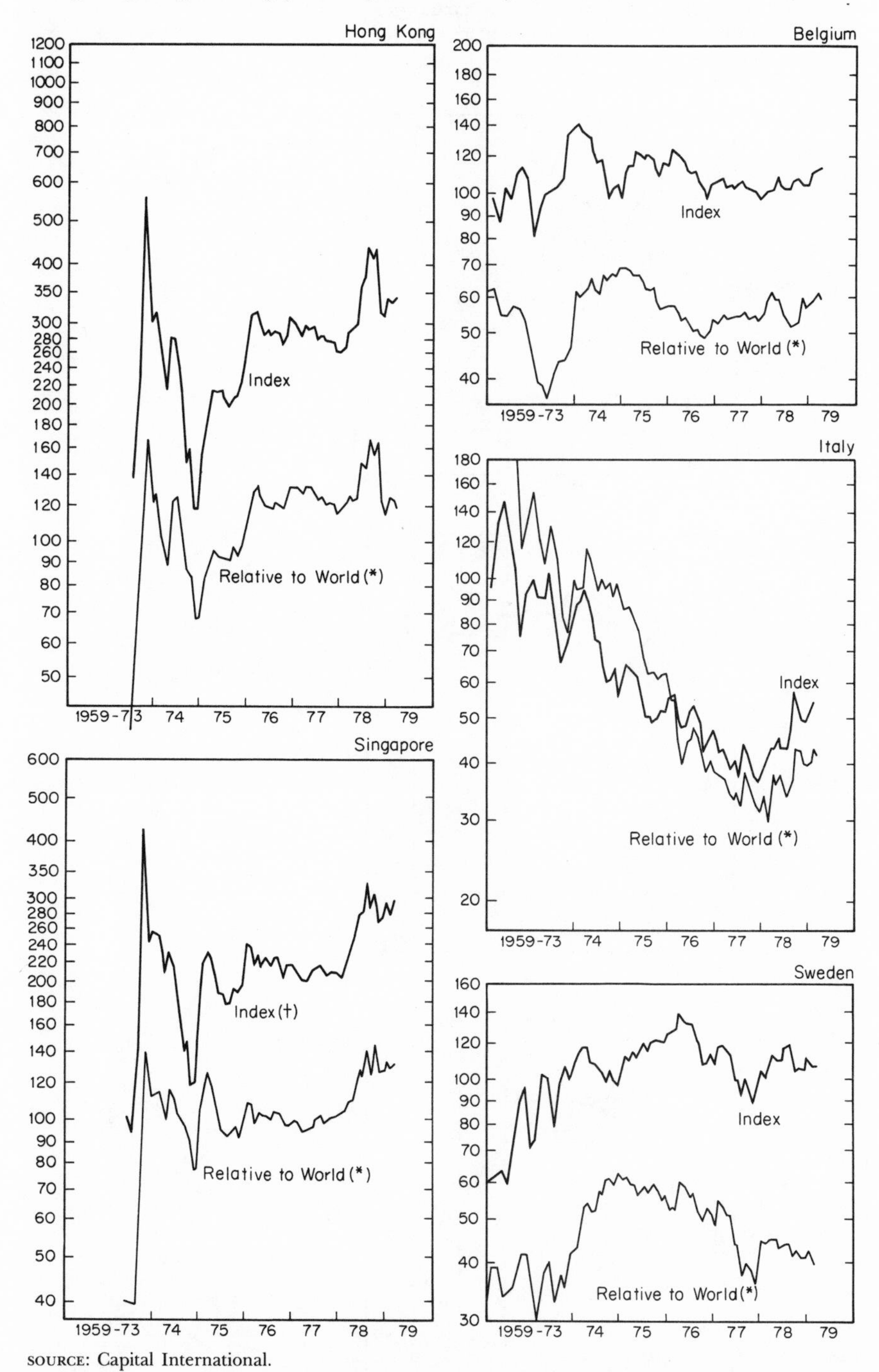

SOURCE: Capital International.

* All "Relative to World" curves take into account exchange gains and losses relative to the U.S. dollar.

† The Capital International Index of Singapore was developed in cooperation with the "Oversea Chinese Banking Corporation, Limited," which published this same index under the name "O.C.B.C. index." The figure shown as market value is an estimate of the total aggregate market value for the country.

CHART A1-7 Principal Stock Exchanges and Relative Strength (Showing indexes for Denmark, Austria, and Norway)

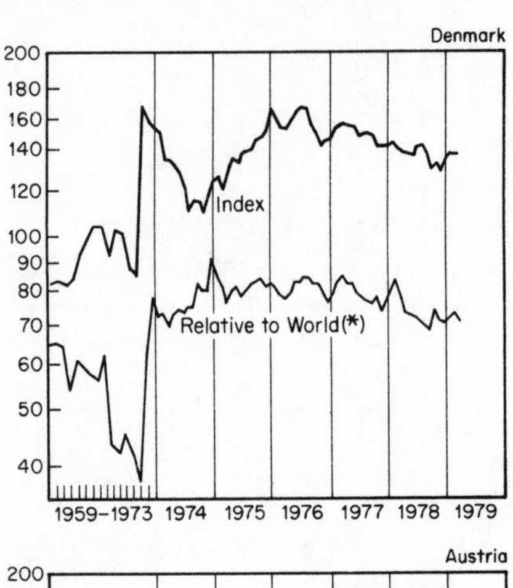

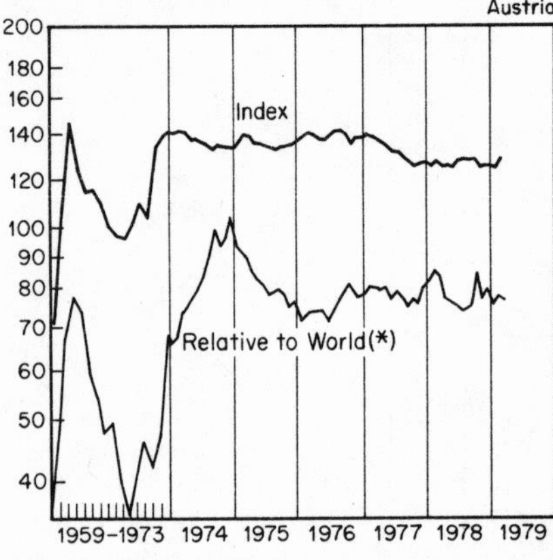

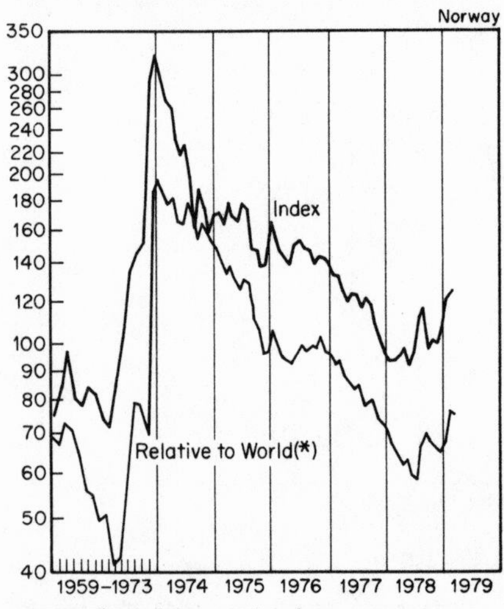

SOURCE: Capital International.

* All "Relative to World" curves take into account exchange gains and losses relative to the U.S. dollar.

CHART A1-8 London Financial Times Ordinary Index versus Financial Times Government Securities Index

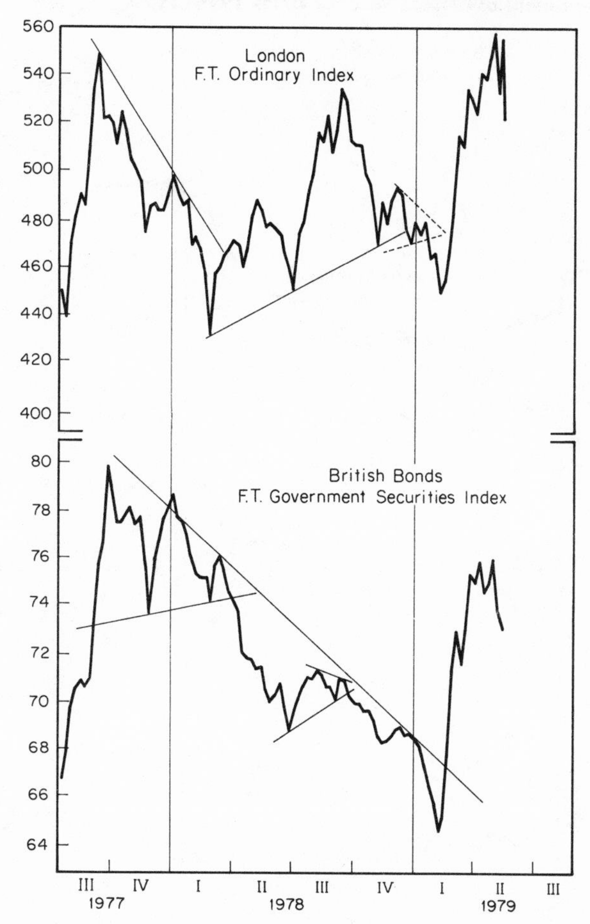

Courtesy of *Deliberations.*

CHART A1-9 Financial Times Actuaries Gilt Stock Index 1970–1979

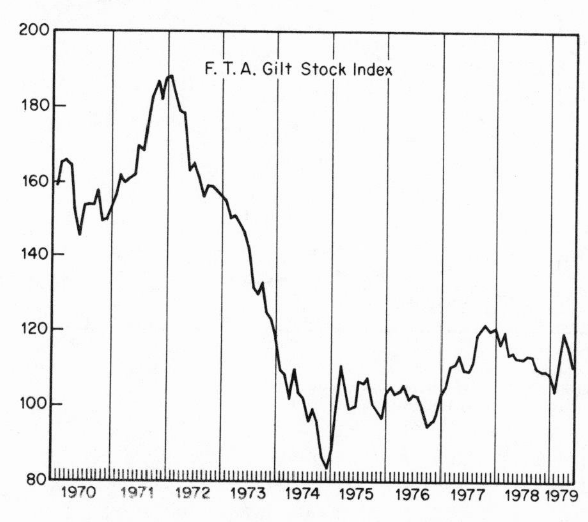

CHART A1-10 Government of Canada Security Yields 1976–1979

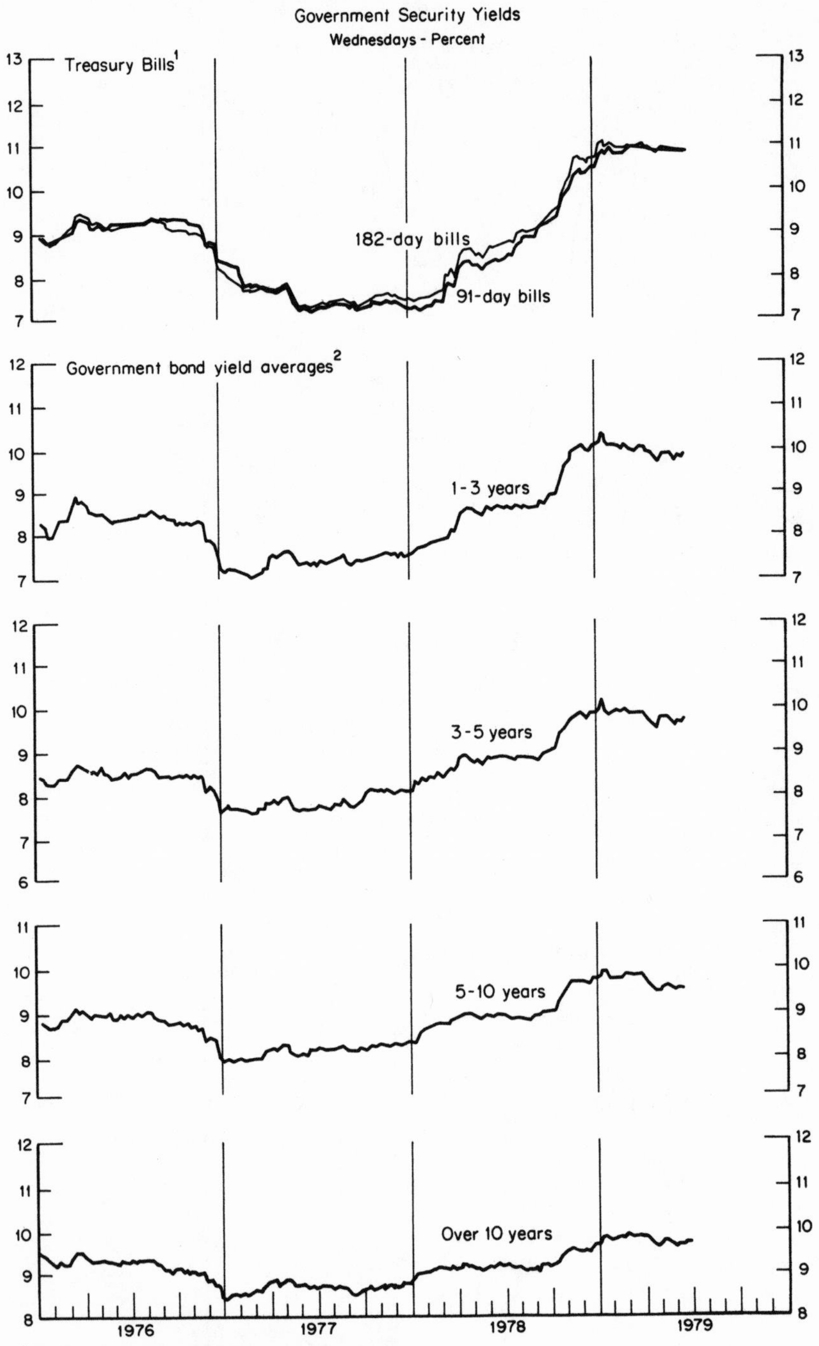

[1] Weekly tender rate on Thursday date.
[2] Based on Wednesday closing mid-market prices. Averages are not weighted and include extendible issues.

CHART A1-11 Weekly Interest Rate Futures (Nearest contract)

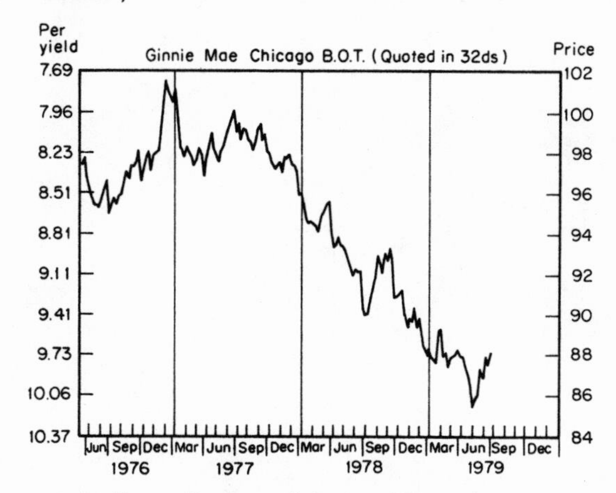

SOURCE: Commodity Research Bureau, Inc.

CHART A1-12 Gold Bullion versus three Gold Share Indexes

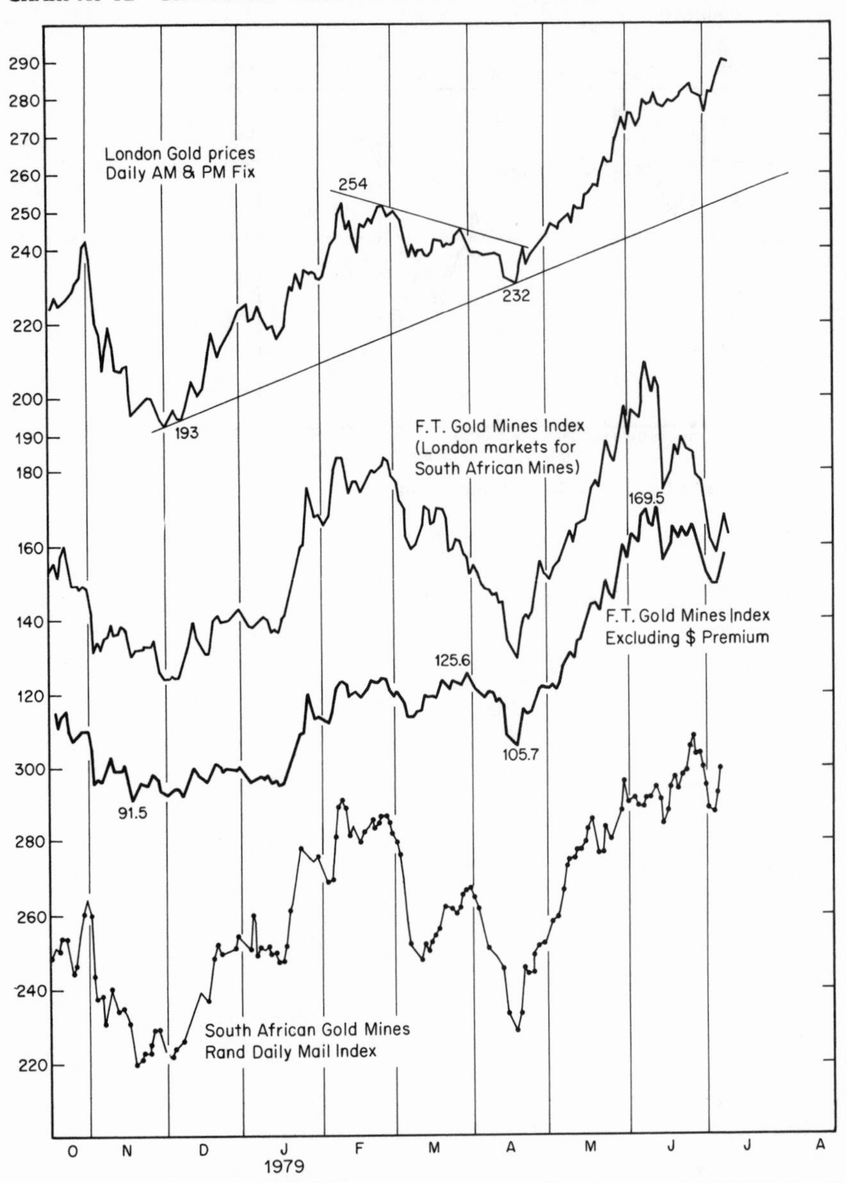

Courtesy of *Deliberations,* P.O. Box 182, Adelaide Street Station, Toronto, Ontario MSC 2J1, Canada.

CHART A1-13 Gold Futures 1975–1979 (Nearest contract)

SOURCE: Commodity Research Bureau, Inc.

CHART A1-14 Trade-Weighted Swiss Franc versus 12-month Rate of Change

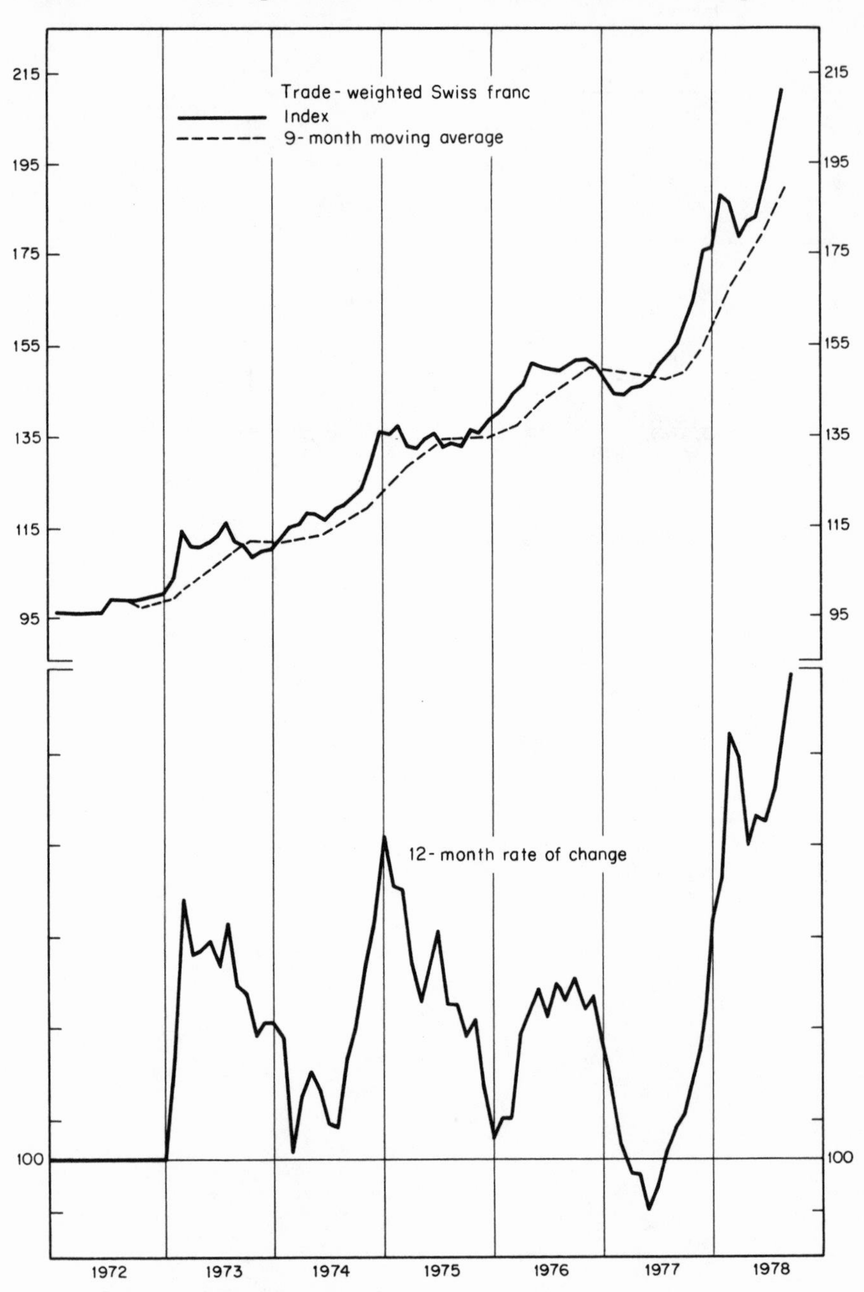

Courtesy of *The International Bank Credit Analyst.*

CHART A1-15 Trade-Weighted Deutschemark versus 12-month Rate of Change

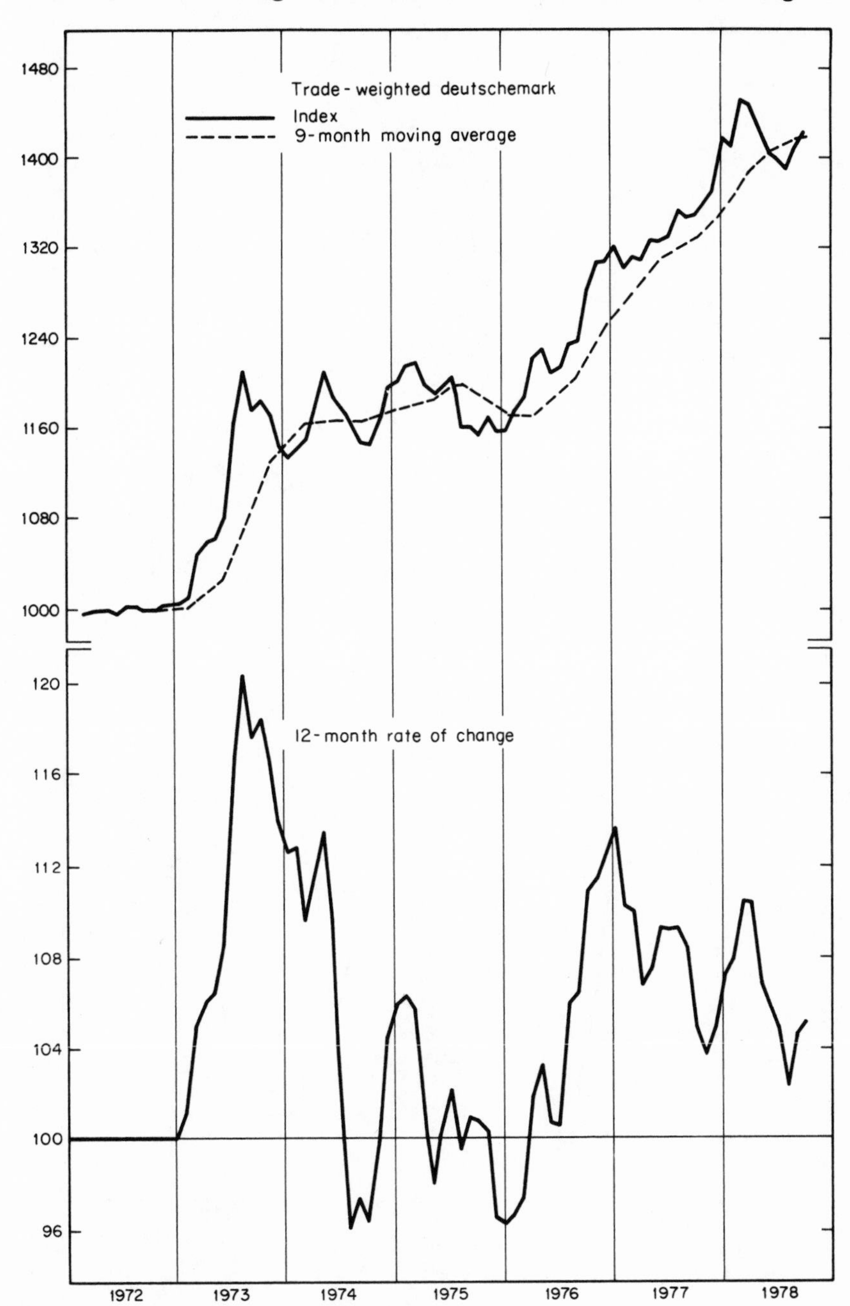

Courtesy of *The International Bank Credit Analyst.*

CHART A1-16 Trade-Weighted French Franc versus 12-month Rate of Change

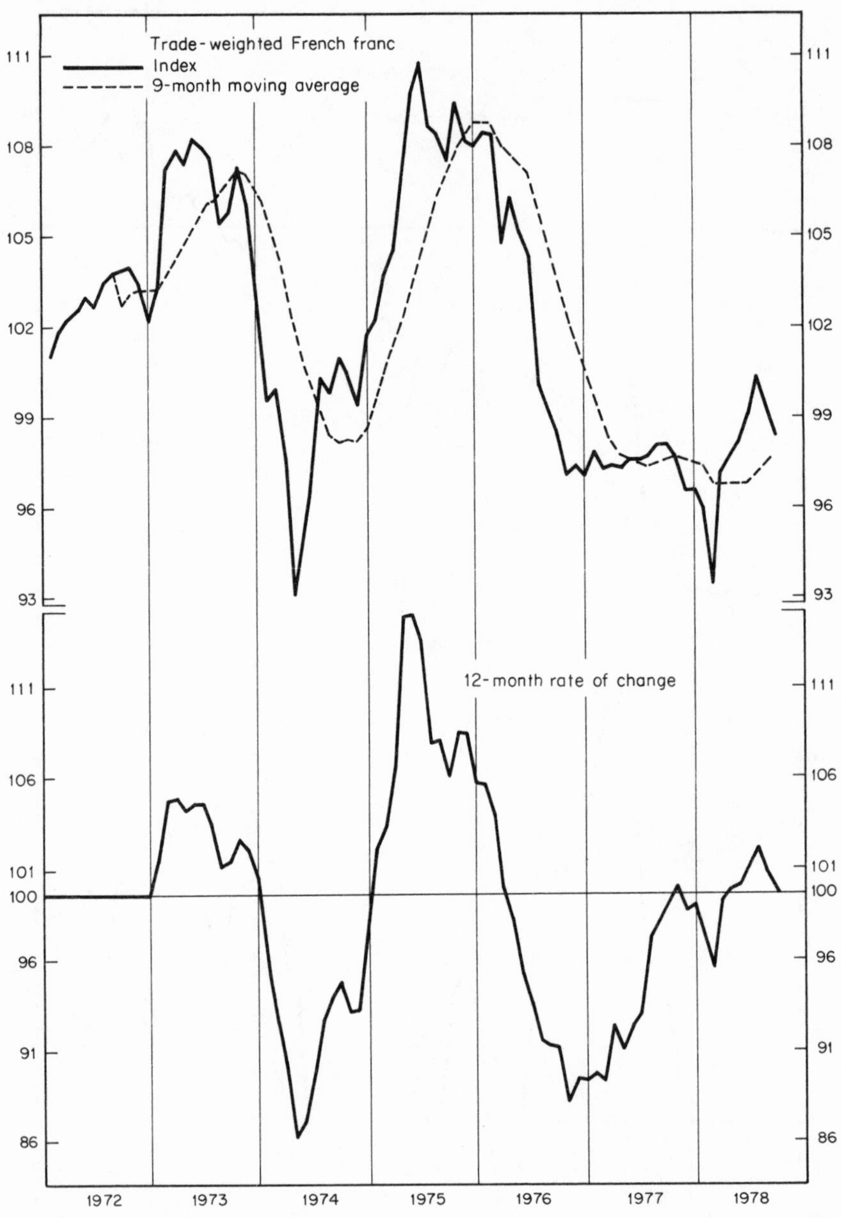

Courtesy of *The International Bank Credit Analyst.*

CHART A1-17 Selected Currency Futures

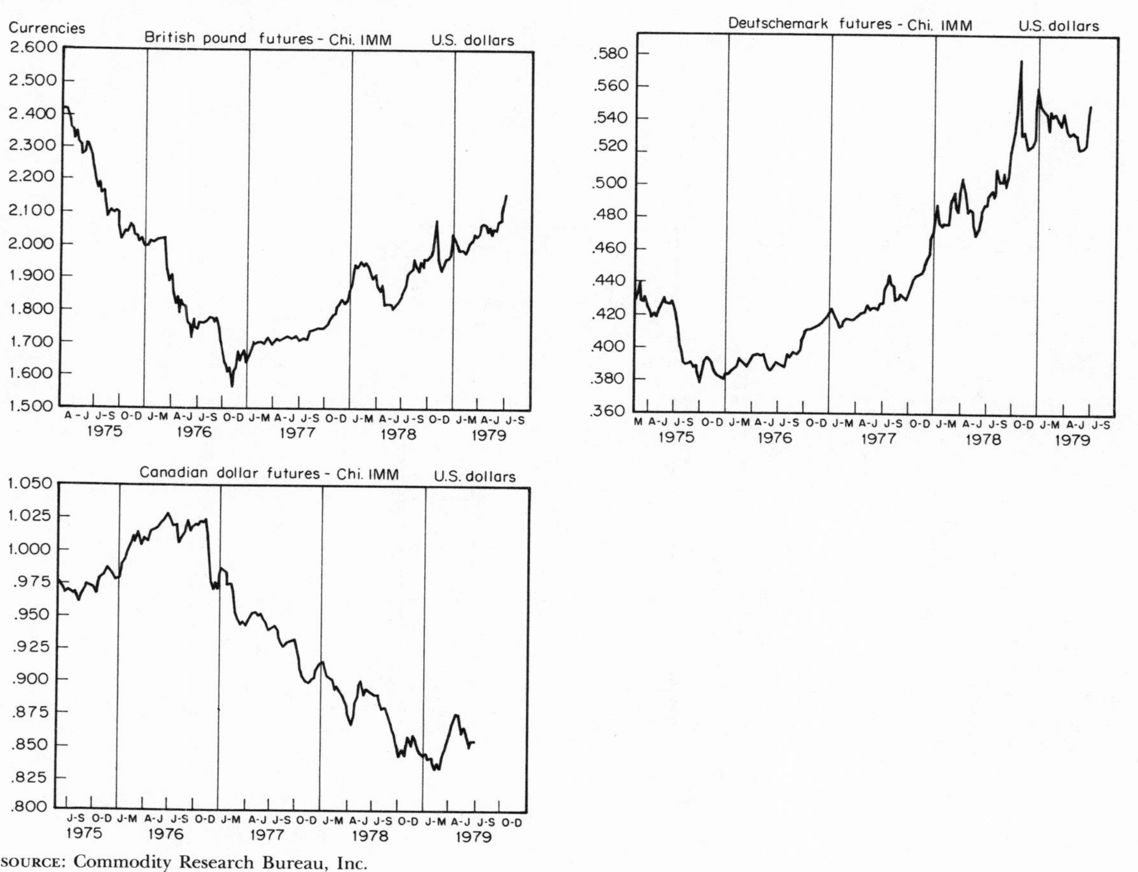

SOURCE: Commodity Research Bureau, Inc.

CHART A1-18 Selected Currency Futures

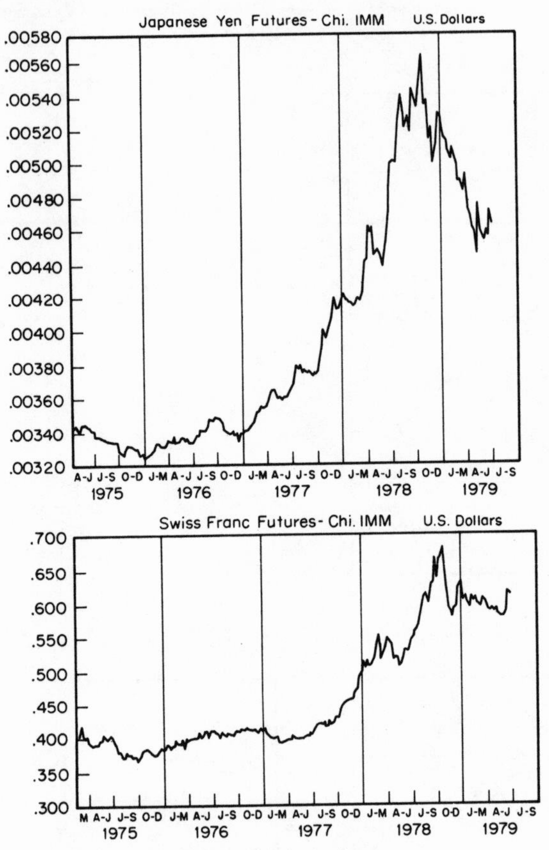

SOURCE: Commodity Research Bureau, Inc.

CHART A1-19 The U.S. Dollar versus Selected Currencies

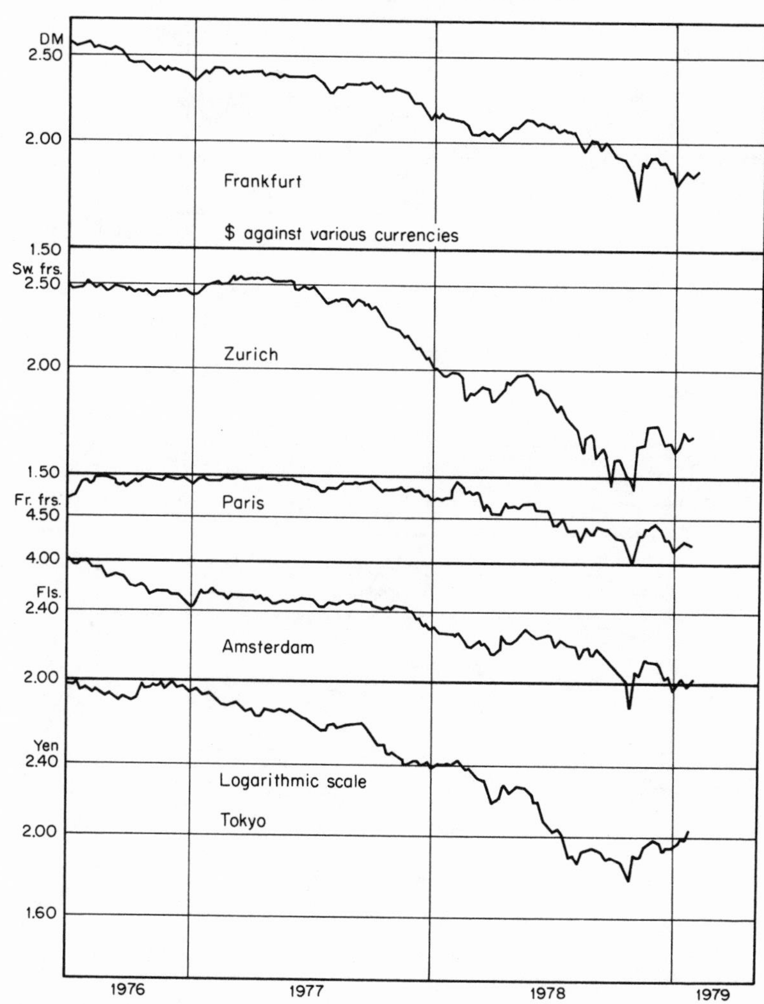

SOURCE: Investment Research.

CHART A1-20 The Pound Sterling versus Selected Currencies

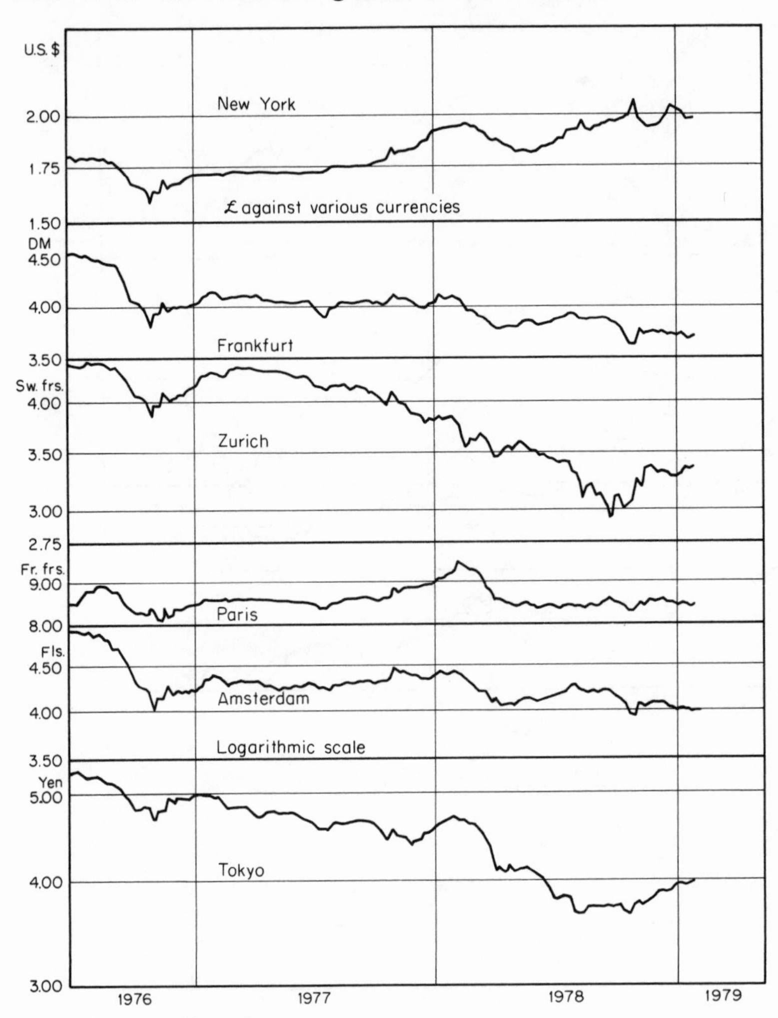

SOURCE: Investment Research.

CHART A1-21 The German Deutschemark versus Selected Currencies

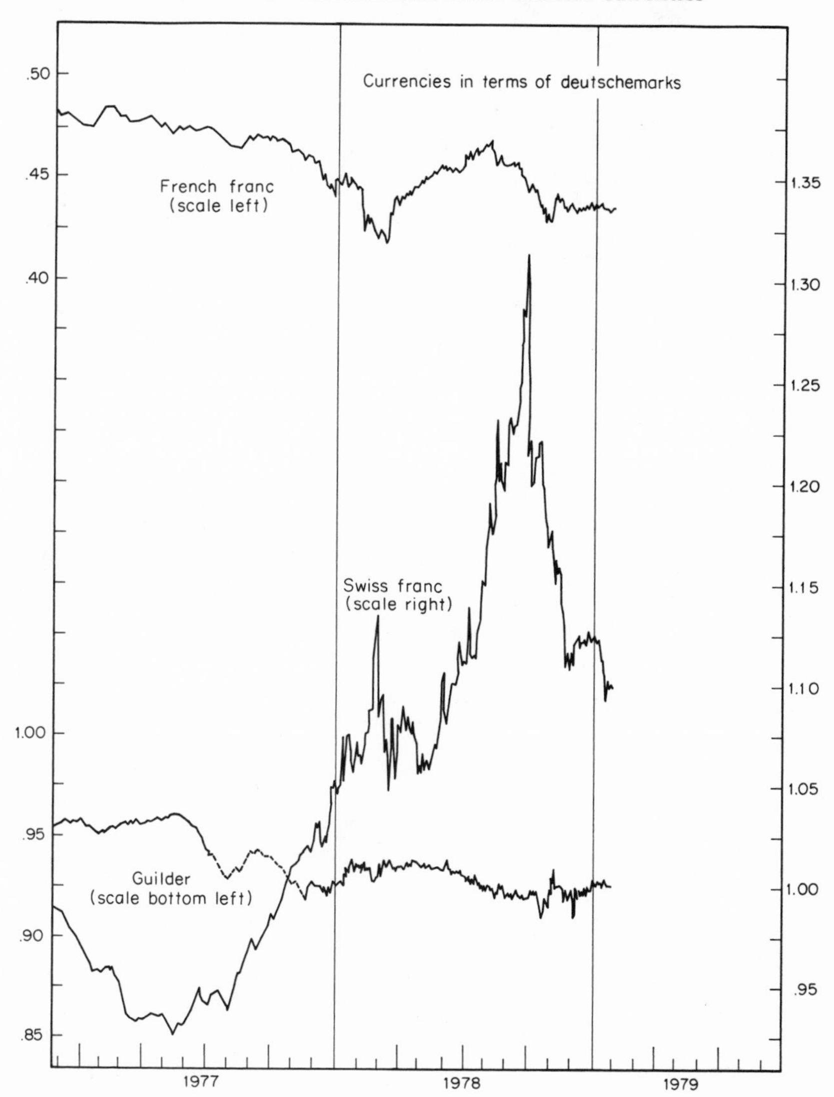

SOURCE: Investment Research.

APPENDIX 2

SOME UNITED STATES NO-LOAD MUTUAL FUNDS

Reproduced from the 1979 *NOLOAD Mutual Fund Directory,* published annually by the NOLOAD Mutual Fund Association, Valley Forge, Pa.

EXPLANATION OF COLUMN HEADINGS AND SHAREOWNER SERVICES OFFERED

- **Fund Name**, Address and Telephone Number with its Investment Adviser/Management Company in smaller type. Telephone number from many areas must be preceded by "1". Also "800" numbers are toll-free but can only be used if calling from out of state. Call the local number collect if calling from same state as the Fund.
- **Investment Objective and Policy** — a capsule description of the fund's objective. Also the investment policies practiced by the adviser to achieve that goal are briefly described. The prospectus contains further details.
- **Year First Offered** — the year in which shares of the fund were first offered to the public.
- **Assets (Mil.) December 31, 1978** — the fund's size in millions of dollars.
- **Purchase Requirements** — Each fund's prospectus describes the procedures to be followed when purchasing shares. The minimum dollar amounts accepted on initial and subsequent purchases are noted. If telephone or wire orders are accepted, they are noted by (Tel.) or (Wire).
- **Redemption Procedures** — each fund's prospectus should be consulted for specific redemption procedures required by the fund.

  Most funds require liquidation requests in writing. Generally a signature guarantee (Sig. Guar.) will be required. A signature guarantee is also needed when a payment is to be made to someone other than the registered shareowner or perhaps just when the proceeds exceed a specified dollar amount. Signature guarantees must be obtained from a member firm of the New York Stock Exchange or from a commercial bank or trust company and they do not charge for stamping your signature.

  Some funds allow liquidation by telephone where pre-arranged and approved agreements have been signed. These are noted by (Tel.) or (Wire).

  Some municipal bond and most money funds offer redemptions through check writing privileges (Ck. Writing).

SERVICES

Dividends — Funds will automatically reinvest income dividends and capital gains distributions in additional shares and fractional shares (Auto.). Funds will also pay either income dividends or capital gains distributions in cash if you elect such an option. The frequency with which income dividends are paid to shareowners are noted: A = annually; S/A = semi-annually; Q = quarterly; M = monthly.

Retirement Plans (Ret. Plans) Master or Prototype Plans are available for adoption with minimum time and expense. These plans generally allow tax-deductible contributions and at the same time shelter current income dividends and capital gains distributions from current tax liability.

(Keo.) This plan is for the self-employed individual.

(Corp.) These pension or profit-sharing plans are in prototype form for use by corporations for corporate employees.

(IRA) An individual not covered by any other qualified retirement plan or who receives a distribution from such a plan can set up an Individual Retirement Account.

403(b) Individuals employed by school districts, hospitals, municipalities, and other non-profit organizations or associations may be eligible to adopt this plan.

OTHER:

Systematic Withdrawal Plans (Syst. With.) If you wish to receive a check from your investment in the fund on a regular monthly or quarterly basis, you can give such standing instructions to the fund. The instructions can be changed at any time and usually a minimum initial investment and a withdrawal amount is required.

Automatic Purchasing (Auto. Pur.) Many funds offer an arrangement for investments to be made either through payroll deductions or from automatic monthly or quarterly bank drafts drawn against your checking account. Also, some funds accept checks from a source, such as military pay or Social Security checks, and deposit them directly in your account.

Exchange These funds will permit you to shift your investment from one fund to another. This generally is permitted only among funds under the same management or with an outside fund under a mutual agreement between the funds. Some funds allow exchanges by telephone (Exchange-Tel.); others require such instructions in writing (Exchange-Writ.). This is a convenience for the shareowner whose investment objective or current needs change.

Group Sub-Accounting (Group Sub-Acct.) is a service offered by some funds to maintain individual account records for large groups — a valuable service for many corporate or municipal savings and other employee benefit plans.

NO LOAD MONEY FUNDS

These funds provide investors with a unique combination of yield, instant liquidity, and safety. The funds invest solely in short-term money market instruments and investors get the benefits of the larger yields available in such investments, as well as the liquidity and services (such as check-writing privileges) of these accounts. These mutual funds are attractive to corporate cash managers, trust departments, and individuals or institutions with any amount of cash that they want to earn current daily interest while waiting to use the cash for some other purpose.

Fund Name (Advisor) Address and Telephone Number	Investment Objective and Policy	Year First Offered	Assets Mil. 12/31/78	Purchase Requirements		Redemption Procedures	Services
				Initial	Subsq.		
ALLIANCE CAPITAL RESERVES, INC. *(Alliance Capital Management Corp.)* 140 Broadway New York, NY 10005 800-221-5672/212-425-4210	Safety of principal, excellent liquidity and maximum current income to the extent consistent with the first two objectives.	1978	$60.4	$0	$0	Writ. with Sig. Guar.	*Dividends:* Auto.; M.
CAPITAL PRESERVATION FUND, INC. *(Benham Management Corp.)* 459 Hamilton Ave. Palo Alto, CA 94301 800-227-8380/800-982-5844 (CA only)	Safety; U.S. Government securities backed by the full faith and credit of the U.S. Treasury and maturing within 1 year.	1972	115.1	1000	0	Writ. with Sig. Guar.; Tel.; Ck. Writ.; Wire	*Dividends:* Auto.; Q. *Ret. Plans:* Keo., IRA, 403(b) *Other:* Syst. With.
CURRENT INTEREST, INC. *(Funds, Inc.)* 711 Polk St. Houston, TX 77002 713-751-2400	Current income consistent with preservation of capital by investing in money market instruments.	1974	7.3	1000	100	Writ. with Sig. Guar.; Tel.; Wire; Ck. Writ.	*Dividends:* Auto.; M. *Ret. Plans:* Keo., IRA *Other:* Syst. With.; Exchange-Tel.
DREYFUS LIQUID ASSETS *(The Dreyfus Corporation)* 600 Madison Ave. New York, NY 10022 800-223-5525/212-935-5700	Maximization of current income to extent consistent with preservation of capital by investing in money market instruments.	1974	881.1	2500	100	Writ. with Sig. Guar.; Ltd. Tel. & Wire; Ck. Writ.	*Dividends:* Auto.; M. *Ret. Plans:* Keo., IRA, Corp., 403(b) *Other:* Syst. With.; Auto. Pur.; Exchange-Tel.
DREYFUS MONEY MKT. INSTRU., INC. *(The Dreyfus Corporation)* 767 Fifth Ave. New York, NY 10022 212-935-6621	Invests in U.S. Gov. securities, bank certificates and repurchase agreements; banker acceptances, and high grade commercial paper.	1975	130.1	1000	500	Writ. with Sig. Guar.; Tel.; Wire; Ck. Writ.	*Dividends:* Auto.; M. *Other:* Syst. With.; Auto. Pur.
FIDELITY CASH RESERVES *(Fidelity Group)* 82 Devonshire St. Boston, MA 02109 800-225-6190/617-726-0650	Current income consistent with stability and liquidity. Invests in high grade money market instruments (including Euro CD's).	1979	0.1	1000	0	Writ. with Sig. Guar.; Tel.; Wire; Ck. Writ.	*Dividends:* Auto.; Q. *Ret. Plans:* Keo., IRA, Corp., 403(b) *Other:* Syst. With.; Exchange-Tel.
FIDELITY DAILY INCOME TRUST *(Fidelity Group)* 82 Devonshire St. Boston, MA 02109 800-225-6190/617-726-0650	Income: invests only in high grade money market instr., U.S. Gov. obligations, prime 1 comm. paper and short term corp. notes rated AA or better.	1974	846.8	5000	500	Writ. with Sig. Guar.; Tel.; Wire; Ck. Writ.	*Dividends:* Auto.; M. *Ret. Plans:* Keo., IRA, Corp., 403(b) *Other:* Syst. With.; Exchange-Tel.
FIDELITY MONEY MARKET TRUST *(Fidelity Group)* 82 Devonshire St. Boston, MA 02109 800-225-6190/617-726-0650	Current income — choice of three portfolios of money market securities for the large institutional, corporate and individual investor.	1979	0.1	250M Wire only	0 Wire only	Wire only	*Dividends:* Auto.; M.
FIRST VARIABLE RATE FUND *(Government Securities Management Co.)* 1700 Pennsylvania Ave., NW Washington, DC 20006 800-424-9861/202-393-5330	High yield, stability, liquidity. Invests exclusively in short term and variable rate obligations backed by the U.S. Government.	1977	46.3	1000	250	Writ. with Sig. Guar.; Tel.; Wire; Ck. Writ.	*Dividends:* Auto.; Q. *Other:* Syst. With.
HOLDING TRUST *(Fundpack Mgt., Inc.)* 3200 Ponce de Leon Blvd. Coral Gables, FL 33134 800-327-2868/305-444-7461	Provide quick entry and withdrawal to investors seeking preservation of capital, liquidity, and high income through high grade money market instr.	1974	12.6	1000	100	Writ. with Sig. Guar.; Tel.; Wire; Ck. Writ.	*Dividends:* Auto.; M. *Ret. Plans:* IRA, Keo., Corp., 403(b) *Other:* Syst. With.; Exchange-Tel.
INTERCAPITAL LIQ. ASSET FUND *(Dean Witter, Reynolds Intercapital Inc.)* 1 Battery Park Plaza New York, NY 10004 800-221-2685/212-422-6700	High current income, preservation of capital, and liquidity thru investment in money market instruments.	1975	442.4	5000	100	Writ. with Sig. Guar.; Wire; Tel.; Ck. Writ.	*Dividends:* Auto.; M. *Ret. Plans:* IRA *Other:* Syst. With.

Fund Name (Advisor) Address and Telephone Number	Investment Objective and Policy	Year First Offered	Assets Mil. 12/31/78	Purchase Requirements		Redemption Procedures	Services
				Initial	Subsq.		
ROWE PRICE PRIME RESERVE FUND *(T. Rowe Price Associates, Inc.)* 100 East Pratt St. Baltimore, MD 21202 800-638-1527/301-547-2000	Preservation of capital, liquidity, and high income in that order through prime money market instruments.	1976	$151	$2000	$100	Written; Sig. Guar. over $5M; Tel.; Wire.; Ck. Writ.	*Dividends:* Auto.; M. *Ret. Plans:* Keo., IRA, Corp., 403(b) *Other:* Syst. With.; Auto. Pur.; Group Sub-Acct.; Exch.-Tel.
SCUDDER MANAGED RESERVES, INC. *(Scudder, Stevens & Clark, Inv. Counsel)* 175 Federal St. Boston, MA 02110 800-225-2470/617-482-3990	Income: Purchases commercial paper; certificates of deposits; banker's acceptance; etc.	1974	259.0	1000	0	Writ. with Sig. Guar.; Tel.; Ck. Writ.	*Dividends:* Auto.; M. *Ret. Plans:* IRA, 403(b), Keo., Corp. *Other:* Syst. With.; Group Sub-Acct.; Exchange-Tel.
SCUDDER CASH INVESTMENT TRUST *(Scudder, Stevens & Clark, Inv. Counsel)* 175 Federal St. Boston, MA 02110 800-225-2470/617-482-3990	Income: Invests in debt securities with maturities not more than one year. Best suited for banks, corporations, fiduciaries, etc. Constant N.A.V.	1975	26.7	1000	0	Writ. with Sig. Guar.; Tel.; Ck. Writ.	*Dividends:* Auto.; M. *Ret. Plans:* Keo., IRA, Corp. 403(b) *Other:* Syst. With.; Exchange-Tel.; Ck. Writ.
SELECTED MONEY MKT FUND, INC. *(Lincoln Nat'l. Investment Mgt. Co.)* 111 W. Washington St. Chicago, IL 60602 800-621-7321/312-630-2762	Maximize current income to the extent consistent with preservation of capital by investing in money market instruments.	1977	2.9	1000	100	Writ. with Sig. Guar.; Tel.; Wire.; Ck. Writ.	*Dividends:* Auto.; M. *Ret. Plans:* Keo., IRA, Corp. *Other:* Syst. With.; Exchange-Writ.
STEINROE CASH RESERVES, INC. *(Stein Roe & Farnham)* 150 S. Wacker Dr. Chicago, IL 60606 800-621-1142/312-368-7822	Maximum current income — Invests in short-term money market instruments maturing in 1 year or less.	1976	55.9	2500	500 Tel., Wire.	Writ. with Sig. Guar.; Tel.; Wire.; Ck. Writ.	*Dividends:* Auto.; M. *Ret. Plans:* Keo., IRA *Other:* Syst. With.; Auto. Pur.; Group Sub-Acct.; Exchange-Writ.
VALUE LINE CASH FUND, INC. *(Arnold Bernhard & Co., Inc.)* 711 Third Ave. New York, NY 10017 212-687-3965	As high a level of current income as is consistent with liquidity and preservation of capital by investing in high grade money market insts.	1979	0.1	1000 Tel., Wire.	100 Tel., Wire.	Writ. with Sig. Guar.; Tel.; Wire.; Ck. Writ.	*Dividends:* Auto.; M. *Other:* Syst. With.; Exchange-Tel.
WHITEHALL MONEY MARKET TRUST *(Wellington Management Company)* The Vanguard Group/Box 1100 Valley Forge, PA 19482 800-523-7910/215-293-1100	Current income, consistent with preservation of capital, through investing in short-term money market obligations.	1975	53.1	3000	100	Ck. Writ.; Tel.; Wire.	*Dividends:* Auto.; M. *Ret. Plans:* Keo., IRA, Corp., 403(b) *Other:* Syst. With.; Auto. Pur.; Exch.-Writ.; Grp. Sub-Acct.

NO LOAD BOND FUNDS

While these funds invest in corporate bonds, they may also buy high dividend-paying common stocks. The primary purpose of most of them is to produce high current income. Each fund approaches the production of this income a little differently and, again, the investment policies should be studied to match up with each person's own wishes. Investors use these funds for long-term investments to take advantage of the compounding effect of the re-invested income dividends or use them to provide or supplement current income.

Fund Name (Advisor) Address and Telephone Number	Investment Objective and Policy	Year First Offered	Assets Mil. 12/31/78	Purchase Requirements		Redemption Procedures	Services
				Initial	Subsq.		
ALLIANCE BOND FUND, INC. *(Alliance Cap. Mgt. Corp.)* 140 Broadway New York, NY 10005 800-221-5672/212-943-0300	High level of total return. Mainly gov't. & corp. bonds. Rated AA-BBB by S&P, or Aaa-Baa by Moody's, Prime 1-2-3 C.P.	1973	$26.7	$5000	$0	Written	*Dividends:* Auto.; S/A
ALPHA INCOME FUND, INC. *(Montag & Caldwell, Inc.)* Suite 500, 2 Piedmont Center, N.E. Atlanta, GA 30305 800-241-1662/404-262-3480	Highest inv. income consistent with preservation of principal. At least 70% in higher rated debt sec. and 90% in income producing securities.	1970	7.0	200	50	Written; Sig. Guar. over 50 shs.	*Dividends:* Auto.; Q. *Ret. Plans:* Keo., IRA, Corp. *Other:* Syst. With.; Auto. Pur.; Exchange-Writ.
AMERICAN INVESTORS INCOME *(American Investors Corp.)* 88 Field Point Rd. P.O. Box 2500 Greenwich, CT 06830 203-622-1600	High current income. Capital appreciation secondary objective. Diversified investments in generous yielding lower rated bonds and pfd. stocks.	1976	8.7	400	20	Written; Sig. Guar. over $5,000; Tel.	*Dividends:* Auto.; Q. *Ret. Plans:* Keo., IRA, Corp. *Other:* Syst. With.; Auto. Pur.; Exchange-Tel.
DREYFUS A BONDS PLUS, INC. *(The Dreyfus Corporation)* 600 Madison Ave. New York, NY 10022 800-223-5525/212-935-6662	Current income with preservation of capital and liquidity— 80% in debt obligations maturing in 4 to 7 years.	1976	7.7	2500	100	Writ. with Sig. Guar.	*Dividends:* Auto.; M. *Ret. Plans:* Keo., IRA, Corp., 403(b) *Other:* Syst. With.; Auto. Pur.; Exchange-Tel.
DREYFUS SPECIAL INCOME FUND *(The Dreyfus Corporation)* 600 Madison Ave. New York, NY 10022 800-223-5525/212-935-5700	Current income with capital appreciation secondary—invests in both bonds and stocks with high current div. and appr. potential.	1971	93.7	500	50	Writ. with Sig. Guar.	*Dividends:* Auto.; M. *Ret. Plans:* Keo., IRA, Corp., 403(b) *Other:* Syst. With.; Auto. Pur.; Exchange-Tel.
FIDELITY AGGRESSIVE INCOME *(Fidelity Group)* 82 Devonshire St. Boston, MA 02109 800-225-6190/617-726-0650	High current income diversified portfolio of high-yielding, fixed-income corporate securities.	1977	56.7	2500	0	Writ. with Sig. Guar.; Tel.	*Dividends:* Auto.; M. *Ret. Plans:* Keo., IRA, Corp., 403(b) *Other:* Syst. With.; Exchange-Tel.
FIDELITY CORPORATE BOND FUND *(Fidelity Group)* 82 Devonshire St. Boston, MA 02109 800-225-6190/617-726-0650	Income: At least 80% of assets in investment-grade (rated BBB or better) debt securities.	1977	97.7	2500	0	Writ. with Sig. Guar.; Tel.	*Dividends:* Auto.; M. *Ret. Plans:* Keo., IRA, Corp., 403(b) *Other:* Syst. With.; Exchange-Tel.
FIDELITY GOV. SECURITIES *(Fidelity Group)* 82 Devonshire St. Boston, MA 02109 800-225-6190/617-726-0650	Income from obligations issued by U.S. Govt., its agencies, or instrumentalities; income is exempt from state and local income taxes.	1979	0.1	1000	0	Writ. with Sig. Guar.; Tel. Wire.	*Dividends:* Auto.; M. *Ret. Plans:* Keo., IRA, Corp., 403(b) *Other:* Syst. With.; Exchange-Tel.
FIDELITY THRIFT TRUST *(Fidelity Group)* 82 Devonshire St. Boston, MA 02109 800-225-6190/617-726-0650	Income: Corporate obligations (AA or better), Gov. securities, and money market instruments; maturity not to exceed ten years.	1975	29.8	1000	100	Writ. with Sig. Guar.; Tel.	*Dividends:* Auto.; M. *Ret. Plans:* Keo., IRA, Corp., 403(b) *Other:* Syst. With.; Exchange-Tel.
HOLDINGS OF US GOV. SEC. *(Fundpack Mgmt., Inc.)* 3200 Ponce de Leon Blvd. Coral Gables, FL 33134 800-327-2868/305-444-7461	High current income with safety of principal in Gov. securities or mortgage backed certificates guar. by U.S. Govt. or its agencies.	1977	5.1	1000	100	Writ. with Sig. Guar.; Tel.	*Dividends:* Auto.; M. *Ret. Plans:* Keo., IRA, Corp., 403(b) *Other:* Syst. With.; Exchange-Tel.
LIBERTY FUND, INC. *(Neuberger & Berman Management Inc.)* 522 Fifth Ave. New York, NY 10036 212-790-9800	Liberal current income.	1956	11	250 Tel.	25 Tel.	Writ. with Sig. Guar.	*Dividends:* Auto.; Q. *Ret. Plans:* Keo., Corp. *Other:* Syst. With.; Exchange-Tel.

Fund Name (Advisor) Address and Telephone Number	Investment Objective and Policy	Year First Offered	Assets Mil. 12/31/78	Purchase Requirements Initial	Subsq.	Redemption Procedures	Services
NEWTON INCOME FUND, INC. *(Heritage Investment Advisors, Inc.)* 733 N. Van Buren St. Milwaukee, WI 53202 414-347-1141	Above-average current income consistent with preservation of capital.	1970	$8.1	$500	$25	Writ. with Sig. Guar.	*Dividends:* Auto.; Q. *Ret. Plans:* Keo.; IRA, 403(b) *Other:* Syst. With.; Auto. Pur.
NORTH STAR BOND FUND INC. *(Investment Advisers Inc.)* 600 Dain Tower Minneapolis, MN 55402 612-371-7780	Taxable income, corporate and government bonds.	1977	5.5	1000	100	Written	*Dividends:* Auto.; Q. *Ret. Plans:* Keo., IRA, Corp., 403(b) *Other:* Exchange-Writ.
PRO INCOME FUND, INC. *(PRO Services, Inc.)* 1107 Bethlehem Pike Flourtown, PA 19409 215-836-1300/212-431-7355	Income: Seeks the highest income available consistent with preservation of principal.	1974	17.6	300	0 Tel.	Writ. with Sig. Guar.; Tel.	*Dividends:* Auto.; Q. *Ret. Plans:* Keo., IRA, Corp., 403(b) *Other:* Syst. With.; Auto. Pur.; Exchange-Writ.
QUALIFIED DIVIDEND PORTFOLIO I *(Wellington Management Company)* The Vanguard Group/Box 1100 Valley Forge, PA 19482 800-523-7910/215-293-1100	Maximize income (from all sources) which qualifies for the 85% corporate dividend exclusion, by investing in common stocks.	1975	13.4	3000	50	Writ. with Sig. Guar.	*Dividends:* Auto.; Q. *Ret. Plans:* Keo., IRA, Corp., 403(b) *Other:* Syst. With.; Auto. Pur.; Exch.-Writ.; Grp. Sub-Acct.
QUALIFIED DIVIDEND PORTFOLIO II *(Wellington Management Company)* The Vanguard Group/Box 1100 Valley Forge, PA 19482 800-523-7910/215-293-1100	Maximize income (from all sources) which qualifies for the 85% corporate dividend exclusion, by investing in preferred stocks.	1975	19.2	3000	50	Writ. with Sig. Guar.	*Dividends:* Auto.; Q. *Ret. Plans:* Keo., IRA, Corp., 403(b) *Other:* Syst. With.; Auto. Pur.; Exch.-Writ.; Grp. Sub-Acct.
ROWE PRICE NEW INCOME FUND *(T. Rowe Price Associates, Inc.)* 100 East Pratt St. Baltimore, MD 21202 800-638-1527/301-547-2000	High current income with reasonable stability through investment grade fixed income securities.	1973	282	1000	100	Written; Sig. Guar. over $5,000; Tel., Ck. Writ.	*Dividends:* Auto.; Q. *Ret. Plans:* Keo., IRA, Corp., 403(b) *Other:* Syst. With.; Auto. Pur.; Group Sub-Acct. Exch.-Tel.
SCUDDER INCOME FUND, INC. *(Scudder, Stevens & Clark, Inv. Counsel)* 175 Federal St. Boston, MA 02110 800-225-2470/617-482-3990	Income: To provide income with due consideration to the prudent investment of the capital.	1928	61.8	500	0 Tel. over 500	Writ. with Sig. Guar.; Tel.	*Dividends:* Auto.; Q. *Ret. Plans:* Keo., IRA, 403(b) *Other:* Syst. With.; Exchange-Tel.
STEINROE BOND FUND, INC. *(Stein Roe & Farnham)* 150 S. Wacker Drive Chicago, IL 60606 800-621-1142/312-368-7848	High current income. Invests primarily in marketable debt securities.	1978	3.4	2500	100	Writ. with Sig. Guar.	*Dividends:* Auto.; Q. *Ret. Plans:* Keo., IRA *Other:* Syst. With.; Auto. Pur.; Group Sub-Acct.; Exchange-Writ.
UNIFIED ACCUMULATION FUND, INC. *(Unified Management Corporation)* 207 Guaranty Bldg. Indianapolis, IN 46204 317-634-3301	Tax shel. capital appreciation. Flexible invest. in high-yield stocks, corp. and gov. bonds. Income and capital gains accumulate tax-free.	1978	.8	1000	25	Written; Tel.	*Dividends:* None Paid *Ret. Plans:* Keo., IRA, Corp. 403(b), *Other:* Syst. With.; Auto. Pur.; Exchange-Tel.
UNIFIED INCOME FUND, INC. *(Unified Management Corporation)* 207 Guaranty Bldg. Indianapolis, IN 46204 317-634-3301	Current income and capital appreciation. Invests without quality restrictions. May buy stock and write options.	1977	.8	500	25	Written; Tel.	*Dividends:* Auto.; S/A. *Ret. Plans:* Keo., IRA, Corp. 403(b), *Other:* Syst. With.; Auto. Pur.; Exchange-Tel.
WELLESLEY INCOME FUND *(Wellington Management Company)* The Vanguard Group/Box 1100 Valley Forge, PA 19482 800-523-7910/215-293-1100	Seeks as much current income as is consistent with reasonable risk; primarily in fixed-income securities; balance in high-yielding stocks.	1970	122.6	500	50	Writ. with Sig. Guar.	*Dividends:* Auto.; Q. *Ret. Plans:* Keo., IRA, Corp., 403(b) *Other:* Syst. With.; Auto. Pur.; Exch.-Writ.; Grp. Sub-Acct.
WESTMINSTER BOND FUND *(Wellington Management Company)* The Vanguard Group/Box 1100 Valley Forge, PA 19482 800-523-7910/215-293-1100	Current income, primarily from corporate bonds. Two separate portfolios: investment-grade and high-yield.	1973	47.0	500	50	Writ. with Sig. Guar.	*Dividends:* Auto.; M. *Ret. Plans:* Keo., IRA, Corp., 403(b) *Other:* Syst. With.; Auto. Pur.; Exchange-Writ.
WISCONSIN INCOME FUND, INC. *(Nicholas Company, Inc.)* 312 East Wisconsin Ave. Milwaukee, WI 53202 414-272-6133	High current income consistent with conservation of capital.	1929	15.0	500	50	Written; Sig. Guar. on Certificates only	*Dividends:* Auto.; Q. *Ret. Plans:* Keo., IRA *Other:* Syst. With.; Exchange-Writ.

NO-LOAD MUNICIPAL BOND FUNDS

These funds invest in bonds issued by state and local government agencies and the income received by investors is generally free from Federal income taxes. These funds are purchased by investors in higher tax brackets who are seeking current income free of Federal income tax or who wish to compound interest on a tax-free basis.

Fund Name (Advisor) Address and Telephone Number	Investment Objective and Policy	Year First Offered	Assets Mil. 12/31/78	Purchase Requirements		Redemption Procedures	Services
				Initial	Subsq.		
ALPHA TAX-EXEMPT BOND FUND *(Montag & Caldwell, Inc.)* 2 Piedmont Center, N.E., Suite 500 Atlanta, GA 30305 800-241-1662/404-262-3480	Highest interest income exempt from Federal taxes with preservation of principal by investing in a diversified portfolio of marketable muni. bonds.	1977	$2.1	$1000	$50	Written; Sig. Guar. over 50 shs.	*Dividends:* Auto.; M. *Other:* Syst. With.; Auto. Pur.; Exchange-Writ.
DREYFUS TAX EXEMPT BOND FUND *(The Dreyfus Corporation)* 600 Madison Ave. New York, NY 10022 800-223-5525/212-935-5700	Highest interest income exempt from Federal income taxes consistent with preservation of capital by investing in a diversified list of municipal securities.	1976	603.4	2500	100	Writ. with Sig. Guar.	*Dividends:* Auto.; M. *Other:* Syst. With.; Auto. Pur.; Exchange-Tel.
FIDELITY HIGH YIELD MUNICIPALS *(Fidelity Group)* 82 Devonshire St. Boston, MA 02109 800-225-6190/617-726-0650	Tax-free income: Carefully selected long-term municipal bonds of medium quality.	1977	106.1	2500	0	Writ. with Sig. Guar., Tel.	*Dividends:* Auto.; M. *Other:* Syst. With. Exchange-Tel.
FIDELITY LTD. TERM MUNICIPALS *(Fidelity Group)* 82 Devonshire St. Boston, MA 02109 800-225-6190/617-726-0650	Tax-free income: Tax-exempt obligations maturing in 15 years or less, with average maturity of 12 years or less.	1977	67.2	10M	1000	Writ. with Sig. Guar.; Tel.; Ck.-Writ.	*Dividends:* Auto; M. *Other:* Syst. With.; Exchange-Tel.
FIDELITY MUNICIPAL BOND FUND *(Fidelity Group)* 82 Devonshire St. Boston, MA 02109 800-225-6190/617-726-0650	Tax-free income: invests primarily in high grade or upper medium grade, long-term municipal bonds.	1976	583.7	2500	0	Writ. with Sig. Guar.; Tel.	*Dividends:* Auto; M. *Other:* Syst. With.; Exchange-Tel.
ROWE PRICE TAX-FREE INCOME *(T. Rowe Price Associates, Inc.)* 100 East Pratt St. Baltimore, MD 21202 800-638-1527/301-547-2000	High income exempt from Federal income taxes through investment grade municipal bonds.	1976	209	1000	100	Written; Sig. Guar. over $5M; Tel.; Ck. Writ.	*Dividends:* Auto.; Q. *Other:* Syst. With.; Auto. Pur.; Exchange-Tel. Group Sub.-Acct.
SCUDDER MANAGED MUNI. BONDS *(Scudder, Stevens & Clark, Inv. Counsel)* 175 Federal St. Boston, MA 02110 800-225-2472/617-482-3990	Income tax exempt (Federal); invests in a high grade portfolio consisting primarily of municipal bonds.	1976	110.0	1000	0	Writ. with Sig. Guar.; Tel.	*Dividends:* Auto.; M. *Other:* Syst. With.; Exchange-Tel.
SELECTED TAX-EXEMPT BOND FUND *(Lincoln Nat'l. Investment Mgt. Co.)* 111 W. Washington St., Chicago, IL 60602 800-621-7321/312-630-2762	To earn current income exempt from Federal income tax. Invest primarily in a portfolio of "high grade" bonds and notes.	1977	1.6	1000	100	Writ. with Sig. Guar.	*Dividends:* Auto; M. *Other:* Syst. With.; Exchange-Writ.
STEINROE TAX-EXEMPT BOND FUND *(Stein Roe & Farnham)* 150 S. Wacker Dr. Chicago, IL 60606 800-621-1142/312-368-7831	High current income. Invests primarily in municipal bonds so that at least 80% of income is exempt from Federal income taxes.	1976	23.4	2500	100	Writ. with Sig. Guar.	*Dividends:* Auto; Q. *Other:* Exchange-Writ.; Syst. With.; Group Sub-Acct.
WARWICK MUNICIPAL BOND FUND *(Citibank, N.A.)* The Vanguard Group/Box 1100 Valley Forge, PA 19482 800-523-7910/215-293-1100	Tax-free income, 4 portfolios to choose from: 3 investment grade (short; intermediate; and long-term); plus a high-yield portfolio.	1977	55.0	3000	50	Ck. Writ.; Tel.; Wire	*Dividends:* Auto.; M. *Other:* Syst. With.; Auto. Pur.; Exchange-Tel.; Group Sub-Acct.

NO LOAD BALANCED FUNDS

The name of this category of mutual funds indicates that the funds "balance" fixed income investments (bonds) and common stocks. These funds tend to provide a general or basic approach to investing and are used by investors seeking long-term commitments that provide a complete package of common stocks and bonds.

Fund Name (Advisor) Address and Telephone Number	Investment Objective and Policy	Year First Offered	Assets Mil. 12/31/78	Purchase Requirements		Redemption Procedures	Services
				Initial	Subsq.		
DODGE & COX BALANCED FUND *(Dodge & Cox)* One Post St., 35th Fl. San Francisco, CA 94104 415-981-1710	Regular income, conservation of principal long-term growth balanced between common stocks & fixed-income securities.	1931	$15.2	$250	$50 Tel.	Written	*Dividends:* Auto.; Q. *Ret. Plans:* Keo.. *Other:* Syst. With.; Exchange-Writ.
EVERGREEN TOTAL RETURN FUND *(Saxon Wood Mgt. Corp.)* 600 Mamaroneck Ave. Harrison, NY 10528 914-698-5711/212-828-7700	Income production and growth achieved through undervalued common stocks, convertible securities, bonds, limited sale of options and security loans.	1978	6.5	1500 Tel.	0 Tel.	Writ. with Sig. Guar.	*Dividends:* Auto.; Q.
LINDNER FUND FOR INCOME, INC. *(Lindner Management Corp.)* 200 South Bemiston St. Louis, MO 63105 314-727-5305	Income. Invests largely in common stocks with above-average yield and potential for future dividend increases.	1976	1.2	1000	100	Written; Tel.	*Dividends:* Auto.; Q. *Other:* Syst. With.; Exchange-Tel.
LOOMIS-SAYLES MUTUAL FUND *(Loomis, Sayles & Co.)* Box 449, Back Bay Annex Boston, MA 02117 617-267-6600	Reasonable long-term capital appreciation and current income return, without undue risk.	1929	89.5	250	50 Tel.	Written; Sig. Guar. over $5,000	*Dividends:* Auto.; Q. *Ret. Plans:* Keo., IRA, Corp. *Other:* Syst. With.; Auto. Pur.
MUTUAL SHARES CORP. *(Heine Securities Corp.)* 170 Broadway New York, NY 10038 212-267-4200	Capital gains. May be short term. Income secondary. Invest in common, preferred & debt securities at prices less than intrinsic value.	1949	47	1000	0 Tel.	Writ. with Sig. Guar.	*Dividends:* Auto.; S/A *Ret. Plans:* Keo., IRA *Other:* Syst. With.
STEIN ROE & FARNHAM BAL. FUND *(Stein Roe & Farnham)* 150 S. Wacker Dr. Chicago, IL 60606 312-368-7810	Maintain and increase capital while providing income. Diversified investments: bonds, preferred and common stocks.	1949	103.3	300	50	Writ. with Sig. Guar.; Tel.	*Dividends:* Auto.; Q. *Ret. Plans:* Keo., IRA *Other:* Exchange-Writ. Syst. With.; Group Sub-Acct.; Auto. Pur.
UNIFIED MUTUAL SHARES, INC. *(Unified Management Corporation)* 207 Guaranty Bldg. Indianapolis, IN 46204 317-634-3301	Capital growth and current income. Flexible with emphasis on high quality stocks and convertibles; uses covered option writing.	1963	7.8	200	25	Written; Tel.	*Dividends:* Auto.; S/A *Ret. Plans:* Keo., IRA, 403(b), Corp. *Other:* Syst. With.; Auto. Pur.; Exchange-Tel,
WELLINGTON FUND *(Wellington Management Company)* The Vanguard Group/Box 1100 Valley Forge, PA 19482 800-523-7910/215-293-1100	Conservation of principal; reasonable income; profits without undue risk. 60-70% in common stocks; balance in fixed-income securities.	1928	639.5	500	50	Writ. with Sig. Guar.	*Dividends:* Auto.; Q. *Ret. Plans:* Keo., IRA, Corp, 403(b) *Other:* Syst. With.; Auto. Pur.; Exch.-Writ.; Grp. Sub-Acct.

COMMON STOCK FUNDS

Common stock funds are the best known type of no-load mutual funds. Investors using these funds generally are seeking growth of capital and perhaps growth of income also. The funds listed below will give different degrees of aggressiveness in seeking this growth. The objectives and policies should be read carefully to match up with your own. Investors generally use these types of funds for long-term investments, to build assets for retirement, cover college costs, to try to offset inflation, and as general equity-type investments after basic financial needs have been met.

Fund Name *(Advisor)* Address and Telephone Number	Investment Objective and Policy	Year First Offered	Assets Mil. 12/31/78	Purchase Requirements		Redemption Procedures	Services
				Initial	Subsq.		
ACORN FUND *(Harris Associates, Inc.)* 120 S. La Salle St. Chicago, Il. 60603 312-621-0630	Capital growth—Seeks smaller growth companies with financial strength whose investment qualities have not been widely recognized.	1970	$41.0	$1000	$200	Writ. with Sig. Guar.	*Dividends:* Auto.; S/A *Ret. Plans:* Keo.; IRA *Other:* Auto. Pur.; Syst. With.
AFUTURE FUND, INC. *(Carlisle-Asher Management Co.)* 8 N. Pennell Rd. Lima, PA. 19037 800-523-7594/215-565-3131	Growth—appreciation of capital.	1968	22.0	500	30	Writ. with Sig. Guar.	*Dividends:* Auto.; A. *Ret. Plans:* Keo.; IRA *Other:* Syst. With.
ALPHA FUND, INC. *(Montag & Caldwell, Inc.)* 2 Piedmont Center, Suite 500, N.E. Atlanta, GA. 30305 800-241-1662/404-262-3480	Growth of capital invests primarily in common stocks or securities exchangeable for common stocks.	1968	13.7	200	50	Written; Sig. Guar. over 50 shs.	*Dividends:* Auto.; A. *Ret. Plans:* Keo.; IRA, Corp. *Other:* Syst. With.; Auto. Pur.; Exchange-Writ.
AMERICAN INVESTORS FUND, INC. *(American Investors Corp.)* 88 Field Point Rd. P.O. Box 2500, Greenwich, CT. 06830 203-622-1600	Growth of investment capital. Emphasis on timing and selecting securities believed to have best potential for capital appreciation.	1958	108.3	400	20	Written; Sig. Guar. over $5,000; Tel.	*Dividends:* Auto.; A. *Ret. Plans:* Keo.; IRA, Corp. *Other:* Syst. With.; Auto. Pur.; Exchange-Tel.
ANALYTIC OPTIONED EQUITY FUND *(Analytic Investment Mgt.)* Box 19274 Irvine, CA. 92715 714-833-0294	Seeks greater total return with less risk by writing covered call options on its diversified, high quality stocks.	1978	0.5	25M	1000	Writ. with Sig. Guar.; Tel., Wire	*Dividends:* Auto.; Q. *Ret. Plans:* Keo., Corp. *Other:* Syst. With.
ARMSTRONG ASSOCIATES INC. *(Portfolios Inc.)* 2400 First International Bldg. Dallas, TX. 75270 214-744-5558	Capital growth by investing primarily in common stocks and securities convertible into common stock.	1967	4.2	500	50	Written.	*Dividends:* Auto.; A. *Ret. Plans:* Keo., IRA, Corp. *Other:* Sys. With.; Auto. Pur.
BEACON HILL MUTUAL FUND, INC. *(Beacon Hill Management, Inc.)* 75 Federal St. Boston, MA. 02110 617-482-0795	Growth—specialize in quality growth stocks—flexible but generally investing in common stocks.	1964	2.2	0	0	Writ. with Sig. Guar.	*Dividends:* Auto.; A. *Ret. Plans:* Keo., IRA *Other:* Syst. With.
BULL & BEAR INCORPORATED *(Bull & Bear Management Corp., Inc.)* 111 Broadway New York, NY. 10006 212-267-5100	Two Funds: Bear Fund for apprec. in down mkts., always has short pos. and puts. Bull Fund for apprec. in up mkts., always has com. stk. and calls.	1977	0.7	5000	500	Written; Sig. Guar. over $1,000	*Dividends:* Auto.; A. *Other:* Exchange between Bull & Bear Funds by phone.
CAPAMERICA FUND, INC. *(Bull & Bear Group, Inc.)* 111 Broadway New York, NY. 10006 212-267-5100	Investing for long term growth of capital and current income.	1961	2.8	500	25	Written; Sig. Guar. over $1,000	*Dividends:* Auto.; Q. *Ret. plans:* Keo., IRA
CAPITAL SHARES, INC. *(Bull & Bear Group, Inc.)* 111 Broadway New York, N.Y. 10006 212-267-5100	Investing for long term capital appreciation.	1959	25.8	500	25	Written; Sig. Guar. over $1,000	*Dividends:* Auto.; A. *Ret. Plans:* Keo., IRA
COMMERCE INCOME SHARES, INC. *(Funds, Inc.)* 711 Polk St. Houston, TX. 77002 713-751-2400	Income/growth—high level of current income with reasonable safety of capital, and secondarily seeking growth of income and capital.	1949	44.0	3500	50 Tel. over 500	Writ. with Sig. Guar.	*Dividends:* Auto.; Q. *Ret. Plans:* Keo., IRA *Other:* Syst. With.; Auto. Pur., Exchange-Tel.

Fund Name (Advisor) Address and Telephone Number	Investment Objective and Policy	Year First Offered	Assets Mil. 12/31/78	Purchase Requirements		Redemption Procedures	Services
				Initial	Subsq.		
CONSTELLATION GROWTH FUND *(Weingarten Management Corp.)* 331 Madison Ave. New York, NY. 10017 212-557-8787	Growth—emphasis on issues with rapid earnings growth and use of aggresive investment techniques.	1966	$ 3.6	$500	$50 Tel.	Written; Sig. Guar. on certificates only	*Dividends:* Auto.; A. *Ret. Plans:* Keo., IRA
CONTRAFUND, INC. *(Fidelity Group)* 82 Devonshire St. Boston, MA. 02109 800-225-6190/617-726-0650	Growth: seeks solid investment values among industry groups and stocks currently out of favor.	1967	43.8	500	50	Writ. with Sig. Guar.	*Dividends:* Auto; A. *Ret. Plans:* Keo., IRA; Corp.; 403(b) *Other:* Syst. With.; Auto. Pur.; Exchange-Tel.
DE VEGH MUTUAL FUND, INC. *(Wood Struthers & Winthrop Mgt. Corp.)* 14 Wall St. New York, NY 10005 800-221-5672/212-344-9200	Long term capital appreciation.	1950	54	250	100	Writ. With Sig. Guar.	*Dividends:* Auto.; S/A *Ret. Plans:* Keo., IRA *Other:* Syst. With.; Auto. Pur.
DODGE & COX STOCK FUND *(Dodge & Cox)* One Post St., 35th Fl. San Francisco, CA 94104 415-981-1710	Long term growth of principal and income with current income secondary-primarily in diversified list of high-grade common stocks.	1965	13.9	250	50 Tel.	Written	*Dividends:* Auto; Q. *Ret. Plans:* Keo. *Other:* Syst. With.; Exchange-Writ.
THE DREXEL BURNHAM FUND *(Drexel Burnham Lambert Mgt. Corp.)* 60 Broad St. New York, NY 10004 212-483-1436	Capital appreciation mainly long term with income secondary emphasizing a flexible approach but generally common stocks.	1960	35.4	1000	250	Writ. with Sig. Guar.	*Div.:* Auto; Q. *Ret. Plans:* Keo., IRA *Other:* Syst. With.
DREYFUS NUMBER NINE, INC. *(The Dreyfus Corporation)* 600 Madison Ave. New York, NY 10022 800-223-5525/212-935-5700	Long term capital growth with current income secondary thru common stocks.	1972	14.6	500	50	Writ. with Sig. Guar.	*Dividends:* Auto.; A. *Ret. Plans:* Keo., IRA, Corp., 403(b) *Other:* Syst. With.; Auto. Pur.; Exchange-Tel.
DREYFUS THIRD CENTURY FUND *(The Dreyfus Corporation)* 600 Madison Ave. New York, NY 10022 800-223-5525/212-935-5700	Long term capital growth with current income secondary thru purchase of common stocks.	1971	24.9	500	50	Writ. with Sig. Guar.	*Dividends:* Auto.; A. *Ret. Plans:* IRA, Corp., 403(b) *Other:* Syst. With.; Auto. Pur.; Exchange-Tel.
ELDORADO FUND, INC. *(Cedric Fricke Associates, Inc)* 18158 Westover Southfield, MI 48075 313-569-4150	Long term capital growth—using primarily common stocks with flexibility to go in many areas.	1970	0.3	100	50	Written	*Dividends:* Auto.; A.
ENERGY FUND INCORPORATED *(Neuberger & Berman Management Inc.)* 522 Fifth Ave. New York, NY 10036 212-790-9800	Long-term capital appreciation; primarily investing in common stocks whose activities are related to the field of energy.	1955	184	100 Tel.	25 Tel.	Writ. with Sig. Guar.	*Dividends:* Auto.; A. *Ret. Plans:* Keo., IRA, Corp. *Other:* Syst. With.; Exchange-Tel.
THE EVERGREEN FUND, INC. *(Saxon Wood Mgt. Corp.)* 600 Mamaroneck Ave. Harrison, NY 10528 914-698-5711/212-828-7700	Capital appreciation-predominantly stocks of smaller companies analyzed as under-valued based on growth trends and finances.	1971	11.9	1500 Tel.	0 Tel.	Written	*Dividends:* Auto.; A.
EXPLORER FUND *(Wellington Management Company)* The Vanguard Group/Box 1100 Valley Forge, PA 19482 800-523-7910/215-293-1100	Long term capital growth by investing in small, unseasoned or embryonic companies.	1967	10.4	500	50	Writ. with Sig. Guar.	*Dividends:* Auto.; A. *Ret. Plans:* Keo., IRA, Corp., 403(b) *Other:* Syst. With.; Auto. Pur.; Exch.-Writ; Grp. Sub-Acct.
FIDELITY ASSET INVEST. TRUST *(Fidelity Group)* 82 Devonshire St. Boston, MA 02109 800-225-6190/617-726-0650	Growth: specialize in securities of companies whose market value is less than their book value.	1978	0.2	1000	50	Writ. with Sig. Guar.	*Dividends:* Auto.; A. *Ret. Plans:* Keo; IRA, Corp.,. 403(b) *Other:* Syst. With.; Auto. Pur.; Exchange-Tel.
FIDELITY EQUITY-INCOME FUND *(Fidelity Group)* 82 Devonshire St. Boston, MA 02109 800-225-6190/617-726-0650	Growth and Income: at least 80% in income-producing equity securities with remainder generally in convertible securities.	1966	63.9	500 Tel.	50 Tel.	Writ. with Sig. Guar.	*Dividends:* Auto.; Q. *Ret. Plans:* Keo, IRA. Corp., 403(b) *Other:* Syst. With.; Auto. Pur.; Exchange-Tel.
FINOMIC INVESTMENT FUND *(Investment Advisors Inc.)* 600 Jefferson Houston, TX 77002 713-659-2611	Capital appreciation. Primarily in common stocks of small to medium size companies generally located in the Sun-Belt.	1972	0.4	750	50	Writ. with Sig. Guar.	*Dividends:* Auto.; A. *Ret. Plans:* Keo., IRA, Corp *Other:* Syst. With.; Auto. Pur.

Fund Name (Advisor) Address and Telephone Number	Investment Objective and Policy	Year First Offered	Assets Mil. 12/31/78	Purchase Requirements		Redemption Procedures	Services
				Initial	Subsq.		
THE 44 WALL STREET FUND, INC. *(Forty Four Mgt. Ltd.)* 150 Broadway New York, NY 10038 212-374-1146	Long-term capital appreciation — using limited no. of common stk. companies with above aver. potential and are fundamentally attractive.	1969	$30.6	$1000	$100 Tel.	Writ. with Sig. Guar.; Tel.	*Dividends:* Auto.; A. *Ret. Plans:* Keo., IRA, 403 (b) *Other:* Syst. With.; Auto. Pur.; Exchange-Tel.
FIRST INDEX INVESTMENT TRUST *(none)* The Vanguard Group/Box 1100 Valley Forge, PA 19482 800-523-7910/215-293-1100	Seeks to provide investment results that correspond to the price and yield performance of the S & P 500 Index, by owning all stocks in the S & P 500.	1976	66.2	1500	50	Writ. with Sig. Guar.	*Dividends:* Auto.; Q. *Ret. Plans:* Keo., IRA, Corp., 403 (b) *Other:* Syst. With.; Auto. Pur.; Exch.-Writ; Grp. Sub-Acct.
FIRST MUTUAL FUND, INC. *(The Providence Group)* 50 South Main St. Providence, RI 02903 401-272-3800	Growth with income secondary; investments made in companies with growth characteristics and some attention given to market timing.	1959	0.8	100	100 Tel.	Writ. with Sig. Guar.	*Dividends:* Auto,; S/A.
THE FUNDPACK, INC. *(Fundpack Mgt., Inc.)* 3200 Ponce de Leon Blvd. Coral Gables, FL 33134 800-327-2868/305-444-7461	Capital appreciation — Invests in shares of other growth mutual funds.	1970	5.8	1000	100	Writ. with Sig. Guar.; Tel.	*Dividends:* Auto; A. *Ret. Plans:* Keo., IRA, Corp., 403 (b) *Other:* Syst. With.; Auto. Pur.; Exchange-Tel.
GAMING, SPORTS & GROWTH FUND *(Stuart Management Inc.)* 1700 Market St. Phila., PA 19103 215-864-7777	Growth — specialize in gaming and sports related companies.	1979	0.1	2500	250	Writ. with Sig. Guar.	*Dividends:* Auto.; A.
GATEWAY OPTION INCOME FUND *(Gateway Investment Advisers, Inc.)* 330 Dixie Terminal Bldg. Cincinnati, OH 45202 513-621-7774	High current income — Invests in diversified portfolio of common stocks and sells covered call options on those stocks.	1977	10.2	1500	500	Writ. with Sig. Guar.	*Dividends:* Auto.; Q. *Ret. Plans:* Keo., IRA *Other:* Syst. With.
G. T. PACIFIC FUND, INC. *(G. T. Capital Management, Inc.)* 555 California St. San Francisco, CA 94104 415-392-6181	Long-term growth through investment in diversified portfolio of Japanese securities, primarily common stocks.	1977	17.7	1000	100	Writ. with Sig. Guar.	*Dividends:* Auto.; A.
GENERAL SECURITIES, INC. *(Craig-Hallum, Inc.)* 133 South Seventh St. Minneapolis, MN 55402 612-332-1212	Capital appreciation and security of principal — Flexible to use stocks and sometimes fixed income securities — also covered options.	1951	9.1	100	10 Tel.	Writ. with Sig. Guar.	*Dividends:* Auto.; Q. *Ret. Plans:* Keo., IRA., 403 (b) *Other:* Syst. With.; Auto. Pur.
GOLCONDA INVESTORS, LTD. *(Golconda Management Corp.)* 111 Broadway, New York, NY 10006 212-267-5100	Growth — Specialize in gold bullion and mining stocks.	1974	1.5	0	0	Written; Sig. Guar. over 1,000	*Dividends:* Auto.; A.
GROWTH INDUSTRY SHARES *(William Blair & Company)* 135 S. LaSalle St. Chicago, IL 60603 312-346-4830	Appreciation of capital & growing income thru growth companies; diversification among different size companies.	1946	27.4	200	25	Written; Sig. Guar. over 5,000	*Dividends:* Auto.; Q. *Ret. Plans:* Keo., IRA, Corp. *Other:* Auto. Pur.; Syst. With.
GUARDIAN MUTUAL FUND, INC. *(Neuberger & Berman Management Inc.)* 522 Fifth Ave. New York, NY 10036 212-790-9800	Capital appreciation with income secondary; common stocks of seasoned companies, flexibility to shift to fixed income securities.	1950	93	200 Tel.	50 Tel.	Writ. with Sig. Guar.	*Dividends:* Auto., Q. *Ret. Plans:* Keo., IRA, Corp. *Other:* Syst. With.; Exchange-Tel.
THE EDSON GOULD FUND, INC. *(Anametrics Fund Advisors, Inc.)* 30 Rockefeller Plaza New York, NY 10020 212-246-1000	Growth of capital. Current income secondary. Will sell common stocks & switch to highly defensive position when appropriate.	1976	4.7	1000	50	Writ. with Sig. Guar.	*Dividends:* Auto.; A. *Ret. Plans:* Keo., IRA, Corp. *Other:* Syst. With.
HARTWELL GROWTH FUND, INC. *(Hartwell Management Co., Inc.)* 50 Rockefeller Plaza New York, NY 10020 212-247-8740	Capital appreciation. Invests primarily in intermediate size growth companies.	1965	4.5	300	50	Writ. with Sig. Guar.	*Div.:* Auto.; A. *Ret. Plans:* IRA *Other:* Syst. With.; Auto. Pur.
HARTWELL LEVERAGE FUND, INC. *(Hartwell Management Co., Inc.)* 50 Rockefeller Plaza New York, NY 10020 212-247-8740	Capital appreciation. Flexible policy emphasizing appreciation potential.	1968	5.1	5000	50	Writ. with Sig. Guar.	*Div.:* Auto.; A. *Ret. Plans:* IRA *Other:* Auto. Pur.

Fund Name (Advisor) Address and Telephone Number	Investment Objective and Policy	Year First Offered	Assets Mil. 12/31/78	Purchase Requirements Initial	Subsq.	Redemption Procedures	Services
INVESTMENT GUIDANCE FUND, INC. *(Roulston & Company, Inc.)* 1801 E. Ninth St. Cleveland, OH 44114 216-696-3070	Capital appreciation. Value oriented selection.	1968	$ 2.5	$10 Shares Tel.	$0 Tel.	Writ. with Sig. Guar.	*Dividends:* Auto.; A. *Ret. Plans:* Keo., IRA *Other:* Auto. Pur.
IVEST FUND *(Wellington Management Company)* The Vanguard Group/Box 1100 Valley Forge, PA 19482 800-523-7910/215-293-1100	Seeks long-term capital growth, by investing in common stocks believed to have potential for appreciation.	1961	151. 8	500	50	Writ. with Sig. Guar.	*Dividends:* Auto.; A. *Ret. Plans:* Keo., IRA, Corp., 403(b) *Other:* Syst. With.; Auto. Pur.; Exch.-Writ; Grp. Sub-Acct.
IVY FUND, INC. *(Furman Selz, et.al.; Grantham, Mayo, et.al.; SCNC Advis. Corp.)* 201 Devonshire St., Boston, MA 02110 617-426-0636	Growth. The fund seeks to achieve long-term growth of capital through investment in equity securities.	1961	29.2	500	100	Writ. with Sig. Guar.	*Dividends:* Auto.; A. *Ret. Plans:* Keo., IRA *Other:* Syst. With.
JANUS FUND, INC. *(Janus Management Corp.)* 789 Sherman St. Denver, CO 80203 800-525-3713/303-837-1774	Growth of capital. Takes positions in a limited number of securities and may use leveraging.	1970	18.8	500	100	Writ. with Sig. Guar.	*Dividends:* Auto.; A *Ret. Plans:* Keo., IRA *Other:* Exchange-Tel.; Syst. With.; Auto. Pur.
THE JOHNSTON MUTUAL FUND INC. *(Douglas T. Johnston & Co., Inc.)* One Boston Place Boston, MA 02106 800-343-6324/617-722-7250	Long term capital growth with moderate risk—well selected and supervised portfolio of growth stocks.	1947	210.6	250	50	Written; Sig. Guar. over $5,000	*Dividends:* Auto.; S/A *Ret. Plans:* Keo., IRA, Corp. *Other:* Syst. With., Auto. Pur.
LINDNER FUND, INC. *(Lindner Management Corp.)* 200 South Bemiston St. Louis, MO 63105 314-727-5305	Growth. Seeks optimum combination of low price-earnings ratio and growth. Majority of holdings are over-the-counter stocks.	1973	9.1	1000	100	Written; Tel.	*Dividends:* Auto.; A. *Ret. Plans:* IRA *Other:* Syst. With; Exchange-Tel.
NEUWIRTH FUND, INC. *(Wood, Struthers & Winthrop Mgt. Corp.)* 14 Wall St. New York, NY 10005 800-221-5672/212-344-9200	Capital growth. Common stock of established companies with growth characteristics; also emerging growth companies.	1966	13.7	500	50	Writ. with Sig. Guar.	*Dividends:* Auto.; A. *Ret. Plans:* IRA, Keo. *Other:* Syst. With.
MANHATTAN FUND, INC. *(Neuberger & Berman Management Inc.)* 522 Fifth Ave. New York, NY 10036 212-790-9800	Capital appreciation.	1966	44	250 Tel.	25 Tel.	Writ. with Sig. Guar.	*Dividends:* Auto.; A. *Ret. Plans:* Keo., Corp. *Other:* Syst. With.; Exchange-Tel.
NEWTON GROWTH FUND, INC. *(Heritage Investment Advisors, Inc.)* 733 N. Van Buren St. Milwaukee, WI 53202 414-347-1141	Long term growth of capital, current income of lessor importance.	1960	13.9	500	25	Writ. with Sig. Guar.	*Dividends:* Auto.; A. *Ret. Plans:* Keo., IRA, 403(b) *Other:* Syst. With.; Auto . Pur.
NICHOLAS FUND, INC. *(Nicholas Company, Inc.)* 312 East Wisconsin Ave. Milwaukee, WI 53202 414-272-6133	Growth. Concentrates in common stocks of small and medium size companies.	1969	40.0	500	100	Written; Sig. Guar. on certificates only	*Dividends:* Auto.; A. *Ret. Plans:* Keo., IRA *Other:* Exchange-Tel.
NORTH STAR STOCK FUND, INC. *(Investment Advisers, Inc.)* 600 Dain Tower Minneapolis, MN 55402 612-371-7780	Growth with a secondary emphasis on income. Common stocks.	1971	6.5	1000	100	Written	*Dividends:* Auto.; S/A *Ret. Plans:* Keo., IRA, Corp., 403 (b) *Other:* Exchange-Writ.
ONE WILLIAM STREET FUND *(Lehman Management Co., Inc.)* 55 Water St. New York, NY 10041 212-558-2020	Long-term growth of capital; income secondary, through common stock investment.	1958	246	250	50	Written; Sig. Guar. over $5,000	*Dividends:* Auto.; Q. *Ret. Plans:* Keo. *Other:* Syst. With.; Auto. Pur.
THE PARTNERS FUND, INC. *(Neuberger & Berman Management Inc.)* 522 Fifth Ave. New York, NY 10036 212-790-9800	Capital growth. Emphasis on common stocks with a portion of assets in stocks selected for short-term gain potential.	1968	28	250 Tel.	0 Tel.	Writ. with Sig. Guar.	*Dividends:* Auto.; A. *Ret. Plans:* Keo., IRA, Corp. *Other:* Syst. With.; Exchange-Tel.
PENN SQUARE MUTUAL FUND *(Penn Square Mgmt. Corp.)* 451 Penn Sq. Reading, PA 19603 800-523-8400/215-376-6771	Long term capital growth. Investments principally in common stocks of larger companies considered under-valued on a fundamental basis.	1958	140.1	250	0	Written	*Dividends:* Auto.; Q. *Ret. Plans:* Keo., IRA, Corp., 403 (b) *Other:* Syst. With.

Fund Name (Advisor) Address and Telephone Number	Investment Objective and Policy	Year First Offered	Assets Mil. 12/31/78	Purchase Requirements Initial	Subsq.	Redemption Procedures	Services
PENNSYLVANIA MUTUAL FUND, INC. *(Quest Advisory Corp.)* 127 John St. New York, NY 10038 800-221-4268/212-269-8533	Capital appreciation. Invests in common stocks generally, with special emphasis on securities of medium-sized companies.	1962	$42.1	$ 500	$50	Writ. with Sig. Guar.; Tel.	*Dividends:* Auto.; A. *Ret. Plans:* Keo., IRA, 403 (b) *Other:* Syst. With.; Auto. Pur.; Exchange-Tel.
PILOT FUND, INC. *(Funds, Inc.)* 711 Polk St. Houston, TX 77002 713-751-2400	Growth. Capital appreciation through investments in companies expected to benefit from significant new developments.	1967	18.1	2000	50	Writ. with Sig. Guar.	*Dividends:* Auto.; A. *Ret. Plans:* Keo., IRA *Other:* Syst. With.; Auto. Pur; Exchange-Tel.
PINE STREET FUND INC. *(Wood, Struthers & Winthrop Mgmt. Corp.)* 14 Wall St. New York, NY 10005 800-221-5672/212-344-9200	Income & Growth. Emphasis on stocks but also use Gov't. agency and corporate bonds & money market instruments.	1949	38.5	500 Tel.	50 Tel.	Written; Sig. Guar. over 500	*Dividends:* Auto.; Q. *Ret. Plans:* Keo., IRA *Other:* Syst. With.
PRO FUND, INC. *(PRO Services, Inc.)* 1107 Bethlehem Pike Flourtown, PA 19409 215-836-1300/212-431-7355	Growth. Invests primarily in common stocks believed by management to have potential for capital appreciation.	1967	35.3	300	0 Tel.	Writ. with Sig. Guar.	*Dividends:* Auto.; Q. *Ret. Plans:* Keo., IRA, Corp., 403 (b) *Other:* Syst. With.; Auto. Pur.; Exchange-Writ.
THE RAINBOW FUND, INC. *(Robert Furman)* 55 Water St., RM. 4260 New York, NY 10041 212-964-7989	Growth of capital. A non-diversified fund primarily investing in common stocks.	1967	1.4	300	50	Writ. with Sig. Guar.	*Dividends:* Auto.; A. *Ret. Plans:* Keo., IRA *Other:* Syst. With.
REVERE FUND, INC. *(Berkshire Investment Mgt. Co.)* 209 Lancaster Ave. Reading, PA 19611 215-375-0170	Appreciation of capital. Investment selection assisted by the use of Modern Portfolio Theory.	1959	4.3	500	50	Writ. with Sig. Guar.	*Dividends:* Auto.; A. *Ret. Plans:* Keo., IRA *Other:* Syst. With.; Auto. Pur.
THE ROCHESTER FUND INC. *(Rochester Shares Mgt.)* 183 E. Main St. Rochester, NY 14604 716-244-8790	Long-term growth.	1967	0.9	250	25	Written	*Dividends:* Auto.; A. *Ret. Plans:* Keo *Other:* Syst. With.
ROWE PRICE NEW ERA FUND *(T. Rowe Price Associates, Inc.)* 100 East Pratt St. Baltimore, MD 21202 800-638-1527/301-547-2000	Long-term capital appreciation through investment primarily in common stocks of companies that own or develop natural resources.	1969	177	1000	100	Written; Sig. Guar. over $5,000	*Dividends:* Auto.; A. *Ret. Plans:* Keo., IRA, Corp. 403(b) *Other:* Syst. With.; Auto. Pur.; Group Sub-Acct.; Exch.-Tel.
T. ROWE PRICE GROWTH STOCK *(T. Rowe Price Associates, Inc.)* 100 East Pratt St. Baltimore, MD 21202 800-638-1527/301-547-2000	Long-term capital appreciation and future income through investment in stocks of well-established growth companies.	1950	935	500	50	Written; Sig. Guar. over $5,000	*Dividends:* Auto.; A. *Ret. Plans:* Keo., IRA, Corp. 403(b) *Other:* Syst. With.; Auto. Pur.; Group Sub-Acct.; Exch.-Tel.
ROWE PRICE NEW HORIZONS FUND *(T. Rowe Price Associates, Inc.)* 100 East Pratt St. Baltimore, MD 21202 800-638-1527/301-547-2000	Long-term capital appreciation through investment in newer smaller companies with potential to become major growth companies.	1960	442	1000	100	Written; Sig. Guar. over $5,000	*Dividends:* Auto.; A. *Ret. Plans:* Keo., IRA, Corp., 403(b) *Other:* Syst. With.; Auto. Pur.; Group Sub-Acct.; Exch.-Tel.
SCHUSTER FUND, INC. *(Neuberger & Berman Mangement Inc.)* 522 Fifth Ave. New York, NY 10036 212-790-9800	Appreciation of capital.	1967	13	250 Tel.	25 Tel.	Writ. with Sig. Guar.	*Dividends:* Auto.; A. *Ret. Plans:* Keo., Corp. *Other:* Syst. With.; Exchange-Tel.
SCUDDER DEVELOPMENT FUND *(Scudder, Stevens & Clark, Inv. Counsel)* 345 Park Ave. New York, NY 10022 212-350-8200	Growth. Consists primarily of marketable equity securities of small or little known companies.	1971	31.5	2000	0 Tel.	Writ. with Sig. Guar.	*Dividends:* Auto.; A.
SCUDDER INTERNATIONAL FUND *(Scudder, Stevens & Clark, Inv. Counsel)* 345 Park Ave. New York, NY 10022 212-350-8200	Growth. Specializes in common stocks of non-U.S. companies and economies.	1954	18.1	1000	0 Tel.	Writ. with Sig. Guar.; Tel.	*Dividends:* Auto.; A. *Other:* Syst. With.; Exchange-Tel.
SCUDDER SPECIAL FUND, INC. *(Scudder, Stevens & Clark, Inv. Counsel)* 345 Park Ave. New York, NY 10022 212-350-8200	Growth. Emphasizes common stocks of above-average risk.	1956	91.4	500	0 Tel.	Writ. with Sig. Guar.; Tel.	*Dividends:* Auto.; A. *Ret. Plans:* Keo., IRA, 403(b), Corp. *Other:* Syst. With.; Auto. Pur.; Exchange-Tel.

Fund Name (Advisor) Address and Telephone Number	Investment Objective and Policy	Year First Offered	Assets Mil. 12/31/78	Purchase Requirements Initial	Subsq.	Redemption Procedures	Services
SCUDDER COMMON STOCK FUND *(Scudder, Stevens & Clark, Inv. Counsel)* 175 Federal St. Boston, MA 02110 800-225-2470/617-482-3990	Growth. Common stocks, readily marketable securities of leading companies.	1929	$130.6	$500	$0 Tel.	Writ. with Sig. Guar. Tel.	*Dividends:* Auto.; S/A *Ret. Plans:* Keo., IRA, 403(b), Corp. *Other:* Syst. With.; Auto. Pur.; Exchange-Tel.
SELECTED AMERICAN SHARES, INC. *(Lincoln Nat'l. Investment Mgt. Co.)* 111 W. Washington St. Chicago, IL 60602 800-621-7321/312-630-2762	Combination of growth of capital and income. Investment among common and preferred stocks, and bonds.	1933	97.9	200 Tel.	50 Tel.	Writ. with Sig. Guar.	*Dividends:* Auto.; Q. *Ret. Plans:* Keo., IRA, Corp. *Other:* Syst. With.; Auto. Pur.; Exchange-Writ.
SELECTED SPECIAL SHARES, INC. *(Lincoln Nat'l. Investment Mgt. Co.)* 111 W. Washington St. Chicago, Il 60602 800-621-7321/312-630-2762	Capital growth. Investing in securities which afford maximum opportunity for appreciation.	1968	36.2	200 Tel.	50 Tel.	Writ. with Sig. Guar.	*Dividends:* Auto.; A. *Ret. Plans:* Keo., IRA, Corp. *Other:* Syst. With.; Auto. Pur.; Exchange-Writ.
SHERMAN, DEAN FUND *(Sherman, Dean Mgmt. & Res. Corp.)* 120 Broadway, New York, NY 10005 212-577-3850	The primary objective of the fund is capital appreciation. Income is of secondary importance.	1968	3.9	1000	100	Writ. with Sig. Guar.	*Dividends:* Auto.; A. *Ret. Plans:* IRA
STEIN ROE & FARN. CAP. OPPOR. *(Stein Roe & Farnham)* 150 S. Wacker Dr., Chicago, IL 60606 312-368-7820	Long-term capital appreciation. Invests in common stocks of both seasoned and smaller companies.	1963	21.3	300	50	Writ. with Sig. Guar.; Tel.	*Dividends:* Auto.; A. *Ret. Plans:* Keo., IRA *Other:* Syst. With.; Auto Pur.; Group Sub-Acct.; Exchange-Writ.
STEIN ROE & FARNHAM STOCK FUND *(Stein Roe & Farnham)* 150 S. Wacker Dr. Chicago, IL 60606 312-368-7800	Long-term capital appreciation. Invests substantially all assets in common stocks a:d other equity-type securities.	1958	137.7	300	50	Writ. with Sig. Guar., Tel.	*Dividends:* Auto.; Q. *Ret. Plans:* Keo., IRA *Other:* Syst. With.; Auto Pur.; Group Sub-Acct.; Exchange-Writ.
STRATTON GROWTH FUND *(Stratton Management Co.)* Butler & Skippack Pikes Blue Bell, PA 19422 215-542-0363	Growth-primary; income-secondary. Value-oriented high yield, low P/E common stocks; turnaround and takeover situations.	1972	4.6	1000	100 Tel.	Writ. with Sig. Guar.	*Dividends:* Auto.; A. *Ret. Plans:* Keo., IRA, 403 (b) *Other:* Syst. With.
TUDOR HEDGE FUND *(Tudor Management Co., Inc.)* 30 Wall St. New York, NY 10005 212-422-7216	Capital appreciation. Sell short, leverage, write covered call options.	1969	11.0	1000	250	Writ. with Sig. Guar.	*Dividends:* Auto.; A. *Ret. Plans:* Keo., IRA *Other:* Syst. With.
TWENTIETH CENTURY GROWTH *(Investors Research Corporation)* 605 W. 47th St. Kansas City, MO 64112 816-531-5575	Capital growth. Common stocks believed to have above-average appreciation potential.	1958	27.4	0	0	Writ. with Sig. Guar.	*Dividends:* Auto.; A. *Ret. Plans:* Keo., IRA, Corp. *Other:* Syst. With.; Auto. Pur.; Exchange-Writ.
TWENTIETH CENTURY INCOME *(Investors Research Corporation)* 605 W. 47th St. Kansas City, MO 64112 816-531-5575	Satisfactory rate of return through dividend paying common stocks selected for appreciation potential.	1958	4.0	0	0	Writ. with Sig. Guar.	*Dividends:* Auto.; A. *Ret. Plans:* Keo., IRA, Corp. *Other:* Syst. With.; Auto. Pur.; Exchange-Writ.
UNIFIED GROWTH FUND, INC. *(Unified Management Corporation)* 207 Guaranty Building Indianapolis, IN 46204 317-634-3301	Capital appreciation. Medium to smaller companies with above average growth in sales and earnings. Attention to timing.	1970	1.7	200	25	Written; Tel.	*Dividends:* Auto.; A. *Ret. Plans:* Keo., IRA, 403 (b), Corp. *Other:* Syst. With.; Auto. Pur.; Exchange-Tel.
UNITED SERVICES FUND, INC. *(Growth Research and Management, Inc.)* 110 E. Byrd Blvd., Universal City, TX 78148 800-531-7510/512-658-3562	Growth, Income. Specializes in gold shares and other precious metals.	1970	19.0	500	50	Written; Sig. Guar. over $5,000	*Dividends:* Auto.; S/A *Ret. Plans:* Keo., IRA *Other:* Syst. With.; Auto. Pur.
VALLEY FORGE FUND, INC. *(Valley Forge Management Corp.)* P.O. Box 262 Valley Forge, PA 19481 215-688-6839	Capital appreciation through market timing. We periodically move into C.D.'s and/or debt securities to defend capital.	1971	0.3	300	100 Tel.	Writ. with Sig. Guar.; Tel.; Wire	*Dividends:* Auto.; A. *Other:* Auto. Pur.
WEINGARTEN EQUITY FUND, INC. *(Weingarten Management Corp.)* 331 Madison Ave. New York, NY 10017 212-557-8787	Growth. Emphasis on companies with above-average earnings growth.	1967	14.4	500	50 Tel.	Written; Sig. Guar. on Certificates only.	*Dividends:* Auto.; A. *Ret. Plans:* Keo., IRA

Fund Name (Advisor) Address and Telephone Number	Investment Objective and Policy	Year First Offered	Assets Mil. 12/31/78	Purchase Requirements		Redemption Procedures	Services
				Initial	Subsq.		
CLARENCE M. WHIPPLE FUND *(Stonehenge Asset Management)* 2405 Church Rd. Cherry Hill, NJ 08002 609-667-6120	At least 90% income oriented securities with an emphasis on fundamentally sound bonds and stocks.	1968	$ 1.5	$ 50	$ 0	Writ. with Sig. Guar.	*Dividends:* Auto.; A. *Ret. Plans:* Keo., IRA *Other:* Syst. With.
WINDSOR FUND *(Wellington Management Company)* The Vanguard Group/Box 1100 Valley Forge, PA 19482 800-523-7910/215-293-1100	Long-term growth of capital and income, by investing in companies with favorable prospects but currently under-valued in the market.	1958	598.8	500	50	Writ. with Sig. Guar.	*Dividends:* Auto.; S/A *Ret. Plans:* Keo., IRA, Corp, 403 (b) *Other:* Syst. With.; Auto. Pur.; Exch.-Writ.; Grp. Sub-Acct.
W. L. MORGAN GROWTH FUND *(Wellington Management Company)* The Vanguard Group/Box 1100 Valley Forge, PA 19482 800-523-7910/215-293-1100	Seeks long-term growth of capital, by investing in companies believed to have above-average growth potential.	1968	81.6	500	50	Writ. with Sig. Guar.	*Dividends:* Auto.; A. *Ret. Plans:* Keo., IRA, Corp., 403 (b) *Other:* Syst. With.; Auto. Pur.; Exch.-Writ.; Grp. Sub-Acct.

APPENDIX 3

A PARTIAL LIST OF INTERNATIONAL MUTUAL FUNDS

This appendix lists just some of the major international mutual funds. The funds are divided in two general categories—equity funds and bond funds—according to the country in which the investments are made. Countries are discussed in the following order.

1. United Kingdom
2. West Germany
3. Japan
4. Canada
5. Australia
6. Switzerland
7. France
8. Italy
9. Spain
10. Europe
11. South Africa
12. Hong Kong and Singapore
13. Philippines

EQUITY FUNDS

United Kingdom

STRATTON TRUST (*See Chart 10-2*)

Stratton trust is an authorized U.K. united trust managed by Baring Bros., a British merchant bank, which started in November 1968. Net assets under management were almost $11m in early 1979. It is listed under Authorised Unit Trusts in the *Financial Times* of London.

Baring Bros. & Co. Ltd., 88 Leadenhall Street, London E.C.3., U.K. Tel. 01-588-2830

BRITANNIA GROWTH INVESTORS TRUST

This offshore mutual fund specializes in U.K. equities. At the beginning of 1969 the fund had $12m under management. There is a loading charge of 5 percent with an annual management fee of 1 percent. Minimum investment is $500. Switching privileges between other Britannia Funds exist. Quotations are listed in the *Financial Times, Times* of London, and the *International Herald Tribune.*

Britannia Trust Management (C.I.) Ltd., 30 Bath St., St. Helier, Jersey. Tel. 0534-73114

UNICORN GROWTH ACCUMULATOR TRUST

This trust is managed by Barclays Bank. Invests in U.K. growth equities. Total asset value in early 1979 was $40m. Minimum purchase is £250. Acquisition charges may be obtained on request. A small negotiated charge enables switching to any of the other Barclay Unicorn funds. Quoted in the Authorised Unit Trust section of the *Financial Times.*

Barclays Unicorn Ltd., Unicorn House, 252 Romford Rd., London E77, U.K. Tel. 01-534-5544

M&G RECOVERY FUND (*See Chart 10-8*)

The M&G Recovery Fund is designed as a speculative vehicle in U.K. companies that have fallen on bad times. There is an acquisition charge of 3¼ percent of the value of each unit included in the unit price plus an annual management fee of ½ percent which is deducted from the Fund's gross income. Minimum holding is 200 units. The Fund is quoted in the Unit Trust section of the *Financial Times.*

M&G Group, Three Quays, Tower Hill, London, EC3R 6BQ, U.K. Tel. 01-626-4586

Germany

UNIFONDS

Unifonds has been in existence for at least 14 years and is oriented to German equities and subject to German law on investment companies. Initial investment charge is 5 percent; no fee on redemption. A management fee not to exceed 0.5 per mill is calculated on the fund's assets at the end of the month. Issuing and redemption prices are calculated daily and published under Offshore and Overseas Funds in the *Financial Times* and the *International Herald Tribune.*

Union Investment Gesellschaft, Postfach 16767D 6,000 Frankfurt 16, W. Germany.

ADIRENTA

Adirenta specializes in German equities and is managed by ADIG, the oldest German unit trust managers. At the beginning of 1979 net assets under management were almost 4 bn.DM. Commission costs are 3 percent. Minimum investment is the cost of one quoted unit. Switching between the other eight funds under ADIG is not permitted. Bid and ask prices for the fund are quoted in the *Financial Times.*

ADIG Investment, Von-der-Tann-Strassell, 8,000 Munchen 22, W. Germany. Tel.089-2396-1 Telex 05/24269

CONCENTRA

Concentra is an open-end investment fund which was organized in 1956 and specializes in German shares. A loading charge of 6 percent is based on net asset value. Units issued in bearer form in denominations of 1, 5, 10, and 100 units. A management fee of ⅛ percent is to be paid every 3 months, plus a quarterly fee of 0.01 percent paid to the Depository Bank. The fund is exempt from all German taxes on income and property. There is no witholding tax. Prices are quoted in the Offshore and Overseas Fund section of the *Financial Times* and the *International Herald Tribune.*

Deutscher Investment Trust, Postfach 2685 Biebergasse 6-10 6,000 Frankfurt, W. Germany.

INVESTA

Incorporated in 1956. Investa specializes in German equities and is controlled by DWS, who have $8.5bn under management in private accounts and other open-ended mutual funds (2.5bnDM for Investa). There is a sales charge of 5 percent, a management fee of ⅛ percent paid each quarter, and a custodian fee of about 0.0005 percent of net asset value per annum. Minimum investment is $500. Prices are quoted in the *Financial Times* under Offshore and Overseas Funds, and in the *International Herald Tribune.*

D.W.S. Deutsche Ges F. Wertpapiersp, Gruneburgweg 113, 6,000 Frankfurt, W. Germany.
Tel. 7114-1 Telex 411916

Japan

HENDERSON-BARING JAPAN (*See Chart 10-3*)

The Henderson-Baring Fund was incorporated in 1976 with the objective of long-term growth in Japanese equities. Total assets were $38m in 1979. The subscription charge of up to 2½ percent is reduced on a sliding scale for investments of more than $75,000. The manager is entitled to an annual fee of .75 percent of the net asset value, and the trustee .25 percent per annum of the first $10,000,-000 of net assets reducing thereafter. Prices are quoted in the Offshore and Overseas section of the *Financial Times.*

Henderson-Baring Fund, Claughton House, Shirley Street, P. O. Box N4723, Nassau, Bahamas.
Tel. 809-28134 Telex 297156

JARDINE JAPAN FUND

This fund was established in 1969 with the objective of long-term capital growth through investment primarily in Japanese securities. Total net asset value was in excess of $80m in early 1979. Minimum investment is HK$10,000. Acquisition charge is 2½ percent of net asset value. There is also a redemption charge of 1.5 percent and an annual management fee of 0.6 percent of the value of the fund and a small performance fee. Quoted in the *South China Morning Post,* the Offshore and Overseas section of the *Financial Times,* and the *International Herald Tribune*

Jardine Fleming & Co. Ltd., 46th Floor, Connaught Centre, Hong Kong. Tel. 5-228011

JAPAN FUND

The Japan Fund is a closed-end investment fund invested in Japanese securities listed on the New York Stock Exchange. Purchase is made as with any other listed stock through a broker. The Japan Fund is quoted with other NYSE issues in the U.S. financial press.

NOMURA CAPITAL FUND OF JAPAN

This fund is registered with the SEC and was first offered in 1976. It is an open-ended fund with an objective of long-term capital gain with at least an 80 percent exposure to Japanese equities. Assets under management are approximately $16m. There is an acquisition fee of 7.0 percent of the NAV, less for investments over $10,000. A management fee of ½ percent per annum is also charged. The minimum initial purchase is $500. There is no charge for redemptions, which are obtained on written request. Prices are quoted daily in *The Wall Street Journal* and other major financial papers.

Nomura Capital Fund of Japan Inc., 100 Wall St., New York, N.Y., 10005. Tel. 212-425-9294 (call collect in New York. Elsewhere can toll free 800-221-3513)

M&G JAPAN (*See Chart 10-6*)

M&G Japan is designed to invest in a wide range of Japanese securities embracing all aspects of the economy. There is an acquisition fee of 5 percent included in the quoted price plus an annual management charge of ⅜ percent deducted from the fund's gross income. Minimum holding is $250 units. Prices are quoted in the Unit Trust section of the *Financial Times.*

M&G Group, Three Quays, Tower Hill, London EC3 R6BQ, U.K. Tel. 01-626-4586

GT PACIFIC FUND

This is a no-load, U.S.-based fund that invests in Japanese securities, primarily common stocks. There were $17.7m of assets under management at December 31, 1978. Minimum initial investment is $1000.

GT Management Inc., 555 California Street, San Francisco, Ca., 94104. Tel. 415-392-6181

Canada

PHILLIPS, HAGER AND NORTH CANADIAN FUND

Phillips, Hager and North operates a common stock fund investing its assets in Canadian securities. $2.2mCan. was under management in 1975. Maximum acquisition charge is 2 percent, management fee is 1 percent per annum. Shares may be redeemed at NAV on the day following receipt of notice to redeem. Quoted in the *Toronto Globe and Mail* business section.

Phillips, Hager and North, Suite 1700, 1055 West Hastings Street, Vancouver V6E 2H3, B.C., Canada.

ROY FUND EQUITY

Roy Fund operates a mutual fund primarily in equities. Assets under management were $54m in 1975. The acquisition fee is 4 percent with discounts available over $25m. There is no charge at any time for redemption upon receipt of written request. Transfer privileges are available to Roy Fund Income Trust. Prices are quoted in the business section of the *Toronoto Globe and Mail.*

United Bond and Share, Suite 2615, 800 Dorchester Blvd. West, Montreal, Quebec, Canada H3B 1X9.

Australia

M&G AUSTRALASIAN AND GENERAL FUND (*See Chart 10-5*)

This fund is designed to invest in Australian and New Zealand securities. There is an acquisition fee of 3¼ percent of the value of each unit included in the quoted price, with an annual management fee of ½ percent, which is deducted from gross income. Minimum holding is 500 units. Prices are quoted in the Unit Trust section of the *Financial Times.*

M&G Group, Three Quays, Tower Hill, London EC3 R6BQ, U.K. Tel. 01-626-4586

BARCLAYS UNICORN AUSTRALIA

Barclays Unicorn Australia is an authorized unit trust managed by Barclays Bank and invested in Australian securities. Total assets in the fund were about $30m at the beginning of 1979. The minimum investment is £250. Acquisition charges may be obtained on request. Prices are quoted in the Authorised Unit Trust section of the *Financial Times.*

Barclays Unicorn Ltd., Unicorn House, 252 Romford Road, London E.7. Tel. 01-534-5544

THE AUSTRALIAN AND GENERAL EXEMPT FUND (*See Chart 10-4a*)

This fund is designed to invest primarily in Australian securities embracing all aspects of the economy. Acquisition cost is not to exceed 5 percent of NAV. There is an annual management fee of ¾ percent. Minimum holding is 500 units. In August 1978 the fund had $3.4m U.S. under management. Prices are quoted in the Offshore Mutual Fund section of the *Financial Times.* For performance see Chart 10-4*a*.

M&G (Cayman) Ltd., P.O. Box 706, Cardinal Ave, Grand Cayman, B.W.I.

AUSTRALIAN SELECTION FUND

The Australian Selection Fund was founded in 1969 with the objective of capital growth in Australian equities. It pays no dividends. Minimum subscription is 100 shares. Acquisition cost: (U.S.) $1–24,999, 8½ percent; $25,000–$49,999, 6 percent; $50,000–$99,999, 4 percent. Redemption charge is not to exceed 2 percent of net asset value. Management fee is ⅜ percent semiannually plus 4 percent of the increase in the net asset value per share. If there is a reduction in value, no fee is paid. Prices are quoted in the Offshore and Overseas Funds section of the *Financial Times.*

Market Opportunities, c/o Irish Young and Outhwaite, 127 Kent St., Sydney, Australia.

ANCHOR AUSTRALIAN TRUST

This trust was founded in 1969 with the objective of steady growth in Australian securities. It has assets in excess of $5m. Minimum purchase is 300 units. Purchase charges are A$33,00 or less 5 percent; A$33,000–A$59,999, 4 percent; A$60,000–A$119,999, 3 percent. Management fee is 1 percent of the capital value per annum. Valuations are made weekly and published in the *Financial Times* under Offshore and Overseas Funds, and in Channel Island newspapers.

Management International Ltd., International Centre, P.O. Box 464, Hamilton, Bermuda.

Switzerland

FONSA

Fonsa was established in Switzerland in 1949 with the objective of capital growth and regular dividends in Swiss securities. It can be purchased on the Zurich Stock Exchange or through the Union Bank of Switzerland at net asset value plus expenses incurred in purchasing securities as well as a 4 percent placement charge and Federal Stamp Duty of 0.6 percent. There is a small redemption charge and a management fee of 3 percent of the gross revenue. Prices are quoted in the *International Herald Tribune.*

Union Bank of Switzerland, Bahnhofstrasse 45, Zurich, Switzerland.

France

FRANCIT

Established in 1949 with the objective of capital growth through investment in French equities, Francit can be purchased on the Zurich Stock Exchange or through the Union Bank of Switzerland at net asset value plus the expenses incurred in purchasing securities as well as a 4 percent placement charge and Federal Stamp Duty of 0.6 percent. There is a small redemption charge and an annual management fee of 5 percent of the gross revenue.

Union Bank of Switzerland, Bahnhofstrasse 45, Zurich, Switzerland.

Italy

ITAC

Itac is an open-ended investment fund established in 1958 with the objective of capital growth and regular income through investment in Italian securities. Shares can be purchased on the Zurich Stock Exchange or through the Union Bank of Switzerland at net asset value plus the expenses involved in purchasing securities, as well as a 4 percent placement charge and Federal Stamp Duty of 0.6 percent. There is a small redemption charge and a management fee of 5 percent of the gross revenue.

Union Bank of Switzerland, Bahnhofstrasse 45, Zurich, Switzerland.

Spain

INESPA FONDO DE INVERSION MOBILARIA

This is a Spanish growth fund founded in 1966. Acquisition cost is the net asset value price plus a sales commission which starts at 6 percent for purchases under 100,000 pesetas, reducing to 2 percent for purchases over 5,000,000 pesetas. These charges are only for systematic and automatic withdrawal plans. Commission is reduced by 50 percent for cash investments. There is also a charge of 1½ per thousand of the amount invested plus 5 pesetas for stockbroker charges. The management fee is 2 percent per annum. Prices are quoted in the large Spanish newspapers as well as the *Journal de Genève.*

Gestinver, SA Marqués de Valgeiglesias 6, Madrid 4 Spain.

ESPAC

Quoted since 1961 and run by the Union Bank of Switzerland, Espac has net assets in excess of $5.2m. Can be obtained on the Zurich Stock Exchange or through the Union Bank at net asset value plus the expenses incurred in purchasing securities as well as a 4 percent placement charge and Federal Stamp Duty of 0.6 percent. An annual management fee of 5 percent of the gross income is charged.

Union Bank of Switzerland, Bahnhofstrasse 45, Zurich, Switzerland.

Europe

EUROPEAN GROWTH FUND (*See Chart 10-1*)

The European Growth Fund is an authorized U.K. Unit trust with about £8.5m in total assets oriented to continental European securities. Acquisition charges range from 7½ to 1½ percent, depending on the amount invested. There are no redemption charges but there is a nominal management fee. Quoted under the Authorised Unit Trust section of the *Financial Times.*

Save & Prosper Group Ltd., 4 Great St. Helens, London EC3P 3EP, U.K.

M&G EUROPEAN FUND (*See Chart 10-4b*)

This fund is designed to invest in a wide range of European securities for long-term capital growth. There is an acquisition charge of 3¼ percent of the value of each unit included in the quoted price, with a management fee of ½ percent of the value of the fund deducted from gross income. Minimum holding is 500 units. Quoted in the Unit Trust section of the *Financial Times.*

M&G Group, Three Quays, Tower Hill, London EC3R6BQ, U.K.

South Africa

SAFIT

Founded in 1948, Safit invests in South African equities with a high proportion of the portfolio oriented to gold shares. Assets are in excess of $37m. Shares can be purchased through the Union Bank of Switzerland at net asset value plus the expenses entailed in purchasing securities as well as a 4 percent placement charge and Federal Stamp Duty of 0.6 percent. It is also possible to obtain them on the Zurich Stock Exchange. There is a .96 percent annual management fee. Quoted in the *International Herald Tribune.*

Union Bank of Switzerland, Bahnhofstrasse 45, Zurich, Switzerland.

Hong Kong and Singapore

M&G FAR EASTERN (*See Chart 10-7*)

The fund is designed to invest in far-eastern securities but reference to Chart 10-7 shows a high correlation to the Straits Times Index (Singapore) and the Hang Seng Index (Hong Kong). There is an acquisition charge of 3¼ percent included in the quoted price. An annual management fee of ½ percent of the value of the fund is deducted from its gross income. Minimum holding is 500 units. Quoted in the Unit Trust section of the *Financial Times.*

M&G Group, Three Quays, Tower Hill, London EC3R6BQ U.K.
Tel. 01-626-4586

The Philippines

G.T. PHILIPPINE FUND

This fund is a unit trust specializing in investments in the Republic of the Philippines. The fund was incorporated in 1978 ($1.2m under management). There is an acquisition charge of not more than 5 percent and a management and trustee fee of 2½ percent of NAV. There is no minimum subscription. The trust is valued at the close of business on each Dealing Day and units may be realized through the managers. Prices are published in the *Financial Times, South China Morning Post,* and the *Hong Kong Standard.*

G.T. Management (Asia) Ltd. 1008, 1010 Hutchison House, Harcourt Road, Hong Kong.

BOND FUNDS

United Kingdom

ANCHOR GILT EDGED FUND

The Anchor Gilt Edged Fund was incorporated in 1972 to enable international investors to benefit from a managed tax-free portfolio of British government securities. Minimum purchase is 50 shares. Acquisition charge is £7.50 per £1000 on the first £10,00; £3.75 on the next £20,000; £1.25 per £1000 on the next £40,-000; and £0.625 per £1000 over £70,000. Management fee is 0.3125 percent of the net asset value payable semiannually. Quoted weekly in the *Financial Times* under Offshore and Overseas Funds and in the Channel Island Press.

Management International (Jersey) Ltd., 37 Broad Street, St. Helier, Jersey, Channel Islands, U.K.

BRITANNIA HIGH INTEREST STERLING TRUST

This is an offshore mutual fund specializing in British government securities. Assets under management in early 1969 were $6m. Initial charge is 3½ percent with an annual management fee of ¾ percent. Initial minimum investment is £500. Switching privileges are available with other Britannia Funds (see Growth Investors Trust on page 207). Quoted in the *Financial Times* under Offshore Funds and Overseas Funds, the *Times* of London and the *International Herald Tribune.*

Britannia Trust Management (C.I.) Ltd., 30 Bath Street, St. Helier, Jersey, Channel Islands, U.K.

Germany

RENTEN FUNDS

This German-oriented bond fund is managed by D.I.T. (Deutscher Investment Trust) and has assets under management of 2.2bn DM. The acquisition fee is 2.5 percent. Income distribution is invested free of the loading charge to any D.I.T. mutual fund. Shares are not currently quoted in the English language publications.

Deutscher Investment Trust, Postfach 2685, Biebergasse 6-10 6,000 Frankfurt, West Germany.

Canada

FONDS DESJARDINS OBLIGATIONS

Fonds Desjardins Obligations operates a fully managed bond fund with net assets of $1.8m in 1976. There is no acquisition or redemption fee. Shares may be redeemed at net asset value as of the close of business on the valuation day next following the day on which the redemption request is received. Net asset value is determined each Friday and on the last day of each month. Payment is made within 7 days. There is a small management fee.

Les Placements Collectifs Inc., 511 Place D'Armes, Montreal, Quebec, H2Y 2W7, Canada.

PHILLIPS, HAGER AND NORTH BOND FUND

The assets of this bond mutual fund are invested entirely in fixed income securities. In 1975 assets totaled $7.2m. There is an acquisition charge of 1 percent and a ½ percent management fee per annum. Redemption is net asset value, provided a written request has been received 10 days before the valuation day, which is the last day of the month.

Phillips, Hager & North, Suite 1700, 1055 West Hastings St., Vancouver, B. C., V6E 2H3, Canada.

Switzerland

HELVETINVEST

Helvetinvest was founded in 1971 and is managed by Intrag Ltd. Shares are purchased through the Union Bank of Switzerland at net asset value plus the expenses incurred in purchasing securities in addition to a ¼ percent placement charge. Shares may also be acquired at the prevailing bid and offer prices on the Zurich Stock Exchange. There is a management fee of ¼ percent.

Union Bank of Switzerland, Bahnhofstrasse 45, Zurich, Switzerland.

APPENDIX 4

SUPPLEMENTARY SOURCES OF INFORMATION

AUSTRALIA

Principal Stock Exchanges

The Stock Exchange of Melbourne, 351 Collins St., Melbourne.
The Sydney Stock Exchange, 20–22 O'Connell Street, Sydney.

Australian Stock Brokers (Members of Sydney Exchange)

Hattersley & Maxwell, 105 Pitt St., Sydney.
Meares & Philips, 33 Bligh St., Sydney.
Pring, Dean & Co., 20 O'Connell Street, Sydney.
Ross McFadyen & Co., 17 O'Connell Street, Sydney.

Australian Newspapers with Financial Coverage

Australian Financial Review, Broadway, Sydney. U.S. office: 1501 Broadway, New York, N.Y., 10036.
The Daily Telegraph, 168 Castlereigh, Sydney.
The Sydney Morning Herald, 235 Jones Street, Broadway, Sydney.

FRANCE

Stock Exchange

Bourse de Paris, 4 Place de la Bourse, Paris.

Major French Banks Involved in Purchase of Securities

Banque Française du Commerce Extérieur, 21 Blvd. Haussmann, Paris.
Banque Rothschild, 21 Rue Lafitte, Paris. Affiliate: New Court Securities Corp., 1 Rockefeller Plaza, New York, N.Y., 10020.
Crédit Commercial de France, 103, Ave. des Champs-Élysées, Paris, France.

Daily Newspapers with Good Financial Coverage

Le Figaro, 14 Rond-Point des Champs-Élysées, Paris.
Le Monde, 5 Rue des Italiens, Paris.

GERMANY

Leading Financial Daily

Frankfurter Allgemeine Zeitung, Hellerhofstrasse 2-4, Frankfurt.

Financial Publications

Blict durch die Wirtschaft, Hellerhofstrasse 2-4, Frankfurt.
Börsen Zeitung, Dusseldorferstrasse 16, Frankfurt.
Handelsblatt, Martin-Luther-Platz 27, Düsseldorf.

Information Service

Verlag Hoppenstedt & Co., Postfach 4006, Havelstrasse 9, Darmstadt.

Major Stock Exchanges

Bayerische Börse, Lenbachplatz 2a, Munich.
Frankfurter Wertpapierbörse, Börsenplatz 6, Frankfurt.

Major Banks Involved in the Purchase of Securities

Commerzbank A.G., Neuer-Mainzer Strasse 32-36, Frankfurt, Affiliate: Euro-Partners Securities Corp., 1, World Trade Center, New York, N.Y., 10048.
Deutsche Bank A.G., Grosse Gallustrasse 10-14, Frankfurt. Affiliate: U.B.S.-B.D. Corp., 40 Wall Street, New York, N.Y., 10005.
Dresdner Bank A.G., Gallusanlage 7-8, Frankfurt. Affiliate: A.B.D. Securities Corp., 1 Battery Park Plaza, New York, N.Y., 10004.

HOLLAND

Major Stock Exchange

Vereniging voor de Effectenhandel, Beursplein 5, Amsterdam.

Dutch Banks and Broker-Dealers

Pierson, Heldring and Pierson, Herengracht 206-214, Amsterdam. Affiliate: New Court Securities Corp., 1 Rockefeller Plaza, New York, N.Y., 10020.
Bank de Paris et des Pays-Bas, Herengracht 539-541, Amsterdam.
Barclays Kol and Co. N.V., Herengracht 500, Amsterdam.

Dutch Information Services

Tabel van Laagste en Hoogste Koersen, Weesperstraat 85, Amsterdam.

Newspapers with Financial Coverage

Algemeen Dagblad, Postbus 241, Rotterdam.
Het Parool, Posthus 433, Amsterdam.
De Tijd, Posthus 348, Amsterdam.

HONG KONG

Major Stock Exchanges

Hong Kong Stock Exchange Ltd., 21st floor, Hutchinson House.
Kam Ngan Stock Exchange, 7th Floor, Connaught Centre.

Hong Kong Stock Exchange Foreign Brokerage House Members

Astaire & Co. (Far East), 20th floor, Prince's Building.
James Capel, Room 608, Hong Kong Hilton.
Cazenove & Co. (Far East), Hutchison House.
Richardson Securities of Canada (Pacific) Ltd., Bank of Canton Bldg.

Newspapers with Financial Coverage

Asian Wall Street Journal, 2F South China Morning Post Bldg., Tong Chong Street, Quarry Bay.
South China Morning Post, Taikoo Sugar Refinery Block D, Quarry Bay.
The Star, 19-21 Pennington St., Causeway Bay.

ITALY

Major Stock Exchanges

Borsa Valori di Milano, Piazza degli Affari 6, Milan.

Important Banks Doing Investment Business

Banca Commerciale Italiana, Piazza della Scala 6, Milan.
Credito Italiano, Piazza Cordusio 2, Milan.

Newspapers with Financial Coverage

Corriere della Sera, Via Solferino 28, Milan.
Il Messagero, Via de Tritone 152, Rome.
La Stampa and *Stampa Sera,* Via Roma 80 and Galleria S Federico 16, Turin.

Italian Financial Press

Il Sole-24 Ore, Via Monviso 26, Milan.

JAPAN

Major Stock Exchange

Tokyo Stock Excange, Kabuto-cho, Chuo-Ku, Tokyo.

Japanese Brokerage Houses in the United States

Daiwa Securities Co. America, 1 Liberty Plaza, New York, N.Y., 10005.
Nikko Securities Co. International Inc., 140 Broadway, New York, N.Y., 10005.
Nomura Securities International Inc., 100 Wall St., New York, N.Y., 10005.
Yamaichi International America Inc., 1 World Trade Center, New York, N.Y., 10048.

SPAIN

Major Stock Exchanges

Bolsa Oficial de Comercio de Barcelona, Paseo Isabel II, Consulado 2, Barcelona.
Bolsa de Comercio de Madrid, Plaza de la Lealtad 1, Madrid.

Some Banks Handling Investments

Banco de Bilbao, Alcalá 16, Madrid; 767 Fifth Ave, New York, N.Y., 10022.
Banco Exterior de España, Carrera de San Jeronimo 36, Madrid; and 46 West 55th Street, New York, N.Y., 10019.
Banco Hispano Americano, Serrano 47, Madrid; and 645 Fifth Ave, New York, N.Y., 10017.

Some Newspapers with Financial Coverage

ABC, Serrano 61, Madrid.
Informaciones, San Roque 9, Madrid.
La Vanguardia, Barcelona.

SWITZERLAND

Major Stock Exchanges

Börsenkammer des Kantons Basel-Stadt, Freistrasse 3, Basel.
Chambre de la Bourse de Génève, 8 Rue Petitot, Geneva.
Effektenbörsenverein Zurich, Bleicherweg 5, Zurich.

Major Banks Handling Investments

Schweizerische Bankgesellschaft, Bahnhofstrasse 45, Zurich. Affiliate: UBS-DB Corp. 40 Wall Street, New York, N.Y., 10005.
Schweizerische Kreditanstalt, Paradeplatz 8, Zurich. Affiliate: SoGen Swiss International Corp., 20 Broad St., New York, N.Y., 10005.
Schweizerische Bankverein, Aeschenvorstadt 1, Basel. Affiliate: Basel Securities Corp., 120 Broadway, New York, N.Y., 10005.

Leading Newspapers with Financial Coverage

Basler Nachrichten, Dufourstrasse 40, Basel.
Journal de Génève, 5–7 Rue Général Dufour, Geneva.
Neue Zürcher Zeitung, Falkenstrasse 11, Zurich.

GLOSSARY

American depository receipt (ADR) A certificate issued by an American custodian in lieu of the original shares held in custody abroad. One ADR may represent one underlying share or several.

Arbitrage A financial asset that is purchased or sold simultaneously in different markets so as to profit from the price differences in those markets.

Bear trap A signal which suggests that the rising trend of an index or stock has reversed but which proves to be false.

Bull trap A signal which suggests that the declining trend of an index or stock has reversed but which proves to be false.

Cash market Market for the immediate delivery and payment of financial assets, or commodities.

Closed-end mutual fund Investment companies in which the original capital is raised by selling stocks and/or preferred shares. Attempts to raise additional funds for investment are infrequent so that the capital is for the most part "closed" to a limited number of shares. The outstanding shares are traded on the exchanges, or the over-the-counter markets in much the same way as ordinary shares. The price is determined by supply and demand in the marketplace and can therefore be above or below the breakup value of the fund. Consequently the price of the shares rarely trade exactly at their net asset value but fluctuate around it.

Cross rate The price relationship of two currencies where neither currency is the home currency of the user.

Deferred futures Futures contracts which expire at a more distant month.

Eurobond A bond underwritten by an international syndicate and sold outside the country of the currency in which it is denominated.

Eurocurrency Deposits of a currency held outside the country which originally issued it.

Eurodollar American dollar deposits held outside the United States.

Forward market The buying and selling of currencies for deferred delivery in a foreign exchange market. Prices are determined by dealers in the marketplace.

Futures contract **1**. A regulated contract covering the sale of commodities for delivery at a specified date in the future. **2**. An agreement between a buyer and seller to pay for and deliver a specific financial asset or commodity at a specified future date.

Inverted market A futures market in which earlier months are selling at premiums to the later months.

Loading charge The cost of acquiring a unit of an open-ended mutual fund. The loading charge is usually paid to an agent and is therefore normally a commission. It ranges from 1–8 percent.

Management fee The fee charged by the managers of a mutual fund. The management fee typically ranges between ½ percent and 1 percent p.a. of the net asset value of the fund.

Margin Occurs when an investor pays part of the purchase price of a security and borrows the balance, usually from a broker; the "margin" is the difference between the market value of the security and the loan which is made against it.

Margin call The demand upon a customer to put up money or securities with a broker. The call is made if a customer's equity in a margin account declines below a minimum standard set by the Exchange or brokerage firm. This happens when there is a drop in price of the securities being held as collateral.

Nearbys The earlier delivery months of a financial or commodities futures market.

Net assest value Refers to the total market value of a mutual fund less its liabilities at the close of business on a specified day. *Net asset value per unit* is the total net asset value of a mutual fund divided by the number of outstanding units.

No-load fund A mutual fund for which there is no acquisition charge.

Open-ended mutual fund An investment fund that continually sells its treasury shares and is committed to redeem them upon demand at, or close to, their liquidation value. The fund's shares are bought from and sold to the company itself rather than other shareholders.

Open interest The number of outstanding contracts at any specific time.

Overbought An opinion as to the level of prices. It may refer to a specific indicator or to the market as a whole after a period of vigorous buying, following which it may be argued that prices are overextended for the time being and are in need of a period of downward or horizontal adjustment.

Oversold The opposite of overbought, i.e., a price move that has overextended on the downside.

Over-the-counter market (O.T.C.) An informal collection of brokers and dealers. Securities traded include almost all federal, state, municipal, and corporate bonds, and all widely owned equity issues not listed on the stock exchanges.

Round turn commission A commission charge that includes a broker's fee for both the buying and selling side of a transaction. In futures markets commissions are debited to the customer's account only when both sides of a transaction have been completed.

Short selling Short selling is normally a speculative operation undertaken in the belief that the price of the shares will fall. It is accomplished by selling shares one does not own by borrowing stock from a broker. Most stock exchanges prohibit the short sale of a security below the price at which the last board lot was traded. (Short selling can also take place with other financial assets.)

Short covering The process of buying back stock that has already been sold short.

Short position (interest) The total amount of short sales outstanding on a specific exchange at a particular time. The short position is published monthly.

Spot exchange rate A transaction with delivery of one or two days forward.

Yield Curve The structure of the level of interest rates through various maturities. Usually the shorter the maturity, the lower the interest rate. Thus 3-month Treasury bills usually yield less than 20-year government bonds. The slope of the yield curve relates to the speed with which rates rise as the maturity increases. In periods of tight money, short-term rates usually yield more than longer-term rates, and the curve is then called an inverse yield curve.

BIBLIOGRAPHY

BOOKS

International Investing

Esslen, Rainer: *The Complete Book of International Investing*, McGraw-Hill, New York, 1978.

Kinsman, Robert: *The Robert Kinsman Guide to Tax Havens*, Dow Jones Irwin, Homewood, Ill., 1978

Mutual Funds

Financial Post Survey of (Canadian) Mutual Funds

The International Fund Year Book: Annual Directory of Offshore Funds, Investors' Chronicle, London.

NOLOAD (U.S.) Mutual Fund Directory, NOLOAD Mutual Fund Association, Valley Forge, Pa.

Financial Futures

Dushek, Charles, and Carol Harding: *Trading in Foreign Currencies*, American Trans-Euro Corp., Chicago, 1978.

Powers, Mark J.: *Getting Started in Commodity Futures Trading*, Investor Publications, Waterloo, Iowa, 1973.

Schwarz, Edward: *How to Use the Money Markets Futures Contracts*, Dow Jones Irwin, Homewood, Ill., 1979.

Technical Analysis

Edwards, Robert D., and John Magee: *Technical Analysis of Stock Trends*, John Magee, Springfield, Mass., 1957.

Jiler, William: *How Charts Can Help you in the Stock Market,* Commodity Research Publications, New York, N.Y., 1962.

Pring, Martin J.: *Technical Analysis Explained*, McGraw-Hill, New York, N.Y., 1980.

Contrary Opinion and Mental Attitude

Gann, W. D.: *Truth of the Stock Tape*, Financial Guardian, New York, N.Y., 1932.

Howard, Henry: *The Psychology of Speculation*, Fraser Publishing Co., Wells, Vermont, 1966.

Neill, Humphrey B.: *The Art of Contrary Thinking*, The Caxton Printers Ltd., Caldwell, Idaho, 1971.

Nelson, Samuel: *ABC of Stock Market Speculation*, Taylor, New York, N.Y., 1934.

Sokoloff, Kiril: *The Thinking Investor's Guide to the Stock Market*, McGraw-Hill, New York, N.Y., 1978.

MAGAZINES

Commodities Magazine, 219 Parkade, Cedar Falls, Iowa, 50613.

INDEX

INDEX